Arne is one of tho...
warrior. Having beer
that the power of pro
Mountain Movers!

...rayer
know
those

...eter Fassbender
Minister of Education, MLA Surrey Fleetwood

Arne has ploughed the way.

Rob Parker
National House of Prayer, Ottawa

A good encourager. He's like a dad. Hard worker. Dedicated to making
sure he fulfilled whatever God told him to do.

Fran Parker
National House of Prayer, Ottawa

It has been very rewarding to me as a politician to have my name
weekly lifted up in prayer. God is so good. The Lord did not take me
into a pastoral or prophetic ministry but building the nation. The two
roles cannot independently succeed unless they work together. Arne
and Kathie are good friends—more than parents to me.

Tagak Curley
Inuit leader and former MLA in both NWT
and Nunavut Territories

I don't know of a person I'd rather listen to, or talk to, or have pray for
me. He lifts you up.

Bill White
Board Member, Prayer Canada

He loves the Lord beyond words.

Al Jones,
Friend

My job is to challenge people to do something beyond where they've
been. God's plans are so far beyond man's plans it doesn't matter
where you are, you've got a long ways to go. But you and the Lord are
an unbeatable team!

Arne Bryan

21/8/17.

To my freind & Partner in
God-baseness
Ken Jasper

Arne Bryan
PIONEER OF PRAYER CANADA

Bless You
Arne Bryan

BETH CARSON

14-358-109ave
Sarrey BC V3R0P6

ARNE BRYAN: PIONEER OF PRAYER CANADA

Printed in Canada

ISBN: 978-1-4866-0399-2

Word Alive Press
131 Cordite Road, Winnipeg, MB R3W 1S1
www.wordalivepress.ca

WORD ALIVE
—P R E S S—

MIX
Paper from
responsible sources
FSC
www.fsc.org   FSC® C016245

Cataloguing in Publication information may be obtained from Library and Archives Canada

TABLE OF CONTENTS

INTRODUCTION

We live in a blessed country, in no small part because the Lord God, through Arne Bryan, has called His people to pray for Canada's authorities.

It has been a daunting task to tell Arne Bryan's story. For one thing, it covers many years! It may seem that Arne's life's work didn't start until he was 59 but his early years shaped the man. My goal was not only to describe events but also to capture his winning personality: adventurous, knowledgeable, tenacious (some would say annoying), encouraging, caring, enthusiastic, and full of fun. Arne learned to hear God—in the Bible, in dreams, in visions—and to obey. Obedience has built faith and sharpened his ear to hear more.

The story also had to reflect the quality of the people who have been drawn to work with Arne over the years and who have become his firm friends. I wish I could have spoken with more of you. Please enjoy those who are included. If your name or your community are not mentioned, please forgive me. You are known to the Lord, and Canada values your prayers.

Arne and his wonderful wife Kathie spent hours telling me stories. Those of you who know him well will recognize his style in much of the book. They also gave me access to their archives and photographs. My prayer is that our collaborative effort will bring glory to God and that He will use this book to further His will in Canada.

PROLOGUE

The auction was the easy part. To make it possible, the twenty ranchers had toiled long and hard together, riding out over the vast, undulating Albertan prairies. This was the last round-up of wild horses that wandered free in the ancient water-carved coulees, and the ranchers had hunted the horses out from among the trees in the bluffs where they grazed. Hard experience had taught the cowboys how to be as wily as the wild mustangs they were rounding up. Eventually they were able to drive them towards the fences that would funnel them into a big, secure corral, built strong enough to contain the animal fury. Now the ranchers were hoping for a good profit to share after their hard work. Some were in friendly competition to buy horses for their own farms.

The round-up took place in the Handhills, a high plateau named after a Cree word referring to the five ridges which spread like fingers (although another account says the name came from the name of a famous Blackfoot chief with one small hand, who was killed there). It was about thirty miles east of Drumheller and about five miles south of William Bryan's farm. Will had been breeding and breaking horses for a living for nearly twenty years, mostly to create teams of working horses for local farmers and to ship by train to Ontario.

At this auction, Will knew exactly what sort of horse he wanted and it was not the kind that would pull a plough. Once in a while at these auctions, he would spot one that was suitable to ride and that's what he was looking for this time. He paid ten dollars for a shaggy buckskin cayuse, a nimble "Indian pony," the colour of tanned deerskin, with a black mane and tail.

It was not a big horse but it was unruly and treacherous to handle. It had to be lassoed and, when it was calmed down by the choking effect of the tightened rope, Will wrestled a rawhide halter across its nose and over its ears. He then used a heavy rawhide rope to tie the ring underneath the halter to the tail of a big Belgian mare that he had brought with him for this purpose. When he let the mare loose, she just headed home with the wild horse forced to trot along behind. By the time the two horses reached his farm, the skittish buckskin was getting used to being led.

Will tied his new bronc in the barn, in a box stall with a divider up the middle so that he could get close to the pony to prepare it for training. Then he turned to the lanky boy who had watched him do this any number of times before.

"Well, Doc," he said. "This is your pony. You're going to have to break it yourself and then it'll be your horse."

"Doc" was his ten-year-old son. He was all for this plan. Break and ride his very own saddle horse? He couldn't wait to get going. Doc was big for his age and had been riding since he was three. Tense but confident, he was determined to win this pony over, whatever it took. And he knew what it would take—patience and guts, but mostly patience. Move slowly, stick to his father's plan, persevere through interminable repetitions and dig deep for even more patience and guts.

But, before he could take his new horse out of the stall, he had to watch as his father rigged up the "W" hitch.

Will fastened a heavy surcingle around the girth of the horse, just behind the withers and shoulder area, making it firm enough but not too tight. This was a strong belt-like device with a six-inch steel ring hanging on it under the belly of the horse. The horse was jumpy but there was little room for him to buck around in the narrow stall, and Will was skilful, steady and swift.

Next, around the fetlock of one of the front legs, he fastened a heavy strap with a smaller ring on it. Then he took his lariat, tied it round the fetlock of the other front leg, and threaded it up through the heavy ring under the horse's belly, then down through the smaller ring on the first leg, back up through the ring on the surcingle, and then the rest of the rope was held out behind the horse.

"And there's your W," he announced. "This cayuse won't give us too much trouble out in the field."

Will carefully laid a saddle on the agitated horse, which was all quivering nerves. He used a wire to reach out to grab the belly band underneath to tighten the saddle with great care. The boy knew that process would get the horse jumping. It took time, lots of caution and persistence, but eventually the saddle was firmly in place. Finally Will put the bridle on.

"Is he ready to go out in the yard yet, Dad?"

"Yes, Doc. He is. But I think we'll tie him up to the mare again to keep him under control."

Doc knew his pony needed a lot of work before he would submit to being led by man or boy. After all, if the pony were not stronger than a man he would be of little use. So he was manoeuvred close to the mare again and, once they were tied together, the little procession headed out of the barn.

The boy was eager to mount up straight away.

"Not here, Doc," said Will. "You know why we do this in the ploughed field."

"Softer landing!" grinned the boy.

In the field, Will made sure he had a firm grip on the end of the W lariat before releasing the edgy pony from the steady guide horse. As soon as he began jumping around,

Will yanked hard on the rope, pulling the front feet under the pony, bringing him down on his knees. After two or three of those experiences, the pony smartened up, realizing he'd be tripped immediately if he jumped.

"Now, Doc. Up you go!"

The boy swung himself into the saddle and held the reins firmly. He'd witnessed this often before and knew what was coming. The boy was light but he was the first burden the horse had ever been made to carry. Will let him take a step or two but yanked on the rope at the first sign that he was going to buck, and down the pony went to his knees, nearly catapulting his rider over his ears. But the boy sat back in the saddle and kept his seat. He knew his task was to stay put and wait.

"You're on to it, Doc. Won't take long."

The horse was allowed to his feet again and felt the boy kick his sides. He took a few steps then bucked again to throw his rider. A jerk on the lariat and the shaggy pony was down again.

The boy had to be ready for the sudden dips as they allowed the horse to walk around the field for a while wherever he wanted to go. They were getting him used to walking at the boy's kicks and "Go ahead." Then the boy pulled the reins to the right; the horse's head turned and he walked that way. Then they repeated this to the left. They worked on these simple control exercises for an hour or two, the frequent yanks on the "W" teaching the horse obedience and the boy persistence.

"That's enough for today, Doc. Let's take him in now." So it was back to the barn for the horse. The boy felt great pride. He decided to call his horse "Buck" and couldn't wait for the patient battle to continue the next day.

They repeated this whole procedure day after day. After a few days they tried the pony without the "W." The boy boldly mounted up and set Buck walking, his father alongside on his saddle horse. But Buck was still a wild horse and swift as lightning when spooked. His young rider was bucked off a few times, sampling the "soft landing" of the ploughed field, but got back up again immediately. He was not going to give up. He knew that persistence would master his pony eventually. Sure enough, after each tumble, Buck would stop to let him back into the saddle. He was learning that his young master would not take no for an answer.

The boy did learn to ride Buck, who would be his key saddle horse for about fifteen years, his chief mode of transportation and a vital asset in his business. The boy grew up to be a farmer and rancher alongside his father, and Buck was an excellent horse, always taking care of him. He was fast and could turn on a dime, as they say. He was a great cattle horse because he enjoyed what he was doing. Once trained, he loved to be faster than any cow they were trying to herd. His rider just had to sit tight because Buck knew what was needed and how to do it.

And so the boy and his pony grew into the challenging life of the Albertan rancher, hard-working, independent, and self-reliant, surviving harsh winters, dry summers and blinding dust storms.

Doc broke many horses during those years and never met a horse he couldn't ride. He was not afraid of the wildest pony: "I figured, if my Dad could do it, I could do it."

Doc breaking a horse

The chapters that follow are the story of this daring boy, who was trained, protected and empowered by his heavenly Father, until they could work together as a powerful team, to train, protect and empower others.

PART I: PREPARATION

"...Seek ye first the kingdom of God..."
(Matthew 6:33, KJV)

Arne aged 21

CHAPTER 1

1918—1939:
GROWING UP ON THE FARM

Arne Bryan's grandfather was an Irishman who ran away from home at the age of twelve, stowed away on a freighter bound for Canada and eventually settled on a farm in a little town near Strathroy, Ontario, where he raised a family.

Arne's father, William Jennings Bryan ("W.J."), was born into that family in 1875. He became a teacher and used to travel thirty-nine miles by bicycle to visit Clara Alice Heidt, a legal secretary who lived on a little farm at Southwold. They married in 1901. Clara liked to call her husband Will. In future years they would bring educated conversation to the family dinner table so that their children learned how to speak well. They would also bring a healthy understanding of the difference between hell and heaven, having been saved during the old hellfire and brimstone of the Methodist Church.

Will and Clara's first daughter and son were born during the five years they lived at the Bryan family home. Then in 1906, they set out for the long adventure of homesteading in Alberta.

Under the Dominion Lands Act of 1872, when Crown Land had been surveyed and officially declared available for settlement, individuals could apply to homestead a quarter section of their choice (160 acres) for only the filing fee of ten dollars. After three years, if they had lived on that land for at least six months each year and improved it by building a house and barn, fencing it and cultivating a portion of it, then the homesteaders could apply for the title to the land. At this time the Crown Land being homesteaded was in Alberta so that's where the Bryans headed.

The train brought Will and Clara, their two children and Will's widowed father as far as Stettler, about fifty miles east of Red Deer. Stettler was a small settlement that had been founded only the year before, named after a Swiss immigrant, Carl Stettler. Another daughter and son were born to Will and Clara before they finally settled on their own land.

There was very little on that prairie land to begin with but that was the year settlers were moving in and soon sod shacks and fences started to spring up everywhere. Some lived in their wagons or tents until they could build a house.

Will had registered, not just a quarter-section, but the whole of Section 1-31-17-W4 (640 acres)—a square mile of nothing but grass and a few shrubs, sixty-five miles south-east of Stettler. To find the land where he was going to build his new life, Will had to consult his detailed survey map that showed all the hills and even clumps of bushes, and had to find a peg that marked one corner of his section. Then he had to ride a mile to find the next one, and then two more to complete the square.

This location was not far from a large slough about six hundred feet across. Maybe Will had used the map to identify a spot of higher ground where he would build his house and farmyard. Allowances were marked on the map where roads were planned, bordering his property on three sides. His northern neighbour's land abutted directly on to his, and north of that was a wider allowance that would one day become Highway 9.

When the family moved there from Stettler, it was a three-day journey with the team of horses and wagon they had bought and loaded with all the effects that they would need to set up a household. They named their new home "Ingle Loch Ranch."

Ingle Loch Ranch

Will decided from the beginning that his land was better suited to grazing than growing so, since the settlers coming into this new land all needed horses, horses became his business. He grew some crops and raised cattle for sale, as well as chicken and turkeys, but his chief business was raising horses, or catching wild horses, and breaking them for sale. From the beginning, the new settlers found their way to W.J. at Ingle Loch Ranch to buy horses ready for riding or working.

By the time Arne was born into this community of scattered homesteads in 1918, the nearby village of Delia (named for Delia Davis, the wife of the first post master) had become the market town for the area after the railway finally had come through in 1913.

There had been births and deaths in the family. The family's oldest sons, Quentin and Kermit, had died soon after coming to the property, leaving the family with two daughters. A third and fourth daughter were born. Then Arne came along, born September 29, 1918 (a lovely Sunday morning), in their own home five-and-a-half miles away from a doctor. His three oldest sisters were thrilled to have a brother and they all wanted to name him. So his full name was Gerald Arnold Eugene Bryan. The next year, the second oldest daughter, Zelda, died in the flu epidemic of 1919. Soon after, Will and Clara's last child was born, another daughter.

Will and Clara had worked the ranch for over ten years by then. In about 1920, when Arne was two or three, W.J. arranged for a man to buy the land by making regular payments towards the full price and the Bryan family moved west to Penticton, British Columbia, to the burgeoning orchard area of the Okanagan.

Once the railway made it easier to get fruit to market, many of the cattle ranches in the Okanagan Valley were transformed into apple orchards. It was becoming a profitable industry for those who added know-how and hard work to the hot summers and fertile land of an area often known as the "Garden of Eden."

Penticton (from the Salish for "place to live forever") was a small town between two beautiful lakes. Arne remembers that there was not much for him and his little sister to do there besides playing in the yard with Russell, the neighbour's boy who was the same age as Arne.

Mischievous Doc & little sister Melba, 1922, Penticton

4

However, Arne was developing a mischievous streak. His mother and older sister valiantly tried to keep track of the boys but, as soon as they were distracted, the two boys would vanish. On a good day, they would sneak all the way down to the railroad about five blocks away where Russell's father worked. They liked to try to spot Russell's dad but if he saw them, he would jump off the car he was working on and give them both a licking. Then they'd have to go home, where Arne's dad would give them another licking. These multiple punishments did nothing to diminish Arne's mischievous nature but he grew up to respect discipline.

The family didn't live in Penticton forever—after a few years, the man who had bought their land fell behind on the payments and they had to return to Delia.

Arne's three older sisters: Beryl (behind), Hilda (left) and Edna

Most of Arne's childhood memories are of life on the ranch in Delia. His eldest sister, Beryl, was fifteen years his senior. She became an excellent horsewoman and was able to look after the farm whenever their father went back east delivering horses he had raised or tamed. When they were

5

building roads in the area, Beryl drove a ten-horse team on a road grader. Hilda was seven years and Edna three years older than Arne, and they too drove horses and helped with the farm work whenever they could. There was always plenty of work to do. Like his sisters, Arne learned to ride horseback at about three years of age.

One day, one of the girls shouted, "Wait Daddy, we've lost Arnold!" as the family rode home from Hillview School, two-and-a-half miles from their home. As there was no snow at the time, they had been to the Christmas Concert, a social highlight. They were now all bundled up against the cold in the old democrat wagon with the horses stepping along briskly. With the warmth and the rhythm, Arne had become drowsy and had fallen out from his perch at the back. The family soon gathered him safely up again but he suffered a rude awakening and endless jokes.

The family's Democrat. Arne's mother sits at the front, his uncle Milton and cousin Mark from Ontario in the back (dressed in city clothes). His father took the photo.

Arne's mother told him that he had accepted Jesus when he was three years old and he can't remember a time when he didn't trust in God. Will and Clara made sure that each of their children knew and loved the Lord—young lives were often cut short in those days. They had prayer and Bible reading every morning. It was too far to go to church more than a few times a year, five-and-a-half miles by horse and buggy, so every Sunday after dinner the children had to learn a verse from the Bible. Each one had a scribbler full of verses and they were not allowed to leave the table until they had learned their verse for that week.

"You know, son," Will said to Arne one day. "When I was your age there was a funny paper and in the funny paper there was a Doc Sawbones. And he was always into trouble. So I'm going to call you 'Doc.'" And that was what Arne's family called him from then on. To this day, Arne's relatives call him Doc because their parents before them called him nothing but Doc. He continued to get into mischief and earn many lickings. "Does you good," said his father. "Keeps your hide loose so you can grow good."

Doc and Melba

Arne's younger sister, Melba, died suddenly at the age of eight of a ruptured appendix. It must have been a shocking loss to him. So he grew up with three older sisters who tried their best to keep him out of mischief. His sisters all learned to play the piano. Arne tried to learn the violin but it "didn't sound right." His favourite childhood pastime was to use his binder-twine snare to catch gophers, which were so numerous they had become a pest. If he forgot his snare, he'd unlace his shoes and make one, because he could get half a cent for every gopher tail.

The boys of Hillview School 1924-5
Arne is 4th from right, his friend Jack McCully 2nd from right

Arne and the girls before him all attended Hillview School, covering the two-and-a-half miles there by buggy, saddle horse or walking. As there were only two in his grade, Arne was always either first or last. Often there were not enough children for organized games at noon or recess, so they would go after gophers or, in winter, use rocks from the field to curl on a little slough in the corner of the school yard. Arne, his friend Jack McCully and the other boys all claimed they had the fastest horse and often raced for bragging rights.

Doc and Buck, giving a ride to his nieces and nephew from Oliver

King & Chief, Esther & Elida, Grit & Torey, Nell & Kate, ready for work

Arne's life was full of horses. In the old family photo album, there are more pictures of horses than people, and even now Arne remembers most of their names. From the age of ten, he rode everywhere on Buck, his own saddle horse. The family usually had thirty or forty horses on the land at one time— fifteen or so work horses, plus brood mares raising colts, as well as colts that Will had bought to raise because he had more pasture than most farmers who couldn't pasture more than the six or eight horse teams that they worked. Arne and Edna trained a lot of the colts, which were not too difficult to handle. They made friends with them by feeding them and sometimes giving them sugar, then took them to show at the Agricultural Fair where prizes were given for the best trained colts and calves.

Arne had no way of knowing that this was the beginning of the long drought that would lead to the dustbowl years and tough times for Prairie farmers.

In 1933, Arne, Jack McCully and a couple of others started high school in Delia. Jack remembers "the loose window in the back of Shorty McPherson's boarded-up pool hall; and our first taste of curling in the rink (no lights) while our elders were all attending the annual curlers' banquet and dance uptown." Arne was among the boys who used to sneak out behind the school and smoke "anything that would light."

"Look, Doc," said Will one day, as they were taking a sleigh-load of grain to town with a matched sorrel team. "If you don't smoke until you're twenty-one, I'll give you this team."

"Okay," said Arne, hiding his red face. At fourteen, he thought his dad didn't know about the smoking. He determined never to smoke again and later became the proud owner of the team.

His parents managed to steer him through his youth with a wily mixture of discipline, rewards and lots of prayer.

Arne didn't like high school. When he finished grade nine, his father said, "Well, Doc, you can quit school and work on the farm—I need you to work on the farm. But if you stay at school you've got to cut the mustard."

Arne driving a double disk tiller

Arne didn't think he'd make good grades so he said, "Oh no, I'll work on the farm here, Dad." He quit school to continue working with his father on the farm. Strong and bright, he partnered well with his father. He enjoyed driving the horses in teams of six or eight, pulling the plough, drill or disk tiller. He also learned valuable business lessons.

By the time Arne quit school in 1933, the "Dirty '30s" had begun to affect the prairies. Soon drought conditions struck the Bryans' community. The soil became so dry it turned to dust and the wind whipped up blinding dust storms, turning day to night. Some days it was so dark at noontime that Arne had to light a kerosene lamp indoors.

A Prairie Dust Storm by Arne Bryan

At first you see a haze in sight
   and then the wind springs up in height,
A storm cloud it might easily be
   but coming closer you can see
A dust cloud, with its arms outflung,
   and on its breast a sword is hung;
Its cold keen edge it makes you feel,
   the sand it drives like sharpened steel.
The wind it really has no bounds,
   its might it ever onward hounds.
It seems to hold within its clasp
   an irony no man can grasp.
A winding, grinding, blinding mass,
   with outstretched fingers makes its pass,
And as it goes it picks the dust
   from off the fields with glutinous lust.
Like a maddened dog without a leash,
   its might and strength seem to increase.
The sun it dims with ghastly cloak,
   all else it holds and tries to choke.
Until at last its crest is reached.
   Then, like a waterlogged canoe that's
   beached,
It's held – and there it angrily awaits
   until, with a few gusty blasts, the storm
   abates.

Arne Bryan

Written by Arne during the dustbowl years

During these years, which coincided with the Great Depression, the farmers had diminished crops and diminished markets for what little they could produce. But W.J.'s horse-training business saw them through several years. Arne would help him train horses through the winter. Then W.J. would pair them into teams and ship up to twenty-two at a time, by freight car out of Delia to Hamilton, Ontario. The trip would take four or five days, because every twelve hours or so they would unhitch the freight car at a station where they had stockyards. W.J. would unload the horses overnight and buy hay so he could feed and water them. After cleaning out the box car, the horses would be loaded in again to be picked up by the next train. When they got to the Hamilton stockyards, the horses were auctioned off in teams and brought in some much needed cash during the hard times.

Horses were always more valuable in teams. W.J. knew just about every horse for miles around. If he saw a single horse, whether bay, grey or black, he'd offer to buy it at a reduced price, because that farmer would have no use for an odd horse but W.J. would know that someone else would have a match for it. So he and Arne would ride over and buy that one to make a matched team. Although tractors were beginning to replace horse power, there was still need for teams of horses. People always needed saddle horses as well—there was no other transportation for most. Arne and his father would get hold of unbroken horses and break them for sale, along with many of their own colts.

Arne driving family members in the Democrat

Arne and Buck hunting rabbits

Arne, Jake and a four-seat horse-drawn sled called a cutter

Arne would also shoot jackrabbits in the winter and sell them to feed the foxes that people raised. Then there was the meat ring. Every week someone would donate a steer to kill and Arne's father was the one who did the butchering. He cut up the meat so that everyone got a portion of fresh beef each week, which they would keep down in their cellars to make it last as long as possible. W.J. was also good at smoking meat. They raised their own hogs; W.J. would smoke hams and bacon, wrap them in newspaper and bury them in the oat bin where they would last all summer. Sauerkraut was one of the main dishes during the wintertime. The Bryans had a big garden. During the hard times there wasn't really enough rain for it to thrive but there was always something. In fall they cut up cabbages and made a keg of sauerkraut, which they always enjoyed.

Arne had recruited another member for his team. "Okay, Jake," he would call and the German shepherd he had trained, would jump up behind him, tuck his back paws into the rosette straps on the rear of Buck's saddle and lean against Arne as he rode.

Arne and Buck

Arne was very fond of this yellow shirt and cravat

Arne visiting relatives in Ontario, wearing his yellow silk shirt, a flesh-coloured silk vest and a multi-coloured silk tie

Arne and couple of city cousins, one of them trying out his cowboy hat

"He had a voice that made the pilot lights on your radio jump," one listener said later about William "Bible Bill" Aberhart. These were tough times but, like many other struggling families, the Bryans gathered round Doc's crystal set on Sunday afternoons and drew encouragement from Aberhart's sermons from the Bible Institute Baptist Church in Calgary. He preached the gospel of salvation, Bible prophecy and political economics, in a voice that made some people feel they just had to believe him because he seemed "to be in direct contact with the Supreme Being."

"You remain in the Depression because of a shortage of purchasing power imposed by the banking system," Aberhart told his followers. "Social Credit offers you the remedy. If you have not suffered enough, it is your God-given right to suffer more. But if you wish to elect your own representatives to implement the remedy, this is your only way out."

From 1932, Aberhart's preaching had been combined with the economic theories of British engineer Major C.H. Douglas who held that governments should distribute money to increase spending and stimulate the economy. When the evangelist failed to persuade political parties in Alberta to adopt this policy, the Social Credit Party was formed and Aberhart became Alberta's premier in September 1935. Now he could put into practice the premise that all citizens would have the right to the wealth they jointly produced.

But politics couldn't save the Bryan family farm. Four years of totally dried-out crops were followed by a crop devastated by hail. The hail was so heavy that it broke down the grain that was almost ready to cut until there were only a couple of inches of straw on the whole field—a heartbreaking disaster. It was 1939 and it was time to move on and take advantage of the good deals that the government was offering on some irrigated land eighty miles south at Rosemary, near the Bassano Dam on the Bow River.

The Bassano Dam, completed in 1914, raised the water level fourteen metres, allowing water to be diverted into an irrigation system for many acres of land in the area around and towards Brooks. In 1935 a group of farmers acquired the dam and canals from the CPR and formed the Eastern

Irrigation District. W.J. and Arne bought a quarter (160 acres) each, which they could work together.

They were starting out again on rough, empty land. As part of the deal, they were allowed to take off the land in Delia any building that was not on concrete foundations. So, while they had to leave the house, the granaries built on skids would become valuable building materials.

There were seven of the 12' x 14' granaries standing on two big skids made of 8" x 8" solid timbers. These had been used to store the grain from the threshing machine in the fields. A team of four horses could drag the granary close to the threshing machine and the grain would flow out of its pipe and fill up the granary through a high opening. The farmers had limits on how much grain they were allowed to sell at a time, so the remainder could wait in the granary in the field until it was time to shovel another load onto a wagon for sale.

W.J. and Arne worked hard to demolish and transport these granaries. They took each one apart with crowbars until there were two sides of roof for each granary (complete with shingles), two side walls, two ends with the doors in them, plus the heavy base cut into pieces.

They did the same with the big granary. It had three ten-foot bins down each side and a driveway through the middle that was big enough for a team and wagon. It was built on skids, though it was not a mobile granary, so they could demolish it and take it with them. They had to use a heavy crosscut saw to cut the roof into sections.

They piled the pieces on a hay rack. Normally the hay rack had sides built up high so that they could pile the stooks of grain on it to feed the thrashing machine, but without the sides, it made a perfect flat bed. Neighbours came to help load it and take each load two-and-a-half miles to the closest railway siding. There the pieces could be piled up to eight feet high on top of the flat cars. There was no crane to help with the loading. So they arranged planks and used rollers from a binder to roll each piece up onto the railway car. Then they were all tied down tight for the eighty-mile journey.

When they arrived on their new land, W.J. and Arne had to pick a high spot and work out how to build a barn for the horses and milk cows, using the wood from the granaries. They used the bigger sections to build a house.

All their other equipment and household goods traveled by wagons, while Arne and his friend Jack McCully rode on saddle horses driving the cattle. Jack's mother drove Clara by car and then drove Jack home after he had arrived with the cattle.

And so they left all their good friends and neighbours and the farm where they had homesteaded since 1906. Their hearts were filled, not with complaints, but with gratitude for the new start they had been allowed.

(Note: The old farm in Delia now has three oil wells and a gathering station on it. Some farmers benefitted from the oil but most settlers were not told that they should claim the oil rights at the same time as the land rights.)

CHAPTER 2

1939 — 1946:
FROM THE LAND TO THE SEA

The Bryan family had retreated and regrouped after their battle for survival through the Dust Bowl years, but the whole world was about to be engulfed in a real war. The Canadian government declared war on September 10, 1939, and Arne, aged twenty-one, was the first in his district to be called up. He went to Red Deer, Alberta for a thirty-day training period. However, because he was a farmer, he was sent back home to continue farming. Food production was essential work.

Arne during army training in 1939, aged 21

Their new land in the Eastern Irrigation District at Rosemary didn't look like much, and was basically desert and very meagre pasture, but irrigation enabled W.J. and Arne to cultivate about two hundred of their 320 acres. The water flowed from the dam in ditches controlled by gates. Each farmer had to cut ditches on his own land, piling the earth up on either side. W.J. looked over his land and dug his first ditch along a high ridge so the water would run down from that into other ditches. He broke through the dirt at intervals so that the water flowed out over the land. Arne prepared the earth with a six-foot disk tiller and eight horses. When they saw the alfalfa grow an inch or two a day, this new farm seemed like a miracle (except for the mosquitoes).

W.J. and Arne were used to vast pasture land so they were glad to make use of the ten thousand acres of open range where the community put their cattle to graze all summer. Each farmer had maybe twenty or thirty head grazing there, all branded so the farmers could pick out their own in the fall. The arrangement was that the farmers would go out in turn to make sure everything was going well so every ten days or so, Arne and his horse Buck would take a day to ride out on the range looking out for their cattle and checking up on everything.

At six feet, complete with cowboy hat, leather jacket and boots, Arne must have cut a striking figure, his kerchief fluttering as he rode over the almost treeless acres, free as his own wild pony, with his dog Jake cheerfully perched behind him.

The cattle looked after themselves all summer. All Arne, Buck and Jake had to do was herd them up so that Arne's father could butcher and sell them. On that skimpy grass, ten acres had to be allowed per animal for grazing, but that gave plenty of grass for extra horses as well, which were all branded like the cattle. They could just let them loose on that ten-thousand acre field.

During their first year at Rosemary, the Bryans benefitted from Social Credit "funny money": twenty-five dollar prosperity certificates given monthly by the Alberta government to everyone over eighteen. These were dated and had to be spent within thirty days, after which they were worthless. Some said they were already worthless and refused to accept them in their stores in case the government wouldn't pay for them. But there were plenty of places that were happy to have customers with money to spend.

When Aberhart's new Social Credit Party won the 1935 election, they had discovered that they didn't have enough money for that month's government payroll. In order to fulfill their promises and pay 400,000 Albertans twenty-five dollars each in social credit, they basically printed their own money.

"The spirit of Christ has gripped me," Aberhart responded, when accused of being dictatorial. "I am only seeking to feed, clothe and shelter starving people. If that is what you call a dictator then I am one."

This bit of extra income lasted only about a year but Arne was now firmly committed to the ideals of the Social Credit Party.

Arne's three sisters were all married by now and living on fruit ranches in Oliver in the Okanagan, but there was a close neighbour, Eldon, who was just two years older than Arne. He was a Mormon and he had a car. (This neighbouring family also had a John Deere tractor and didn't use horses at all.) Arne and Eldon became good friends and went places together.

A young Christian man like Arne who wanted company would usually look for a church to attend but Rosemary was a Mormon and Mennonite community, and the Mennonites spoke German at their church. Arne went sometimes with Eldon to the Mormon church, to their entertainment events like films and dances. Now a tall, handsome, twenty-one-year-old rancher, Arne enjoyed going to dances and was very popular among the pretty Mormon girls. They gave him the "Book of Mormon," "The Pearl of Great Price" and "Doctrine and Covenants".

"Oh, Arne," they would say. "You'd make a good Mormon—you don't drink tea or coffee." (Arne hadn't even tasted coffee till he was twenty-one.)

He went occasionally to their services but there was no danger of him becoming a Mormon after a childhood immersed in the Scriptures on the family farm. In fact, Eldon eventually became a Christian and in time Eldon's son became a Pentecostal minister in Vermilion, Alberta.

Arne preferred the United Church at Duchess, the next town about fourteen miles away. Occasionally he would drive a team of horses and the old democrat wagon to take his mother and father to special events but mostly it was just Arne and his horse Buck.

Gaye (right) & her twin sister Phee

Duchess seemed no distance at all once a certain beautiful young lady at the United Church caught his eye towards the end of 1939. Her name was Gaye. Her parents owned Gordon's

Dry Goods and Grocery store in Duchess, and Gaye and her two sisters worked there. Arne would ride to see her on the weekends. Arne and Gaye, along with Gaye's sisters, Phee (Phyllis) and Peg (Margaret) and other young people, enjoyed good times together.

Somebody had written in Arne's childhood autograph book when he was thirteen:

There you stand today, a pretty little figure.
If the girls don't like you now,
they will when you get bigger.

Those comic lines had now come true and Arne was a handsome addition to the company. He could also put rhymes together himself. This poem he wrote catches the lightness of the time and his feelings toward Gaye:

Arne & Gaye

AN ODE TO THE BELLE OF DUCHESS

With ruby lips this handsome lasse
Has enchanting smile and appeal en masse.
Vivacious, stunning, she's got classe,
As refreshing sweet as demi tasse.

Her name is Grayce but Gaye will do,
With twinkling eyes of exotic hue,
Like shadowed light on crystal blue.

Do the light fantastic dance or sing,
From rhumba, schottise, to highland fling.
With charm and laughter, she keeps in swing,
Slight and light as bird on wing.

From tip to toe she's delightful I know,
'Bout first degree for a Hollywood show.
No wonder men's heart like motors go,
First pitter patter, then to and fro.

The old saying goes both looks and brains
Don't go together, but truth sustains.
This gal's got both and plenty remains,
Sportsmanship, dignity, tact she retains.

But listen. I'll tell you something more,
You gents that happen to call at her door.
She's two handsome sisters, that's my idee,
Three Belles of Duchess, Gaye, Peg and Phee.

"I'm going over to Duchess," Arne said one Sunday.
"You're crazy," his dad warned. "It's about thirty-five below."
But Arne didn't have anything else to do and the attractions
of Duchess were calling him so he saddled up. He allowed

Buck to walk or just lope along gently, because that sort of cold can get in a horse's lungs. It took a good two hours to get to Duchess. He was able to leave Buck in a friend's barn on the edge of town, while he was there. By the time evening came, it was at least forty below and Arne set off for another long slow ride toward home. Occasionally he would get off and walk, leading Buck along. He was dressed for the cold and the exercise warmed him a little but he was concerned about his horse's breathing. In the end, they made it home safely. Nothing could stop Arne when he'd made up his mind.

Arne loved to pose with his Model A Ford

In 1940, he paid about two hundred dollars for a Model A Ford and could then speed over to Duchess at thirty miles an hour. Once, he fell asleep at the wheel while driving home and woke up driving along the bottom of the big ditch that ran beside the road. He came to a halt just before a stream. There was no way he could get the car back up the steep bank, so he had to walk home and ask Eldon to come with his car to pull him out. Neither Arne nor his car was hurt.

He wrote a long and tender ode, dreaming of an idyllic marriage to his beautiful Gaye:

Arne & Gaye

I'd want to be beside her
through day and darkest night
To ever guard and keep her
that nothing ere might blight
The love we'd share together
through every wrong and right.
Where I could see her loveliness
and hold her soft warm hand
And hear her sparkling laughter,
like ripples on the diamond sand.

I'd tell her how I loved her and,
with cheek upon her hair,
I'd pray to God in heaven,
that his blessings we might share.

And so as months and years roll by,
and life had meted out its climb,
I'd want the thought forever with me
that we could love each other till the end of time.

By 1942, even farmers were needed in the war effort and Arne wanted to be involved. After the crop was harvested, the folks at the Mormon church threw him a big farewell party and the Bryan family sold their land in Rosemary. A whole way of life, the backdrop to Arne's formative years, was over. New adventures called. Will and Clara moved to Oliver, near their three daughters, where they ran a store and cabins, and Arne was first sent to Edmonton to help build the North West Staging Hangars, which is now an airport in the middle of the city.

On March 11, 1943, Arne and Gaye were married, just before he joined the navy. The wedding was in Banff, Alberta, where they had their honeymoon. Then he reported to the navy in Edmonton.

Arne the sailor

Nellie's Good-Bye Poem to Doc

They say that Arnold's going away
And won't be back for many a day.
So while he's here, we'll only say
Hi! Arnold.

Yes it's true. He's joined the navy
To fight for victory stead of slavery.
I'm sure he'll show a lot of bravery,
Our Arnold.

He'll say good-bye to Mom and Dad
And remember the times when he was bad
And Pop would lick him with a gad.
Poor Arnold.

To Gaye he'll say "Wait till I come back
And don't go marrying some other Jack."
Then give her a good big smack.
Dear Arnold.

He'll say good-bye to each horse and cow
And give a loving pat to the plow
And shed a tear on each old sow,
Sad Arnold.

He'll walk through the house that he helped make.
His mother will make his favourite cake.
Dad will say "Be careful for goodness sake."
My Arnold.

So now I'll only say adieu
And pray God's blessings not a few
Will be with you till you come through.
Bye, Arnold

*Extracts from a good-bye poem written by Nellie
(sister of Arne's good friend Eldon)*

Arne wanted to get into the navy medical branch. His uncle was a doctor in Fort William, Port Arthur on Lake Superior and he used to enjoy hearing how his uncle had to go out with a dog team to visit his patients. However, there was no opening in the medical branch. They suggested Arne sign up as a stoker and then, as soon as there was an opening, he could be transferred to the medical branch. Arne reluctantly agreed but, before he signed, he insisted that they put this promise in writing: "Mr. Bryan gets the first chance on the medical branch that comes up after this date."

He spent two months of basic training in Edmonton, where he enjoyed sleeping in a hammock. It was a good experience until he was talked into playing on the baseball team. He usually avoided sports because his knees would easily slip out of joint, but the team was a man short. Sure enough his knee went out during practice.

That resulted in two weeks of treatment in the navy hospital in Kingston, Ontario. Gaye was able to come to Kingston too. There were plenty of jobs because all the men were away for the war so Gaye started working in the jewellery department of Eaton's.

During his stay there, the medical staff discovered that Arne had AB blood type which had the kind of antigens they needed to keep one of their patients alive. Arne was able to donate blood and save the patient's life.

After his time in the hospital, Arne and others who were recovering from accidents were sent as ambassadors from the navy to a sea cadets' camp in the Thousand Islands in the St. Lawrence River, a beautiful spot in the early summer. They were smartly dressed in their navy uniforms and so the young cadets looked to them for advice about sailing. Arne, the prairie boy, was no sailing expert but he wasn't going to disappoint them. "Oh, you guys are doing great," he said. Instead of teaching them how to sail, he learned it from them.

When he was fit enough, he was sent to Nova Scotia to continue his training as a stoker at HMCS Cornwallis, the largest naval training base in the British Commonwealth. While there, his valuable blood was commandeered regularly to save the life of one person or another.

During Arne's time in Nova Scotia, Gaye transferred to the Eaton's in Halifax, working in the jewellery department where she made some good extra income as a commissioned salesperson. Navy, army and airmen came to her to buy jewellery to take overseas. Some would buy a dozen watches each: clearly they enjoyed buying from this beautiful young lady but they also knew they could sell them in Europe for twice what they paid, because so little was available there. Arne and Gaye lived off base and as a service family were given items free in many stores.

Just as Arne completed his training, there was a call for volunteers to train as commandos, who were much in need at that time. Arne signed up and stayed at Cornwallis for the training. He found some parts of training very hard but what he relished was the absolute, immediate obedience given to all orders and the trust placed in those giving the orders. The experience shaped him. Even today, in his nineties, he is a commando at heart.

However, before long there was an opening for him in the medical branch: his negotiations had borne fruit. He was able to stay in Cornwallis for medical training and was expected to go overseas at any time.

Arne (back row far right) with his graduating class in the Navy Medical Corp

The Royal Canadian Navy was becoming a major force. By the end of the war it would be the fourth largest navy in the world. The Battle of the Atlantic had begun on day one of the war, with the Canadian Navy transporting troops and escorting convoys of merchant ships carrying essential supplies to Europe. They fought off constant attacks from German U-boats and aircraft from Norway while battling the mountainous seas of North Atlantic winters. Canadian ships were also involved in the sea-borne invasions of North Africa, Mediterranean countries and Normandy, France.

Three times Arne was scheduled to ship out, and three times he was left on the wharf in Halifax because the needs had changed. He was put on the medical staff at the base, in charge of the ambulance.

Arne used his time wisely. He realized he wasn't as smart as he had thought he was when he was in grade nine. So he completed several high school courses by correspondence through the Canadian Legion.

As a committed Christian, bold and big-hearted like the outspoken disciple Simon Peter, Arne had a great time in the navy, sharing his faith with all these young men he would otherwise never have met. He became pretty good at cutting hair, only charging twenty-five cents, and he used the five minutes while his client was captive in the chair to talk about the Lord. A lot of fellows accepted the Lord while he was cutting their hair. It was not really hard to talk about God because they must have been all wondering what was coming and even whether they would survive. They had no information about the twenty-seven U-boats that had been sunk or the forty-two enemy surface vessels sunk or captured, nor about the twenty-four ships and 1,797 sailors that the Canadian Navy lost in the North Atlantic. But they all knew they were living through serious and terrible years.

Arne attended church services run by the navy chaplaincy but didn't find them very inspiring. He enjoyed a helpful friendship with a Lutheran pastor but was astounded to learn that his friend had not been required to read the Acts of the Apostles to pass his exams. That part of the Bible had been eliminated from their course because the church felt Acts only spoke to the early church.

Arne still wonders how any Christian could ignore the book of Acts and the secret to the apostles' power: "When you look back and see that the apostles, after three years of personal mentoring with Jesus, when the police came to get Him, they all **forsook** Him and fled. That is the greatest sign of lack of **power** in the spiritual level when the twelve apostles departed and fled when they came to get Jesus. They knew who He was and everything but they had not been filled with Holy Ghost **power**. I think it was a great demonstration of how we're helpless until the Holy **Spirit** comes and dwells within us."

This is Arne's distinctive way of speaking—key words suddenly jumping out, high and loud, full of power and meaning, all softened by his disarming smile.

The war was over in 1945 but it was the following year before Arne was discharged. He was one of the last two people to leave the base at Cornwallis after it was closed. The navy hospital had been turned into a tuberculosis (TB) hospital and Arne and his buddy had to move the TB patients in, using the navy ambulance.

In July 1946 he was sent west to HMCS Naden, near Victoria, to receive his discharge. Then he and Gaye began their new life in the Vancouver area.

CHAPTER 3

1946 — 1965:
BUILDING LIFE IN B.C.

Arne, 1946

Gaye, Cam & Jake

By July 1946 when Arne got his discharge from the navy at age twenty-eight, Gaye's parents had sold their store in Duchess, Alberta, and had moved to British Columbia, where they bought another store, on 6th Street near 16th Avenue, on the Burnaby side of the border with New Westminster. As they were using only the ground floor of a two-storey building, they offered the unfinished upstairs to Arne and Gaye. Arne took that empty space and made it into a living room and a bedroom, with a bed that folded up against the wall in the daytime to give more room.

In 1946 their son Cameron was born. Cam's first few years were spent over the store on 6th Street.

As a newly discharged war vet, Arne had to make a big choice: should he take his navy credits in the form of land, business subsidies, or education? He chose to pursue a degree course at the University of British Columbia (UBC). A grade nine education had been just fine on the farm—Arne had all the smarts to be a successful farmer—but now he knew he needed more. First he took a veterans' course at Jericho Beach in Vancouver, through which he completed his remaining high school courses in just eight months. That qualified him for UBC. His parents wanted him to get some theology training and maybe become a preacher but Arne wasn't convinced about the preaching part and wanted something broader. He enrolled at Union College, then recently established at UBC, where he could take arts and theology together in one place.

Arne & a classmate during the veterans' course in Vancouver

For the next three years he thumbed his way to UBC, more than fifteen miles away and usually requiring several rides, but he was never late for a class. At that time, everyone was friendly towards hitchhikers, wanting to help the young men who had recently been soldiers or sailors. One day a Cadillac stopped for him.

"Nice car," said Arne as he climbed inside.

"Well, I'm the Premier of British Columbia," said the driver. Byron Johnson, nicknamed Boss Johnson, from his Icelandic childhood name "Bjosse," had been elected to represent New Westminster in 1945 and was the twenty-third Premier of British Columbia between December 1947 and August 1952.

There followed an interesting discussion in the car because Arne thought the B.C. government was poorly managed and doing ungodly things. He had joined the small organization known as Social Credit for B.C. and was on their first committee, famed for being the only person who had actually lived under Social Credit. It seemed to the committee that Social Credit had worked immensely well in Alberta, which was prosperous after oil had been found in High River.

In spite of their political differences, Boss Johnson was kind enough to drive Arne all the way to UBC.

Arne still has the journal he kept in 1949, during which time he completed his second year at UBC and began his third. Classes and studying were a priority, but so was church at a United Church where he taught Sunday School and later a Bible Class and occasionally took church services. He seemed to be applying to be accepted as a minister. It was very snowy that winter and he made Cam a sleigh. In the summer he spent three months at Cape Mudge on Quadra Island, building a mission home and church. Gaye and Cam were able to enjoy the summer there too.

Aged thirty, Arne had already been a Christian for many years but his longing to serve Christ with commando obedience had not faded. In his journal, he wrote prayers and aspirations that showed his heart:

Saturday January 1: Lord give me strength, understanding and zeal to speak thy message to someone every day.
Tuesday January 4: When we think we face insur-mountable tasks and seeming sacrifices let us visual-ize how paltry they are beside Christ's sufferings.

Thursday January 6: If our desire and interest is deep enough along the path of Faith in Christ, we can loose His unlimited power within us.

Saturday January 22: Dear Lord give Gaye special strength and understanding that Your work comes first. There is no other way.

Wednesday February 2: There is no time to rest and meditate. The world is ruinously close to facing a Christless era. We must be at the work.

Monday February 21: Materially my future very uncertain – spiritual firm.

Thursday March 10: When things seem hard, think of those who are praying for you. It's a wonderful encouragement.

Wednesday March 30: The work seems limitless but so is the power.

Tuesday April 12: Dear Lord when I attempt something for Thee and my fellow man, may I put all I have into it, sparing nothing.

Monday April 18: I only ask and pray that I may know God's wish.

Saturday April 23: Always look ahead and up, faithfully believing that Christ will direct in every circumstance.

Saturday October 15: God's need is urgent for us all, never falter.

To earn money while at UBC, especially during the summers, Arne and Gaye operated a sales business based in their home, like many other people at the time. They invited people to dinner, where they would demonstrate a range of stainless steel cookware and sell the cookware direct from the manufacturer. They were good at it and encouraged others to sign up too. Arne's career would often feature some sort of sales enterprise, not unlike his father's horse business.

One day one of the UBC lecturers asked the twenty-eight students in front of him, "If any of you believe in healing, please stay afterwards and pray for me, because I've just been told I have cancer." Arne was dismayed that he was the only student who stayed to pray.

After three years at UBC, Arne discovered that two of his other lecturers who were theology professors didn't even believe the Bible. They had just found a good job after the war. He talked to the Lord about it and heard Him say, "I didn't send you there anyway." So Arne quit.

His years of study had given him a stimulating education and the resourceful rancher was well able to support his family with or without a degree.

There was plenty of work to be had in big post-war construction projects. In the fall of 1950, Arne began three-and-a-half years making history in one of those heroic Canadian sagas of engineers conquering geography. During the Korean War it became critical to have a reliable supply of fuel oil. The planning and construction of the Trans-Mountain Pipeline began in order to bring much needed fuel from Edmonton all the way to Vancouver and eventually to the Seattle area, a distance of twelve hundred kilometres, including through the massive Rockies (eleven hundred metres at the highest), and then through the steep and rugged mountains of central British Columbia, crossing scores of streams and rivers on the way.

Arne signed on as a chain-man with a survey crew, measuring the line where the pipe would go with chains a hundred feet long. They began at Three Sisters, just east of Jasper on the B.C.-Alberta border. After a few months, the engineer supervising his survey crew discovered that Arne had learned how to operate a transit during a geology course at UBC and clearly knew what he was doing. So he recommended that Arne take his place to run the crew. That released the engineer to move to head office where his mathematical skills were more useful.

Arne was provided with aerial photographs showing the planned line, but down in the forest it was up to him to survey the detailed lay of the land with the transit and to leave marks on the trees to guide the teams that would follow. As well as two chain-men, there were others on his crew who cut branches off trees and cleared a way through the bush. If their way was blocked by a ravine that was invisible from the air, he had to decide where the line should cross it and then get back to the planned route. He was the pathfinder.

They were followed later by the big machinery that clear-cut thirty feet on either side of his marks. On one stretch near Little Fort, the cutting team had difficulty finding the marks because Arne's crew, fitted out with snow shoes, had worked that stretch on top of four or five feet of snow. By the time the clear-cutters came, the snow had melted leaving the marks way above eye level.

The work meant that Arne was away from Gaye and Cam for twenty-one days at a time, then would be home for four or five days before returning to the wilderness. When they were working in Hope, Gaye and Cam were able to stay with him in a little cabin at Kawkawa Lake.

After a year and a half, when the survey was done, Arne was hired by Canadian Bechtel, the chief contractor for the whole pipeline, as an inspector of river crossings. There were many—in the Coquihala Canyon alone there were twenty-two river crossings in thirty-five miles—so this meant more challenges and adventure for Arne. His job was to take frequent measurements and to confirm they had dug far enough down under the riverbed for the two-foot pipe and a foot of gravel on top as protection. Where there was no access by road, the construction workers used hand cars along the railway and then walked down into the valley but Arne enjoyed commuting between these worksites by helicopter.

One tough spot impressed even the Texans on the crew who had worked all over the world. They had to negotiate a steep bank down to the river; there was no way round it. In order to lower the digging machine safely down they used two other big machines all hooked together with cables. The following description of the project is taken from the Bechtel website: "Construction crews ran into formidable natural barriers: rock-walled canyons, cascading rivers, and slide-prone cliffs.... The first delivery of Alberta crude was made in Vancouver in the fall of 1953." (bechtel.com)

After the pipeline was finished, Arne and a survey crew had to go back and put benchmarks every thousand feet or so along the cleared path of the pipeline, giving the actual level of the pipe, fastening the benchmarks to stumps, trees, rocks or on pegs they drove into the ground. "We walked a long ways," says Arne. "We walked a lot of the miles from Jasper to Vancouver."

*Arne, Will & Cam
- three generations*

*The three generations of
Bryans a little older*

Arne & Cam (aged about 8) in 1954 or 55

After those years of dramatic construction work, Arne returned to more mundane construction, first for other contractors then as a contractor himself because he was good with blueprints. This expanded his business experience.

Arne then turned to financing new construction with the Central Mortgage and Housing Corporation (CMHC). This was a government agency that was set up after the war to lend money for construction. For three-and-a-half years, Arne worked with CMHC as an appraiser, and also became an inspector of housing projects. One project he had to inspect every couple of weeks was a group of several dozen houses being built in Tahsis, then a lumber town on the west coast of Vancouver Island. Tahsis could only be reached by boat or seaplane. On one very rough trip, Arne wished he wasn't so tall as he hit his head on the roof of the little plane every time it dropped into an air pocket.

He was clearly successful in the mortgage industry because he was asked to move to Wolstencroft Agencies, a big real estate organization, as a mortgage manager. The company started several key building subdivisions in Surrey, and Arne arranged mortgages for the contractors. He also became a purchaser during his time working there, buying land on behalf of the company to sell to contractors.

As part of his work with the real estate agency, Arne took an insurance course so that he could make sure that all the houses were insured. That insurance training and experience seems to have been the final piece of the puzzle. After ten or more years in construction and associated industries, it was time for Arne to launch his own venture. In about 1959 he left Wolstencroft and set up his own insurance agency.

"Lord, what would be a good name for this insurance business?" he prayed. The Lord gave him the name: Faith Insurance Agency. So Faith Insurance Agency became his business and ministry for the next nineteen years. He opened up an office in Burnaby on 6th Street at 16th Avenue, about three blocks from where he and Gaye had originally lived. Later he moved his office to Main Street and Broadway. Eventually he had an office downtown through a Christian friend named Don Low, who had rented some offices there for his business and who invited Arne to use one of them and take care of all his insurance.

From the start, Faith Insurance Agency was Arne's mission field. "How did you get that name, Arne?" clients would ask, exactly as Arne hoped they would. He was happy to spend more time talking about the Lord than about insurance.

Arne and his family had been living in Coquitlam for a few years, in a place on King Albert Avenue, and they were attending Blue Mountain Baptist Church nearby, when one Sunday Arne responded to a call for those who wanted to dedicate their lives to the Lord. He went forward to make a public demonstration of the commitment that had been there all his life. He made several such commitments during that period. It solidified his faith, and gave him touchstones he could look back to if doubts attacked.

In 1960, Cam was coming to the end of grade eight at the school down the road and there was a decision to be made—just as there had been for Arne at about the same age. Would

Cam go on to the high school across the street, something he wasn't looking forward to? Or would he take up an offer from his Aunt Phee, Gaye's sister?

Phee and her husband had a furniture store and a grocery store in Trochu, Alberta, and they needed help. "We'd love Cam to come over here and help us at the store," they wrote. "He can go to school here and it would be good for him." So Cam had his own Alberta experience, living with his aunt and uncle for three years and doing his high school years at Three Hills.

Around this time, Arne bought a property and built a house on Porter Street, off Como Lake Avenue in Coquitlam. It was a beautiful brick house, with three bedrooms and a full basement. "It's still a lovely looking house," says Arne, "because it's **brick**. It just looks like a new house yet."

Arne moved on in his Christian life, beginning to worship at the Evangelical Free Church in Burnaby on Rumble Street, although Gaye did not join him there. He was involved in the construction of their new church building. He was soon noticed as a "go-getter," zealously inviting everyone to pray about serving the Lord with this or that, whether a new prayer group or a particular church program. He became a board member of the Evangelical Free Church for B.C., traveling to visit churches around the province. He also arranged insurance for several churches.

Because of his experience in the mortgage industry, Arne was a valuable member of the committee that pioneered Trinity Western University (called Trinity Junior College when it first opened in 1962). The Evangelical Free Churches of America had appointed a committee to establish a liberal arts college in the Fraser Valley. The ten board members each guaranteed five thousand dollars to the bank in order to purchase the ninety-acre Seal Kap dairy farm in Langley. The first year there were seventeen students and eleven staff, with a barn for sports and a house for the office.

Arne was asked to represent the board in keeping an eye on the construction of a large auditorium that was being built at the College. It was difficult to provide all the special elements that the various professors wanted in the building plans but Arne insisted on including a huge stage with all the room backstage necessary to put on plays. The Evangelical Free Church did not agree with this idea to begin with but Arne persisted. He had taken a year of drama at UBC and understood how effective drama could be in communicating the gospel.

A few years later, Arne's son, Cam, became a student at Trinity Western and met his wife, Sharon, there. She was from Stettler, Alberta, near where Arne's parents had home-steaded in 1906. Cam and Sharon first lived in Creston, B.C., where he was a millwright, then moved north to the Yukon, and later returned to Alberta. Cam and Arne look a lot alike but Cam is taller and broader. He has given Arne four grand-children.

Gaye did not follow Arne into a deeper Christian commitment and they began to grow apart. This wasn't how it was supposed to be. Arne felt as if someone was yanking on the lariat of the "W" hitch to bring his life down under him.

Arne had set Gaye up in her own store in New Westminster on 6th Street and 3rd Avenue, about ten blocks from his insurance agency. She was an expert seamstress so she sold knitting yarn and sewing supplies and gave classes to groups of women in a back room. Arne would come from his office and pick her up to take her home for dinner.

One day in 1964 or 1965, Arne came to the store as usual and was surprised when the bell on the door didn't ring. Gaye was not in the store, so he walked through into the back room and surprised her in the arms of another man. It was a moment of shock for all three of them. Arne turned round and walked out. His marriage was a wild pony that had just bucked him off—and it didn't feel like a soft landing.

Arne and Gaye had already been drifting apart but now Arne began to sleep downstairs. He wondered how a Christian man should negotiate this. He came home one day to discover that Gaye had changed the locks. Arne rented an apartment in a highrise on West Hastings, near the Vancouver downtown office where he had relocated his Faith Insurance Agency.

He kept asking the Lord what to do about his marriage and heard the Lord say, "Go to a lawyer and he will tell you what to do." He contacted a lawyer who recommended a private detective. Arne hired the detective to observe the house where Gaye was still living.

The report came back to Arne that the detective had gone to the house at about 7:30 one morning and had seen a car parked outside. His knock was answered by Gaye and the detective saw that there was a man having breakfast with her. The detective told them who he was and what he was doing. When it came to the divorce, Gaye had no reason to argue.

The late 1960s were full of turbulent change for Arne. His twenty-five-year marriage had failed but business and opportunities for ministry were flourishing. Then people started talking about something called the Baptism in the Holy Spirit. Arne knew that Christians needed power in their lives but he did not think that speaking in tongues was the answer.

CHAPTER 4

1966 — 1977:
GETTING READY FOR A NEW CALLING

Arne aged about 40

O ne day, Arne had to tell a Christian friend, "Well, Sam, I don't think you'll be able to get a mortgage on this land." Although Sam Doerksen had trained for the ministry, at this time he was working as an encyclopedia salesman. He and Arne had become friends through the regular meetings of the Christian Business Men's Connection. Sam wanted to buy forty acres in the Aldergrove area for sixteen thousand dollars. He didn't have the money but he knew it was a really good deal.

"You won't be able to get a mortgage because it doesn't suit a house situation and it's too small for a farm loan," explained Arne. "So you'll have to get **private** money...and I know somebody who may be interested."

That "somebody" was a successful and very wealthy entrepreneur Arne had dealt with during his days as Mortgage Manager with Wolstencroft Agencies. Arne would call this entrepreneur when a construction company was financially overstretched and in danger of going bankrupt. They would meet at a coffee shop at six in the morning and often the financier would put up blue chip security in court to cover whatever was owed, giving the builder six months or a year to complete his houses and to raise the money he needed. Arne, an experienced appraiser, would do a thorough inspection of the buildings for this financier—20 houses in Fort St John on foreclosure once, for instance—and also arranged the insurance.

After talking to Sam, Arne called an early coffee shop meeting and his millionaire friend agreed to lend the money to Sam at 18%. Sam was excited and bought the land, planning to pay it off in a couple of years.

Sam didn't know that he would be gone by the next year and Arne had no idea that his friendship with Sam would bring the most important person into his life.

Sam had health problems. After major stomach surgery many years before, he had developed peritonitis and had had a serious allergic reaction to the penicillin. Christians all over Vancouver had prayed for him. A friend with whom he used to go to all-night prayer meetings had said, "Sam, you are not going to die. You're going to live to give praise to the name of the Lord." And he had. Sam worked in the shoe department at Woodward's department store, got married and eventually had five children. When he was younger he had completed a four-year course at Briercrest College in Saskatchewan and, once he felt strong enough after his illness, he took a semester at an Alliance school in San Francisco in order to become a pastor—which was quite an undertaking for his wife and children. But, when the Alliance Church couldn't find a church in Vancouver for a new pastor with a large family, Sam had turned to selling encyclopedias and had been involved with Christian work wherever he could.

He had already had more surgery to deal with scar tissue from the earlier operation but a little bit was left and was beginning to cause more problems.

One day Sam came in to see Arne. "I'm going to have to go to hospital to get an operation, Arne," he said. "But you know more about my business than my wife does. Would you mind if Kathie phoned you and asked what you would do about certain things? Because she wouldn't want to bother me if I'm not feeling well."

"Oh, of course. No problem," said Arne. He had all the statistics about Sam's financial statements through helping with the loan and setting up the insurance on the property.

Arne soon realised that his businessman friend who held the property loan was not pleased about missed payments during the months when Sam was not working. Arne was able to advise Kathie Doerksen and lessen those demands on her but she was worn down by many other stresses while Sam's hospital stay lengthened. She needed to earn money and had gone back to work as a nurse while living on their property in Aldergrove with a few cows and horses, and five children (Brian who was then fifteen; Barry, fourteen; Brenda, twelve; Beryl, eleven; and Barb, six). The children looked after a lot at home but Kathie had a long drive to her work at the Surrey Hospital and then on to visit Sam in the Royal Columbian Hospital in New Westminster.

Sam's surgery was not successful. By the time he passed away on September 18, 1966, Kathie was down to 100 pounds and had to face life without the spiritual covering of her husband.

She sold the property quickly and avoided foreclosure. With the help of her in-laws, Kathie was able to find an older house that she could buy and fix up, on an acre of land near the Surrey Alliance Church. But her father-in-law himself died six months after Sam, and one brother-in-law soon had to return to Winnipeg. She was on her own again. But God had a plan: her insurance man, Arne, was always ready to help.

During these years, a wind of Holy Spirit blessing was beginning to blow through the Christian community and believers who were not in Pentecostal churches were experiencing the "Pentecostal Blessing" and speaking in tongues.

Most churches did not like the turbulence the wind caused. Only St. Margaret's Reformed Episcopal Church in East Vancouver would open its doors to the Holy Spirit hurricane, because their pastor the Reverend Robert Birch himself had searched for and received the baptism in the Holy Spirit. His attitude was, "Shouldn't we see, in our time, the sort of things we read of in the book of Acts?"

These blessings were also being taught and prayed for in inter-church meetings in halls here and there. Kathie needed all the encouragement she could find. In one of her phone calls with Arne soon after Sam's death, the conversation turned to one of these meetings in New Westminster.

"I'm not sure, Arne," said Kathie. "I've never been anywhere like that without Sam,"

"Don't worry. I'll arrange for someone to pick you up," announced Arne, in that tone of voice that meant, "No discussion. It's **settled**!" So she went and the Lord touched her deeply.

It was at that meeting that Arne introduced her to a fellow board member from the Evangelical Free Church, Dolphe Hoffman along with his wife, Gloria. The Hoffmans looked after Kathie and became firm friends. Some of the leading couples at Arne's Evangelical Free Church, including Dolphe and Gloria, experienced the Baptism in the Holy Spirit. Arne had always believed that the Holy Spirit's power was essential for Christian living but doubted that speaking in tongues was necessary. The EFC denominational leaders were more than doubtful about it.

Whenever she could, Kathie attended the Tuesday evening prayer meetings at St. Margaret's, where Pastor Bob Birch would pray for people. She took friends there, who were all filled with the Holy Spirit and spoke in tongues, and before long Kathie herself was freed in tongues.

Brought up in a Christian family, Kathie had given her heart to Jesus in Sunday School at eight years of age and had always known His light in her life. But now she could really receive the Holy Spirit's support in raising her children. Those Tuesday meetings were like a "pep pill" for her, with maybe thirty people there praying her through those painful years. On Sundays, she took her family to the Alliance Church next door to their home.

One day Arne picked Kathie up from work and took her around with him as he visited his insurance clients because he knew she was having a really difficult time. She was suffering through weeks of migraine headaches, trying to continue working and being the mother she wanted to be for her children. She had heard the Lord say, "Quit work" but she was fighting against it because it would mean going on social assistance.

She asked Arne to drive her over to have a talk with Bob Birch. As she talked with the pastor, the Lord promised to help her and gave her a verse from the Psalms, *"Do not be like the horse or the mule, which have no understanding but must* be controlled by bit and bridle..." (Psalm 32:9, NIV). The Lord also gave her a verse from Job, "...*the Almighty shall be thy defence, and thou shalt have plenty of silver*" (Job 22:25, KJV).

With that confidence Kathie quit her job and began to experience the Lord's provision. Her family was never without what they needed, with the help of skilfully made soups and stews and trips across the border for the children to choose their clothes at thrift stores. When her car broke down, Eric (a friend with a repair shop in West Vancouver) fixed it for her but wouldn't let her pay. "I said I'd fix it for you."

"At least let me pay for the parts," Kathie offered.

"I *said* I would fix it for you," he insisted. Eric kept that car going for years.

Two of Kathie's children had car accidents. When Barry was seventeen, he was driving down a side road when a little boy wanting to do tricks on his bicycle collided with the hood of the car and cut his head, needing several stitches. The police came to the house and noticed how agitated Barry was. "Are you on drugs?" they demanded.

"No!" said Barry. "I just hit a kid! And I worked all night at the pizza place!"

"Check him out," offered Kathie. She wasn't worried.

Meanwhile Kathie was teaching Brenda to drive and, with the pastor's permission, Brenda was practising in the parking lot of the church next to their house when she heard a strange hissing sound. It was gas escaping from an unprotected gas stand which the car had grazed while she was parallel parking. When the fire department arrived, they found a fire in the church's furnace room. After all the drama and crowds at the church, Kathie had to go home to calm a hysterical Brenda. "Let's be thankful that it didn't happen when there was a church full of people."

Of course there were complicated insurance claims for Arne to sort out for these accidents. The insurance company tried to avoid paying for the fire damage to the church but

Arne reminded them that they legally had to pay because Brenda was driving with permission on private land. They put a lien on Kathie's house, because she had no money, but the cost of the repairs was covered. "Don't worry about the lien on the house," Arne said. "They'll have to give it up after seven years."

Arne seemed to know how to handle everything that was thrown at Kathie and the kids. When Kathie called to say that the septic tank wasn't working, Arne went right over to her house, knowing exactly what to do after all his years in construction. He thought the two boys were big enough to shovel, so he showed them what to do and the boys worked on it after school, digging the ditch, putting in new tile and fixing it up.

The house was quite small for six people, four of them teenagers, so they decided to fix up a room downstairs for the two boys. Arne was often over at the house to supervise these projects.

Early in 1969, Arne had his own infilling of the Holy Spirit when Bob Birch prayed for him at a charismatic meeting, and a few days later, Arne was speaking in tongues. He had always said that wasn't necessary but he didn't argue with the Holy Spirit! Always a positive, enthusiastic man, Arne now found the Holy Spirit was bubbling up in him in a new and powerful way.

Arne explains, "Luke 10:19 really became alive: '...*I've given you authority over **all**...*'" [and he emphasises the word all with a loud clap] "' *Over **all** the power of the enemy....*'" (Luke 10:19, TLB). "Why are we weeping and wailing," he continues. "When we have all the ***power***?" And then he follows it up with one of his chuckles.

Soon Arne moved to worship at St. Margaret's with Dolphe and Gloria and other friends from the EFC. The Holy Spirit was moving there both on Sundays and midweek. Kathie was already part of the life there with her daughters.

At home, her teenagers were reflecting something of the chaotic hippy culture that was flooding the west coast. Kathie was still attending the church next door when she discovered that Beryl's friend was not allowed to come to her house.

"Well, you know," the mother tried to explain when Kathie phoned about it. "Well, your boys... They don't come to church."

"What's wrong? They're obedient," Kathie explained. "I've told them: I don't mind where you go, if you don't feel welcome in one place, as long as you are getting Christian fellowship once a week somewhere."

"And their hair..." The hair in question was only below Kathie's son's ears.

It wasn't important to Kathie. "You can go on drugs if you want," she told her son. "You can do anything you want. You can go down the left hand side of the road if you want. You'll get killed ... but you can do it!"

Here was the clash of cultures that was exploding in churches everywhere. At St. Margaret's, long haired youth of all types were being welcomed and included in all of church life. Kathie knew that her children would be welcomed and built up at the huge lively Inter-Church Fellowship meetings organized by Pastor Bob with Pentecostal minister, Bernice Gerard, and others. They drew international charismatic speakers to various big halls around the Lower Mainland, in a tent out at Point Roberts or Langley, and then in a spectacular "Air Cathedral" which was held up by the air that was pumped into it. It had a translucent, heavenly feel to it, with the sun streaming through the yellow and green covering. The worship soared through the cloud-like roof and believers learned to sing in the Spirit, like birds set free.

After a few years, Arne and Kathie realised there was more than insurance drawing them together—Arne joked that it was the soup that Kathie had learned from her mother ("Summer Borscht," made with spinach, potatoes, buttermilk and dill seed). The soup was a family favourite and he would often be there around lunch when the pot of soup was on.

According to a journal that Arne kept for a few months in 1971, he was also often at Kathie's home for dinner. On April 4 he says simply, "Dear Lord, thank you for Kathie." (The journal shows that his life was busy with Faith Insurance Agency, attending St. Margaret's Church, meetings of the Christian Business Men's Connection meetings, volunteering with World Vision, coping with lawyers' letters and going with Cam to fetch their things from the house on Porter Street.)

When they talked about it, Arne and Kathie realized they had had very different experiences in their first marriages: Kathie's had been good and Arne's not so good. They didn't want to make any mistakes so they agreed not to see one another for two weeks and pray about it.

When the two weeks were over, Arne asked Kathie, "Are you stuck on diamonds for an engagement ring?"

"Oh, no," she said. "Anything."

Kathie's engagement ring

He didn't tell her about the ring the Lord had shown him in a dream–a dream that happily extinguished any hesitation Arne had about marrying a widow with five children. He went to a jeweller friend of his and had it made, then surprised her with a very special engagement ring: it has two large pearls side by side, for Arne and Kathie, and six smaller ones arranged to represent Arne's son, Kathie's three daughters and two sons.

When Kathie sat down with her kids and showed them her ring, it was an eloquent fulfillment of her promise that they would always be involved in any future second marriage. Beryl, her middle daughter, was delighted to be able to say, "That's me right there in the middle!"

"Are you going to make bread again, Mom?" asked Brian, meaning, *"You won't have to work any more."*

Kathie says, "Arne has been more than a father to all of them. Doesn't matter what the problem is, he's there to help solve it. You wouldn't know they weren't his children."

Arne responds, "Well some people **make** problems and other people **solve** problems!"

One problem to be solved was that his divorce was not yet finalized. He had only filed for it late in 1970, when he realised what was developing with Kathie, and it would take at least a year to be final. There was no difficulty with it—Gaye did not put up any objections—but the timing was wrong. He wasn't free yet to marry in Canada.

In July 1971, six months before they could marry in British Coumbia, Arne and Kathie had a pre-nuptial party for the family and set off for the Oregon coast to marry there and have a three-week honeymoon. Arne bought an eighteen-foot trailer and claimed it was his wedding gift to Kathie. It was the first of many road trips they would take together.

They found a Justice of the Peace who ran a museum for tourists. A party of seniors was there that day.

"We want to get **married**," Arne announced with his infectious enthusiasm. "Who wants to be a **witness**?" Their witnesses were two strangers in their nineties.

"You'll never keep my Dad away from business for three weeks!" Cam said when Kathie phoned him. Arne had just sold

Faith Insurance Agency, because the B.C. government was about to take over his type of insurance, but the new owners asked him to continue for a while to consolidate the connections he had. Arne planned to phone his office every day while he was away but the Lord said, "I want you just to forget about it. You just rejoice. You are being blessed." After that, miraculously, Arne did not phone the office once in three weeks.

Arne and Kathie were married on July 12, 1971, aged fifty-two and forty-two respectively, united in the Lord and ready for a new life together. They had both been trained in the Lord's boot camp of difficulties and struggles. What would be next? Arne was no longer so involved with the insurance business and now began to generate income as a salesman trading with a couple of companies. He was full of faith and power from the Holy Spirit, ready for anything. He had time, strength and boundless energy. How would God fill the empty space of the rest of his life?

They lived in Kathie's house on 96th Avenue and experienced amazing roller-coaster-like years at St. Margaret's, the Holy Spirit moving there in constantly surprising ways, with huge crowds at every service and Pastor Bob speaking God's word with boldness. In 1973 they moved on, with Arne's friends from the Evangelical Free Church, to pioneer the Burnaby Christian Fellowship, which became another powerfully influential centre of Christian ministry.

Beryl and Barb both still lived at home but Arne strongly objected to Beryl smoking. He found smoking a really hard sin to cover with love. One day, when Kathie was down in Florida for the birth of one of Brenda's babies, she began to worry about how Arne and Beryl were getting along at home. Then Arne phoned: "The Lord showed me I can't see the forest for the trees." It was a big revelation for him. After that, he could see Beryl for herself, and not just the cigarette she was holding.

Before he got to know Kathie, Arne had had a few years alone. His long-held political persuasion and contacts had led to a fruitful ministry for the Lord when Bob Thompson, the Social Credit MP for Red Deer Alberta, had suggested Arne as a volunteer for World Vision. Since then Arne had been helping World Vision in the Vancouver area, finding sponsors for needy children all over the world, working under Ron Allen of World Vision Alberta.

In 1973, Ron Allen approached Arne with the offer of a full-time position as World Vision's representative in B.C. "Offer to hire this man," the management had said to Ron when they noticed Arne's success arranging sponsors for children. "Let me pray about it," said Arne. He could easily lay aside his selling business and this was a ministry that appealed to both him and Kathie but they had to know that it was the Lord. That weekend they went down to their property in Sudden Valley at Lake Whatcom just east of Bellingham, Washington, where many Canadians had bought property when the land was being developed.

As they prayed about this job offer, the Lord spoke to him in a vivid dream. He and Kathie were in a big building among crowds of people who took no notice of them. Outside they found a two-seater bicycle and rode off on it down the road until Kathie said, "We've got to turn there!" It was just a cow path leading into a ploughed field, and was no good for a bicycle, but Kathie insisted and Arne knew she was right to take the lead. He turned off the road and soon found that they could ride down the middle of the field where two firm furrows ran side by side. Having ploughed many fields, Arne knew this was the only place they could ride. "Look," said the Lord. "You're not even pedaling." They eventually came to a small house at the end of the field and were invited in by a man playing a beautiful grand piano. Arne stood behind the man to look at the music and recognized a name on the page: Bob Pearce, founder of World Vision. When the man stopped playing, Arne noticed that the last page of music was blank. "It's not finished yet," the man said.

When Arne woke up, the Lord said to him, "World Vision, it's not finished, and you're here. Now what are you going to do about it?" The Lord had led them from a crowd where they made no impression, guiding them effortlessly to a place where Arne saw an important link to World Vision and the evidence that his work with them was not finished yet.

So he signed up with World Vision and began work in September 1973. To start him off, Ron Allen organised a weekend program at Miracle Valley, a beautiful Salvation Army centre near Mission, B.C. Arne made phone calls and about thirty-five people who had already sponsored children agreed to come for a sharing time about how to expand.

In preparation, Arne called Ron: "I want a hundred pictures of children to sponsor for this meeting." He thought he was making a normal marketing request but the request had to go to the head office in Toronto, where they almost laughed because they usually only had ten or so children available for sponsorship. Arne persevered, asking over and over again—he was still the same character who knew how to train wild horses—and eventually the Pasadena office was able to send a hundred pictures. Arne discovered that World Vision had been in Canada for fifteen years but had only found sponsors for 1350 children.

Ron received a telegram on the first day of the weekend and had to leave because of an emergency in Saskatchewan, leaving Arne supervised by a man from the Toronto office. The Toronto official spoke on the Saturday and was ready to speak on the Sunday morning as well. But on Sunday morning, Arne knew that he had to share another significant dream the Lord had given him the night before. He had to ask repeatedly, because the official didn't know him well enough, but he finally got approval.

In this dream he had seen a steam train "just hiking across the nation." It was only box cars, not passenger coaches, and there were children's happy faces completely filling the open doors of the box cars, all singing merrily. Occasionally the train would stop and pick up another car load. But ahead was a brick wall across the track and in the dream Arne said, "Oh, Lord, who would build a **brick wall** across your railroad?" The Lord had answered, "That's the excuses of my people. But I no longer have time to wait." And the train smashed through the wall and scattered the bricks everywhere and on they went.

Then, in Arne's dream, the Lord said, "If you've got a real river to cross, I'll build a bridge." Right ahead of the train was a river and a bridge across it. Next He said, "If you've got a real mountain to deal with, I'll build a tunnel." And there it was—a big mountain with a tunnel going through it.

Sitting at their breakfast table the next morning was the only person Arne didn't know at the weekend and Arne told him about the dream that was still so vivid. The man responded suitably with "Oh!" and "Wow!"

"If there were just an artist here this morning who could put this on a blackboard," continued Arne. "I would love that. Let the people **see** it."

"You know, Arne," said the man after a while. "I happen to be an artist."

"Oh!" gasped Arne. "Well let me tell you ..."

"No," he said. "I know exactly the picture. Just find me a blackboard and I'll draw it."

Blackboard drawing of Arne's dream

When they had found the blackboard, Arne felt the Lord give him the verse: "Where your treasure is there your heart is also." He wrote it at the top of the blackboard, thinking, "Maybe somebody will know where that comes from," because he couldn't remember. It took the artist only about fifteen minutes to draw a striking action picture of Arne's dream.

Arne returned just before the meeting and saw that somebody had added Matthew 6:21 to the Scripture.

"Arne," said a lady standing nearby. "Last night the Lord woke me up and said, 'Get up and read your Bible.' I never had that happen to me before. I couldn't rest, so finally I got up and opened my Bible and saw Matthew 6:21. It was blazing red on the page: 'Where your treasure is there your heart is also.' I just read that and the Lord said, 'Okay you can go back to bed now.' So when I came in here and saw it written on the board with no Scripture identification, I knew I was supposed to put it on there."

When Arne got up to speak, he couldn't say anything. He just stood there, tongue-tied. He had the wall filled with the pictures of the one hundred children. He had the blackboard with the dramatic drawing. But he couldn't speak. "Ten thousand," the Lord said in his mind. "Ten thousand. Ten thousand."

This was a number beyond imagination. He didn't want to talk about ten thousand. One hundred he could talk about but not ten thousand. But finally he went to the board and wrote "10,000." Then he could speak.

"You know," he said. "I had to write this ten thousand on here. I've got a hundred pictures but the Lord said ten thousand. I guess He wants ten thousand sponsored, not one hundred." Then he was able to go on and explain the dream and the Lord's heart for the orphans.

In those years Arne often felt the Lord's passion and longing for these children. Frequently when he got up to speak, he couldn't say a word until he'd wept.

Where your treasure is, there will your heart be also
Matthew 6 : 21

After the conference, Arne talked to another artist, who drew the picture of the dream again and Arne had it printed up as letterhead. It has been his personal stationery ever since.

Using the strategy the Lord had given him, Arne saw every one of those hundred children sponsored during the weekend. He suggested that some people should take ten, some five, and then persuade friends and neighbours at home to take those they couldn't sponsor themselves.

Arne and Kathie worked for World Vision for three-and-a-half years, traveling all around B.C. with their trailer, mostly in the summer months so that Kathie's youngest daughter, Barb, and her friend, the daughter of Dolphe and Gloria, could go with them. They showed a twenty-two-minute World Vision movie *"Cry Bangla."* Then Arne would talk about the film and invite people to sign up to go on a thirty-hour planned famine to raise a hundred dollars each.

In 1976 a prophecy was given for Arne at Burnaby Christian Fellowship: "My son I have seen your heart and I know the cry of your spirit over the lost and dying of this world. I see your compassion for those who are forgotten and down-trodden of this world. I say to you this morning be encouraged do not despair. You have asked Me for a body of people to share your burden with you and I say be patient for I have given you that body. When My people seek My face and spend time learning of Me then they shall learn of the things that concern Me. Then they will not need to be spoken of, for the needs of the hungry and despised of this world, for they will share of my love and compassion."

Arne's tactics didn't fit his employer's policies, however. His vision was much bigger than World Vision's ideas of success. Arne visited seventy-nine high schools that welcomed the educational information on developing countries. Students wanted to raise funds for the world's poor children but the hundred dollars stipulated by World Vision's head office for each child was too much, so Arne and Kathie decided to sign them up if they contributed any amount. The students would ask people to sponsor them for each hour of fasting, even though it was not the charity's policy. This was so popular that in their second year they ran out of materials to distribute and made their own, without approval. The seven thousand students who signed up were more than the World Vision computers could handle at that time. Eventually Arne was fired for his unauthorized initiatives.

About six months later, the Lord said to him, "You never checked on the ten thousand."

Arne called the secretary who was a friend of his. "Could you tell me how many children had been sponsored by World Vision by the date I was hired?"

"I think so," she said. "It'll all be in the records."

"And check how many were sponsored by the day that I left World Vision."

A week later the call came back. "Arne, 1,350 children had been sponsored in Canada in the fifteen years of operation before you were hired. By the time you left, the number was 13,050. Most of them were sponsored in British Columbia."

"Hallelujah!" said Arne.

It was 1977 and he and Kathie now had no specific area of service for the Lord but this would not be for long.

Faithful is he that calleth you, who also will do it.
(1 Thessalonians 5:24, KJV)

Arne and Kathie, 1977

CHAPTER 5

1977:
A PRAYER CENTRE IN AN UPPER ROOM

It was not long after Arne finished with World Vision that he got his next job from the Lord, a job that would animate the rest of his life and affect the whole of Canada, probably what the Lord had been training him for all his life. It was the summer of 1977 and he was fifty-nine years young.

The Lord began to say to Arne in several dreams, "I want a prayer centre in an upper room." Eventually Arne realized that this was something the Lord really wanted him to do. He asked Kathie to go for a walk with him and told her what the Lord had put on his heart. Kathie listened and knew it was from the Lord. Arne said it was time for Canada to obey the command in 1 Timothy, chapter 2, to pray for those in authority:

> I exhort therefore, that, first of all, supplications, prayers, intercessions, and giving of thanks, be made for all men; For kings, and for all that are in authority; that we may lead a quiet and peaceable life in all godliness and honesty. For this is good and acceptable in the sight of God our Saviour; who will have all men to be saved and to come unto the knowledge of the truth (1 Timothy 2:1-4, KJV).

All Arne knew was that he had to find an upper room and his attitude was: "No problem, Lord. I'll find a place. Won't take me long." He knew the real estate of the Lower Mainland very well but three weeks later, in spite of all his knowledge and contacts, he had not found anywhere that could work as an upper room for a prayer centre.

"Darling," he finally said to Kathie, kicking himself for not doing it sooner. "We've got to get down and **pray** about this."

That very night after they prayed, Arne had a dream about a hotel with a beautiful aurora around it like the Northern Lights. Arne recognized the hotel—the Surrey Inn (later Compass Point Inn) on King George Boulevard near the Fraser Highway, about three blocks from where they lived. But he was puzzled as he told Kathie in the morning about his dream.

"Well," Kathie said. "Didn't you ask the Lord where he wanted His office?"

"He doesn't want it in a **hotel**! What Christian goes into a hotel looking for a Prayer Centre? Not this guy!"

"Well, you'd better check it out."

After a quick phone call to ask whether the owner had any commercial space for rent, Arne and Kathie were at the hotel in ten minutes. The owner showed them the rooms on each floor, right up to the sixth floor.

"What's this door?" Arne asked on the sixth floor.

"That goes to an upper room," answered the owner, unaware that he was speaking the Lord's language.

"I want to see that," said Arne and they started up the twenty-one steps that any hotel guests would have to take to the top floor.

"You know, I'll give you a good deal on this," said the hotelier. "I've only had it rented eight months out of three years."

As they climbed the stairs, the Lord spoke into Arne's heart: "This is the Upper Room. Where does prayer emanate from but the Upper Room?" Arne nearly made the deal without even seeing the room.

The Surrey Inn later, when it was known as the Compass Point Inn

The room was sixteen feet by thirty-two feet, fully furnished with a desk and beds. Arne knew this was it but he simply said, "I'll be back to see it again."

As he and Kathie were on their way home he said, "Darling, you know that's the **penthouse** of the Surrey Inn. What he thinks is a good deal and what I think is a good deal might be two different things. That's going to cost money every week or every month." They didn't exactly have a big income.

They prayed about it at home, not waiting three weeks this time, and the Lord said: "Don't worry about paying every month. Just pay the first year in advance then you won't have to worry about it every month." That option didn't sound any better to Arne but he went back the next day and asked how much the room would be. He discussed with the owner the best monthly rate he could get, which came to about six thousand dollars a year. Arne had his hand on the door to leave when the Lord said, "You didn't ask him what reduction you'd get if you paid the first year in advance."

"No, I didn't, Lord. I didn't have that kind of faith." He turned to the hotel owner and asked, "How much reduction do I get if I pay the first year in advance?"

The owner immediately reduced it to five thousand dollars for the full year.

"I'll be back," said Arne. "I'm interested."

He and Kathie set to praying again about where the money would come from and what to do next.

Within a week he had a phone call from a client: "Arne, you know that policy of mine that you wrote off because I couldn't pay when I went broke? I've changed horses and everything has been going great. I'm going to pay off that debt."

This client's inability to pay had coincided with Arne selling his insurance business, so this was one policy he couldn't sell and he had had to write it off.

"That's wonderful," said Arne. "How much is it?"

"Five thousand dollars."

"Don't make the cheque out to me. Make it out to the Surrey Inn. I owe them five thousand dollars."

So the rent for Prayer Canada was paid for the first year.

The next question was: who was going to do the praying in this prayer centre? Arne argued a bit with the Lord over this. "Lord, you must have the wrong person," he said. "I'm not a prayer warrior." The Lord answered, "I didn't say you were a prayer warrior. I just said to pray."

All Arne knew was that they had to pray for Canada. With his natural enthusiasm, he asked everyone he ran into, "Do you want to pray for Canada?" and told them about the prayer centre in the Upper Room. In two weeks, he had dozens of different responses along the lines of "Great idea, Arne. Carry on." Or "I would, Arne, but I'm busy right now." Out of this discouragement came faith fuel for the rest of his life.

It was while Arne was not sure what to do and saying "Oh, Lord, You've got the wrong guy, you know," that he read some favourite verses from 1 Thessalonians 5:

Rejoice evermore. Pray without ceasing. In everything give thanks: for this is the will of God in Christ Jesus concerning you. Quench not the Spirit. Despise not prophesyings. Prove all things; hold fast that which is good. Abstain from all appearance of evil. And the very God of peace sanctify you wholly; and I pray God your whole spirit and soul and body be preserved blameless unto the coming of our Lord Jesus Christ. Faithful is he that calleth you, who also will do it (1 Thessalonians 5:16-24, KJV).

Those words became like a power plant in his life. And the promise in the last verse—*"Faithful is he who has called you, who also will do it"*—ruined all his excuses that he wasn't the one to pray for Canada.

Then someone said, "Oh, Arne, I know a guy who loves to pray—Vaughn Galachan. You should phone him. I'll give you his number."

Arne phoned and Vaughn's wife, Mary, answered. "Could I come over and talk to your husband tonight?" Arne asked.

"Oh yes, I think so," she answered. Then she added, "You know, he just retired today."

"Boy, I've hit pay dirt," thought Arne. He went over that evening and found Vaughn sitting in a La-Z-Boy, leaning back reading the paper, definitely retired. Mary introduced Arne and Vaughn just kept on reading. Arne knew Vaughn wasn't interested in whatever this visitor was selling.

"I was told you might be interested in a prayer centre that the Lord told me to create to pray for Canada," Arne began, undaunted. "I've rented a room for a year in the Surrey Inn on the top floor. We call it the Upper Room..."

At that, the newspaper was thrown on the floor and Vaughn jumped up and started dancing in excitement.

"For the last two years," he blurted out. "The Lord's been telling me I'm going to be praying in an upper room. When do we start?"

"Actually we're not going to start right away, because I'm leaving on holidays on Monday," explained Arne. "When I get back we'll start. We've got the room all rented and we can start."

"It's a deal!" said Vaughn.

The vacation was to visit their daughter Brenda in Pasadena, California, but with the new prayer project the Lord was calling them to, Arne and Kathie decided to take the opportunity to visit well known prayer centres to learn how to do it. They went to Ralph Wilkerson's prayer centre at Melody Christian Center near Disneyland in California and the Crystal Cathedral in Garden Grove, California. They were cordially received and shown around, and all their questions were answered. But nothing seemed to answer their question about what to do next.

"Oh, Kathie," said Arne. "We just missed the **biggest**. We've got to go to Oral Roberts' Prayer Tower. That's where we've got to be!"

Arne knew his millionaire investor friend was also in Los Angeles and that he carried with him a small satchel of various air tickets that could be used any time for his frequent journeys. Arne contacted this generous friend at his hotel.

"Kathie and I need to get to Tulsa, Oklahoma," he said. "Do you happen to have tickets from Los Angeles to Tulsa?"

Arne's friend looked in his satchel and found the exact tickets that were needed.

Amazed that a man who lived in New Westminster, B.C., could provide return tickets between Los Angeles and Tulsa, Arne and Kathie gladly accepted them and flew overnight to Tulsa, thanking God for His guidance and provision. The next morning they got a taxi to rush to Oral Roberts University, which seemed quite heavenly to them, beautifully designed in gold, blue and white.

"Just take us right to the Prayer Tower," Arne said to the taxi driver, eager to begin learning what to do.

There was a door in the three-storey tower. It said, "No Access." Walking round the tower, they found two more doors but both said "No Access." They went across the street to the gift shop where they were told they would have to make an appointment to get into the Prayer Tower. They hurried up the street to the office but there was no one there. It was a holiday. Had they heard the Lord right? Across the street was the Tabernacle and the doors were open. Inside was a cleaner who didn't know anything. He suggested they just ask anyone they met on the street. They chased after a number of people who disappeared before they could catch them.

Then the Lord spoke. "It's okay," the Lord said. "You've done your thing. Now get back home and I'll tell you what to do!"

They obeyed.

The day they got back home, Arne began praying with Vaughn Galachan in room 686 of the Surrey Inn, the Upper Room. It was Monday evening, November 21, 1977, the official start of Prayer Canada. The second time the two of them prayed together, they saw in the Spirit a line of shoes across the wall at the entrance. After that, they always removed their shoes when they prayed. And they remembered the vision later when the entrance wall really was lined with shoes as the room was crowded with intercessors.

Arne says that Vaughn taught him to pray. He prayed about the authority of God over all things and he came against any plans that the enemy might have to stop or upset them. Arne listened and learned.

All Arne's friends, of course, knew about the prayer centre in the Upper Room. He'd been talking to everyone about it for weeks. Once he and Vaughn started praying on Monday evenings, people came to pray with them and to see what was going on.

That Monday evening prayer meeting, from seven p.m. to nine p.m., has continued to this day. Every Monday evening, for four-and-a-half years in the Upper Room and then in other locations, faithful intercessors have gathered to pray for Canada according to God's Word:

If my people, which are called by my name, shall humble themselves, and pray, and seek my face, and turn from their wicked ways; then will I hear from heaven, and will forgive their sin, and will heal their land (2 Chronicles 7:14, KJV).

Arne taught from this verse how God could change the nation through the power of their prayers. Then he led them to put it into action, not just talking but praying. He had written to all the premiers in Canada for lists of MLAs and cabinet ministers, and to Prime Minister Trudeau for the names of federal cabinet ministers and MPs. They prayed for each by name.

One early visitor who was struck by Arne's teaching on the power of intercession was John DeVries. In 1969, when John had experienced the life changing power of salvation by receiving Christ into his heart, there had been no mentor to guide him in the Christian life so he read his Bible for hours every night and learned to know the presence of God. He later understood it was the work of the Holy Spirit to bring that presence of God and he recognized that same presence in the Upper Room.

John became a regular. At every meeting, they prayed diligently for the authorities and also for whatever needs were there. The Lord answered prayer for healing. His presence was so thick that every person was on the floor before His glory. John remembers praying for a lady who wanted to have a baby. Faith came into his mind as he prayed for her and he knew nothing could withstand that prayer. She became pregnant soon after.

John was to become a stalwart of the ministry, serving on the board of directors from the beginning until 2008 and lending his Spirit-directed biblical knowledge to writing various policy documents.

Arne shared his excitement with their good friends Dolphe and Gloria Hoffman. Dolphe, who had been one of the founding elders of Burnaby Christian Fellowship, knew how to set things up properly. He explained to Arne and Kathie how to register a charity with the Canadian government and how to become recognised by Victoria as a B.C. society. They named the ministry "Prayer Canada."

One Monday evening as they prayed, Arne was looking out of the big windows over to the North Shore mountains and he had a vision of a giant soldier standing there, wearing a suit of armour.

"Oh, Lord," said Arne. "If I was like that ... no problem."

"You should see who's in there," said the Lord and in his spirit Arne was immediately there. He lifted up the face plate but there was nothing there. The helmet was empty.

"Lord, there's nobody **there**!" he said, back in the prayer room.

"You didn't look enough," the Lord told him.

"That's right. I didn't see what was in the **body** of the suit of armour!"

So the Lord sent him back. He lifted up the face plate again, stuck his head right in and looked down. There, with his arms stretched into the massive arms of the armour, hung a small man. And Arne recognized his own shining bald head.

"Yes," said the Lord. "If you stay within me, I will enable you to take great strides across the land." Arne realised that the Lord would do the striding; he was just along for the ride.

After this, inspired by the suit of armour, Arne wrote the following radical call to war:

The suit of armour represents the Church. *She is totally fitted for war*. She has all the accoutrements necessary to overcome anything in the way. Somehow this army, that has been given all power over the enemy forces, has been tranquilized by one insidious force after another.

Many fires have been started. However, crusaders have listened over the centuries to theological and public opinions. Their fires were quenched. Some were terrorized, some rejected, some excommunicated. The weeds were allowed to grow and the burning coals were many times reduced to ash.

Those that moved into places of authority not being led by the Holy Spirit became power and money hungry and redesigned God's original plans to suit their own personal demands. Yet on the surface, much of it appeared genuine.

The great apostolic movement of Jesus Christ was immobilized, directed into petty denominational bands and social clubs. Though knowing about the power of their Lord, they refused to put it to use in the way it was intended.

Instead of recognizing the great power of unity, each group was misled to go their own way. No one being willing to seek God unequivocally. The flocks were scattered and divided to such an extent that all the world could see, in this great religious conglomerate, was confusion and ineffectiveness. Division is the devil's tool.

God's people must be knit together like a coat of armour mail. Each individual must be linked closely with the next and overlapping each other so that no enemy force can enter in. There is but one God over the universe and only when His directions are followed can His great army move forward as a single force.

I was withdrawn from this great religious conglomerate and set on a path to alert those who could hear. *He* has many coals still glowing, sometimes surrounded by ash and clinkers who are unwilling to be resurrected.

It is these coals across Canada whom we are anxious to make contact with. Are you a coal, willing to be awakened afresh into a flaming sword by the Spirit of God for His purpose, and not your own? Are you willing to come forth as pure gold, letting your heavenly Father burn off the dross and stubble so the world sees you clearly as a shaft of His light that no longer has any designs of your own? How much are you willing to sacrifice that His plans can be accomplished? His aim is to revive His mighty church.

Yes, these bones can be revived, can be reinforced with new light and power to move across the world as His army was intended to do.

In those first few months between twenty and forty believers united in intercession every Monday evening and the Lord's presence was with them, ministering to the needs that were there as the people prayed for each other.

Another friend at the Monday prayer meeting from the beginning was André Checker, a single mother. In 1976, lying in bed and wanting to die, she had looked at a picture on her wall of Jesus with the children sitting on His lap and she heard him say, loudly, "Acts 11:14 to 16." This tells Peter's explanation of how Cornelius and his family had received the gospel, and it led to André's salvation:

He will bring you a message through which you and all your household will be saved. As I began to speak, the Holy Spirit fell upon them just as he did on us at the beginning. Then I remembered what the Lord had said:

'John baptized with water, but you will be baptized with the Holy Spirit' (Acts 11:14-16, NIV).

André stood on that same Scripture when she asked the Lord Jesus to baptize her in the Holy Spirit the following year. She became friends with Arne and Kathie as a result of Full Gospel Businessmen's meetings and it was a delight to her to drive to Surrey to the meetings as often as her shift work would allow.

One Monday evening a newly-saved young man sitting beside her in the crowded room said, "I don't want to be here tonight."

"Well, you are here!" she said, smiling to herself as she wondered what God was up to.

"Yeah, but God won't get off my back. Everywhere I go I get slain in the Spirit. I just don't want to do that anymore."

André put her hand on his shoulder, thinking "Lord, how do You do it when they're sitting down?" She simply blessed him in Jesus' name and he was on the floor on his face for the rest of the meeting.

André was one of those whose friendship with Arne and Kathie, cemented in intercessory prayer, has lasted over the years. Even in later years when she lived in Kelowna, she would manage to see them once a year for fellowship.

Arne knew God had more in mind for Prayer Canada than one weekly prayer meeting but he wasn't sure what the next step was. Then he heard the Lord say, "Go to the authorities. That's where you start praying, with the authorities." So he made some preliminary approaches to their provincial MLA, their federal MP and the mayor of Surrey, Bill Vogel.

Arne believed that somehow they should have a regular time of prayer actually inside municipal halls, in every community of Canada. So he asked the mayor if he could put up a notice in Surrey City Hall, which was in Cloverdale at that time. The notice would announce that there would be a prayer time there one day a week starting in January.

The mayor immediately recognized Arne's name because the mayor's father, Hunter Vogel, had served with Arne on the board of Trinity Western University. He said "That's fine, Arne. That would be great." So Arne followed up by asking for a room to meet in.

"I've got just the room, come with me," said the mayor with no hesitation and took Arne into the board room of City Hall. "This is yours every Tuesday at noon." Prayer Canada has been in Surrey City Hall ever since.

Prayer meetings in government buildings, like this one in Surrey City Hall, were clearly a key part of God's plan—strategically positioned for spiritual impact, regular for consistent building, focusing prayerful blessings on locally elected officials, faithful and loving to serve those who serve. Surrey was the first. But how were they to replicate it in cities and provincial capitals all over the country?

The Lord also spoke to Arne to hold monthly Prayer Canada Prayer Breakfasts, a type of meeting in a neutral venue where elected officials would feel honoured to be guests. He arranged for the first one to be held at the Surrey Inn on Sunday December 18, 1977, from 7 to 9 a.m. so that people would be free to attend their churches afterwards. This was only four weeks after the launch of Prayer Canada in the Upper Room.

He wrote to the churches in Surrey to invite them. On his letterhead paper he had printed "Pray ye therefore the Lord of the Harvest, that He will send forth labourers into His harvest" (Matthew 9:38, KJV). At the bottom was a paraphrase of 1 Timothy 2:1-2: "Pray for all mankind, especially those in authority."

"You know, December 18th, it's the wrong time of year," people advised. "Everybody is so busy at Christmas time."

Never one to be influenced by timid voices, Arne went ahead and a hundred curious people attended, including Mayor Bill Vogel, the local MLA and other government officials. They worshiped the Lord, with Bob Leslie as the soloist, and then Arne outlined how the Lord had called him to establish Prayer Canada. He's a great story teller and his audience enjoyed hearing how the Lord had led him.

He taught that God rules over the nations and commands His people to pray for their rulers, according to 1 Timothy, chapter 2: *"I exhort therefore, that, first of all, supplications, prayers, intercessions, and giving of thanks, be made for all men; for kings, and for all that are in authority..." (1 Timothy 2.1-2, KJV)*.

He pointed out that Christians should not complain about the government if they were not obedient to pray for them. He honoured the elected officials in the gathering and promised to support them in prayer.

He explained the vision of non-denominational prayer groups across the nation, interceding for all levels of government in Canada—federal, provincial and local. He inspired the people to believe that the power of prayer could bring wisdom from God to those who govern and eventually turn the nation toward God.

Everyone could see that Prayer Canada was all the Lord's doing. They could see Arne's enthusiasm, but also his dedication and obedience to the vision. They were stirred in faith and excitement to move on with Arne and be part of a prayer group.

CHAPTER 6

1978:
TWELVE VOLUNTEERS FOR A TRAIN TRIP

"Darling, why don't you quit?" said Kathie a couple of months after the Upper Room had opened.

"I would if I could," Arne answered. "but I can't." The tears in his eyes showed the struggle they were having with finances.

It was still the early days of Prayer Canada so they were not yet receiving many ministry gifts, and Arne was trying to re-establish his business as a salesman, which he had had to put on hold during the World Vision years. At this time he was selling Rebounder mini-trampolines for exercise so he was in the stressful situation of pioneering a new national prayer ministry at the same time as growing a sales business. After Sam had died, Kathie had said that she would never marry another salesman. Now, here they were in this familiar bind.

One day with her Living Bible on her lap Kathie prayed, "God you've got to show me." He gave her this passage from Habakkuk 2:1-3:

I will climb my watchtower now and wait to see what answer God will give to my complaint. And the Lord said to me, "... these things I plan won't happen right away. Slowly, steadily, surely, the time approaches when the vision will be fulfilled. If it seems slow, do not despair. For these things will surely come to pass. Just be patient!

They will not be overdue a single day!" (Habakkuk 2:1-3, TLB)

Arne and Kathie were totally united in the Prayer Canada vision from day one. There would be many difficult times but God always gave strengthening words like these whenever Kathie felt it was all too much.

*Picture specially painted for the Upper Room,
showing the presence of God through the Holy Spirit.
It has hung in the prayer room since the early years.*

The Upper Room was Prayer Canada's command centre, where believing prayer rose to heaven every Monday for Canada's leaders by name and the Lord answered with His presence to bless everyone involved.

The Upper Room also became an office, as Arne and Kathie began to produce a one-page monthly Prayer Canada newsletter which they mailed to churches and other contacts and handed out to everyone they met. People wanted to be involved in prayer or to be prayed for. So in addition to Monday evenings, it was known that the prayer room was open during the day, Monday to Friday, and all night Sunday, on a drop-in basis for prayer or to share a need or an answered prayer. There was a phone line for prayer requests. It soon became a hub of information and communication as Prayer Canada began to grow.

The second prayer breakfast (Sunday January 22, 1978) focused on education. About 150 attended including several school principals.

The third breakfast, on Sunday February 19, had the theme of justice. Prayer Canada asked churches in Surrey to designate that day as Appreciation Sunday for the police who patrolled their neighbourhoods. In Arne's letter inviting police officers to attend, he said, "I for one readily admit and truly realize that our neglect in prayer for you has been extremely serious. However a change is underway." The speaker was Dick Simmons from Seattle who had started a program for prisoners called "M2." The B.C. attorney general and the superintendent of the RCMP were also invited but the superintendent said that Prayer Canada was a little too new for the RCMP to get involved with. "They are a very staid organization," Arne commented later. "We hope that they remain solid and stable but we will pray for them."

The prayer breakfasts were held every month for a number of years and have continued at three-month intervals to the present day—always blessed with good food, heavenly worship, enthusiastic updates from Arne, and a special speaker. Local politicians always find their way to these events and are honoured and prayed for.

André Chequer was occasionally able to attend prayer breakfasts in the early years and says they were usually "pretty awesome" and enthusiastically attended, and that the worship was filled with the presence of God. The centrepiece of each table was the flag of a province or territory of Canada and one person at each table would be designated to pray for that area during the prayer time. Then someone would pray for the federal government and then there would be prayer for individuals.

In March 1978, prayer partners were invited to the Prayer Canada Prayer Centre to pray and fast for three days over the Easter weekend. On the Saturday and Monday there were specific times set aside for prayer, interspersed with teaching and sharing. Sunday had early morning and all night prayer but the main part of the day was free for people to attend their own churches. Monday evening was a "Joyous Celebration Rally." This was developed in subsequent years to become an annual, residential "Three Day Prayer and Fast."

July 19, 1978, was the first official meeting of the board of directors of Prayer Canada. Those present were: Arne Bryan (occupation described as ministry), Kathie Bryan (housewife), Norman Alver (B.C. Hydro Serviceman), Dolphe Hoffman (Chartered Accountant) and John DeVries (contractor, evangelist). The signatures were witnessed by Henriette Versluys (retired).

Many different people since then have served as members of the board of directors of Prayer Canada. The board meetings take their tone from Arne's outgoing, positive personality and his complete dedication to obeying the Lord's guidance. They also pray for one another and enjoy meals together.

It was in July 1978 that Patrick Fisher of Sydney, B.C. sent the following prophecy to Arne:

The Lord has promised to make the hearts of the leaders of this Nation "soft as putty and I will reconstruct them WHOLE. Be thou only accountable to the Lord thy God. Be thou on thy knees in prayer and intercession for the leaders of this Nation. For I have declared it, I have purposed it and thus will I do it, saith the Lord."

Arne was also encouraged by various prophetic words for Canada as a nation, which Patrick Fisher had collected and printed, including these:

My people, I will use you to heal this Nation. Then I will use this Nation to heal the other Nations of this world. And then the whole earth shall know you as people who love the Lord. Revelations 22:2 (Victoria, October 1977)

My people – I am asking you to choose. Will you choose to be with Me or will you stand still? Some of you are standing still. You have not moved one way or another for years. Others have grown up and gone past you. Yet you stand proudly still. ... I can move either through you or around you. Choose now, whether or not you will be with Me as I move. Be not proud. Humble yourselves. (Nanaimo, March 1978)

Patrick also printed something Billy Graham said in Toronto during May 1978: "We are at a unique moment in history, for Canada to take spiritual leadership of the world."

"You know, there's a prayer room right at the top of this hotel, in an Upper Room," said a speaker at a business meeting in the Surrey Inn one day. That sounded interesting to Lynette Fruson, who was attending the meeting with her husband, a pastor. They were going through difficulties in their church at that time and knew they could really use prayer.

They took the elevator up to the sixth floor and with growing anticipation climbed the flight of stairs to the Upper Room, where the group were just coming to the end of their prayer time. Arne welcomed the visitors warmly and showed them around. He showed them the prayer board with the map of Canada and the box where people put their prayer needs.

"Have you any prayer requests?" Arne asked them. They certainly did and put a note in the box without discussing it. Then Arne said, "I believe God wants us to wash your feet" and he proceeded to serve them in this beautiful symbol of God's love.

Afterwards he said, "There is a Scripture that I believe God wants me to give you. It's Isaiah 43." Lynette burst into tears and wept as he read it, because it was the fourth time that day that the Lord had brought that same Scripture to them:

But now the Lord who created you, O Israel, says, Don't be afraid, for I have ransomed you; I have called you by name; you are mine. When you go through rivers of difficulty and great trouble, I will be with you. When you go through rivers of difficulty, you will not drown! When you walk through the fire of oppression, you will not be burned up—the flames will not consume you. ... you are precious to me and honoured, and I love you (Isaiah 43:1-4, TLB).

Arne became a special influence in their lives. Lynette prayed for Prayer Canada in her home in Abbotsford and, more than twenty years later in Kelowna, took up leadership of the prayer post there.

The Upper Room was very active. The Monday evenings in the Upper Room and noon on Tuesdays at the Surrey City Hall were vital prayer times. Prayer Breakfasts were reaching out to different segments of the community. But Arne was calling for more. He knew Christians across the whole country had to be mobilized to pray for governmental leaders at all levels, municipal, provincial and federal. He encouraged his many contacts farther afield to start Prayer Canada prayer groups in their homes. Home groups were the first step, and then they could move into city halls, parliament buildings, and

Ottawa. Reports came of groups started in small places like 100 Mile House B.C. but Arne knew it had to be bigger: he had to reach the capitals. They were busy but that didn't stop Arne from praying and asking God, "What next?"

"I had this dream of a train going across the country," announced Arne one day in August. "And I saw *twelve* people on the train, joyous and laughing and waving."

Here was the next big vision placed by the Lord in Arne's heart. He knew, and anyone listening to him knew, that this was a dream about a real event that was going to happen. Prayer Canada would make a train trip all the way across Canada. The purpose of the journey would be to speak to leadership all across the nation and to pray for them personally. It was so real to him that he asked someone to paint a picture of it.

"Who are the twelve on the train?" people asked.

"I don't know," answered Arne with excitement in his voice. "The Lord will show."

"Arne, am I one of those people?"

"If the Lord has spoken to you, *yes*! But only if the Lord has spoken to you about it."

Of course, the whole idea was impossible. Who would go? How would the costs be covered? Where would they stay each night? How could an unknown organization hope to meet personally with senior government figures in every provincial capital? Arne held on to the promise God had given him: *"Faithful is he that calleth you, who also will do it"* (1 Thessalonians 5:24, KJV). He remembered the vision of the giant suit of armour that would stride across the country with his little figure hanging inside. He just kept praying and talking about this ambitious venture.

The plan was to set off on October 10 for twenty-one days. Letters requesting appointments were sent to premiers and mayors. Arne pursued every opening. Contacts were made to request billeting for them all in the different provincial capital cities. The monthly newsletters explained the vision. One by one people came to Arne saying something like: "Arne, I got information about this from someone and I believe God wants me to go on this train trip." Eventually twelve people submitted a letter explaining how they knew they should join Arne on the "Prayer Train Pilgrimage." Each one was assigned a specific job on the trip.

(left to right) John & Tina DeVries, Harold & Joan Hansen, Sister Aquina
(second row) Chuck Giesbrecht, Mary Ann Carvell, Pauline Karachun
(third row) Barbara Dangerfield, Robert Montpetite, Linda Bowden

Kathie was the first team member. She acted as the timekeeper, making sure everyone had the same time as they crossed all the time zones of Canada.

John DeVries and his wife, Tina, were among the twelve. John had been attracted by the vision of Prayer Canada from the beginning. Then, as he got to know Arne more, he recognized a genuine calling on him to be a prophet as in Ephesians 4:11 – *"And he gave some, apostles; and some, prophets; and some, evangelists; and some, pastors and teachers"* (Ephesians 4.11, KJV).

"There are different flavours of prophet," says John. "Moses and David were so different; Jeremiah was the weeping prophet, Jonah the messenger prophet. Arne is a messenger prophet. He operates in dreams and visions. His strength comes from a sure knowledge that God has spoken. God has shown, so he follows. He has always had a deep heart to accomplish the things the Lord showed him as a mandate."

In their application letter, John wrote, "It is our sure knowledge and belief that we should be part of this 21 day trip... This the #1 mandatory item for prayer for every Christian, to heed 2 Chronicles 7:14 and avert God's judgement."

John was given the role of meeting co-ordinator, working with Arne to plan all the outside meeting commitments of the team.

Harold and Joan Hansen from Golden, B.C. could see the need to pray for Canada's leaders and signed up for the pilgrimage so that they could pray *with* them and not just *for* them. As Roman Catholics, they brought a welcome input to the team. Harold was the official photographer and Joan taped all the interviews and meetings, which meant carrying bulky equipment and enough cassette tapes.

The other Catholic member of the twelve was Sister Aquina, from Grande Prairie AB. She was already sharing the vision of Prayer Canada widely with Women's Aglow meetings and Catholic Charismatic groups in northern Alberta. She declared herself "united in prayer" with Arne and Kathie. She was asked to be the prayer co-ordinator, organizing morning and evening prayer meetings for the whole group.

Chuck Giesbrecht also knew he should be part of the "Prayer Train Pilgrimage." He was given the job of looking after the literature that they were taking with them, including tracts, Gospels of John and 160 French Bibles.

"...For out of Zion shall go forth the law, and the word of the Lord from Jerusalem" (Isaiah 2:3b, KJV) was the Scripture given to Mary Ann Carvell after she met with Arne and Kathie. She wrote about her two great loves: "Israel (spiritual home) and Canada (physical home). It is because of this dual citizenship as it were, the Holy Spirit has directed me to join His Royal Tour October next." Mary Ann was asked to act as treasurer and be responsible to keep a record of all donations and disbursements.

Pauline Karachun was the secretary for the journey. Her job was to keep a daily diary of all activities, list addresses of all contacts, send thank you notes and remind each person to leave a thank you note with their hosts at each stop. She had asked God for a clear word and divine direction about the prayer train pilgrimage. He told her that He wanted her to have a small part in the coming revival in Canada. She said "Yes, Lord".

Red-haired Barbara Dangerfield (now Barbara Blais) from Quesnel, B.C. said that God had told her on several occasions to pray for Canada and its leaders before she heard about Prayer Canada. She wrote: "I believe there are many lonely leaders who need Christ in their hearts and lives." After praying about the train trip, two separate people gave her the verses Colossians 4:1-6, which speak about prayer immediately after saying we are like slaves of our Master in heaven. So she gave up her fully paid registration to the Women's Aglow International Convention, which conflicted with the dates of the trip, thrilled that she would be an answer to the prayer of someone who otherwise couldn't afford to go. Arne asked Barbara to count all the luggage at each transfer or stop-over. That seemed appropriate as she was planning to bring a new guitar and a new song on the trip.

When Robert Montpetite first heard Arne talk about the train trip, he was looking for the fulfillment of a prophecy he had been given the previous year, that the Lord at some time was going to put him on a twenty-one-day fast. He was immediately excited about the train trip but was not sure if he should be part of it, until the evening when Arne outlined the itinerary and said it would be twenty-one days. Robert said he felt a "plunk" at that moment and heard from God that he should join the team. He was put in charge of transportation. He was to count heads at all stops and departures and to designate car rides, etc. He also looked after the lost and found.

Linda Bowden struggled to know whether she should be on the trip. John DeVries had invited her to the Monday prayer meetings months earlier, when she was a relatively new Christian running a drop-in centre for street people with her sister in downtown Vancouver. "John," she said at that time "There are so many prayer meetings here in Vancouver. Why would I want to go all the way out to Surrey?" But he persisted. After she and her sister closed the drop-in centre, Linda finally walked into the Upper Room one Monday evening in May or June of 1978 and she knew something was going on. She sensed that it was more than just another prayer meeting for her. She became a regular and loved it, getting to know Arne and also helping around the office sometimes. However it was a restless transition time for her. "If you by faith walk through the door you believe I'm leading you into," said the Lord, "when you get to the other side, you'll know." When she first heard about the train trip, she thought "Gee, that would be nice," because she loved to travel (her father was an airline pilot) but there was no specific guidance. In faith, she wrote her letter explaining why she believed she was to join the team and then felt a great peace from the Lord. She knew with a jump that she really was to go on the train trip. She felt His anointing when she shared with people about Prayer Canada and about how exciting the trip was going to be, although she didn't see herself as a prayer warrior. Linda's job on the journey was billet coordinator, taking the address and phone number of each person's billet for the night, and on the train keeping track of where each person was, room number or car number.

When it became clear that there were twelve pilgrims in addition to Arne, making thirteen, there was some questioning but they felt it was from the Lord because it caused each of them to double-check their call from God, a healthy exercise in obedience.

Some of the team already knew each other but when the whole team met up on the Monday evening before the start of their epic journey, every person was a stranger to some of the others.

How would Arne lead this disparate group of volunteers who were not trained commandos, when he was more of a visionary than a pastor?

CHAPTER 7

1978:
PRAYER TRAIN PILGRIMAGE

The Prayer Train Pilgrims set off by float plane to Victoria

On Tuesday morning October 10, 1978, Arne ushered his twelve eager disciples on to a tiny sea plane in Vancouver Harbour. The "Prayer Train Pilgrimage" across Canada had to start in Victoria, B.C.'s provincial capital on Vancouver Island, so the first leg was not by train at all.

Most of the twelve were quite intimidated and felt ill-equipped for this venture but they trusted the Lord's leadership through Arne.

"What are you going to say?" John asked him.

"I'm not sure," Arne answered. "The Lord will tell me."

The bold ten-year-old Doc, who had been eager to jump on the wild pony and knew how to lean back and hold on tight when his father pulled the bronco to its knees with the lariat, had grown into a bold leader, who would obediently follow his heavenly Father into unknown territory.

They landed in Victoria Harbour and walked straight into the impressive parliament buildings to a meeting with B.C. Social Credit Party Human Resources Minister, Bill Vander Zalm, who was the MLA from Arne's area and who would become premier in 1986. While introductions were being made, Premier Bill Bennett unexpectedly walked in. "They flew me back," he explained. "I wasn't supposed to be back till tomorrow but they flew me back early."

He was very gracious to the whole group. Arne handed him his card and said, "This is a prayer centre, Bill, and you can phone there most any time. If you have some real serious problems (and once in a while I hear you do get them), don't cast out the possibility that prayer is the answer."

"I've come to ask for forgiveness," he continued, finally knowing what the Lord wanted him to say. "The problems of this province are not your doing. I and the church have failed you by not praying for you as we should." He went on to explain how Christians are commanded, in 1 Timothy chapter 2, to pray for those in authority.

This humble apology, when perhaps the cabinet were used to political demands, led into the promise: "We will pray for you by name and we will intercede before the Lord of heaven that he will give you wisdom to govern this province." Arne explained that this was the first stop in a cross-Canada train trip to repeat this message to as many elected officials as possible.

Just before they left, Premier Bennett said, "Well if you're going to be traveling across Canada, you're going to need some things to give to people." He gave a Canada pin to each of them plus extras to distribute along the way. That became a feature of the trip—they collected pins from almost every office where they were received.

Before the morning was over, they also had some time with Victoria's Mayor Young, who said he believed that Christianity had the only answer to youth delinquency and other problems: "Lack of direction in our youth has been evidenced today in a turning away from materialistic standards, but unfortunately it hasn't been translated into a useful direction... It has been translated into a form of a revulsion against authority... There has been no successful method to convert these people that are the chronic offenders from the course of destruction... save except in those who have actually turned to the Christian faith... and it's extraordinary the success rate that has occurred under those people who have actually made that conversion... So I'm with you... I certainly think that you people have a very appropriate message to carry forward to the persons in authority and others. I counsel you to not despair. It is not an easy task."

They flew back into Vancouver and boarded the train to head east at 3:00 p.m. Stops were planned in Regina, Winnipeg, Toronto, Quebec City, St John's, Halifax, Charlottetown, Fredericton, Ottawa, Edmonton and then back to Vancouver. Traveling by train gave the team of strangers time to build relationships and to share how the Lord had led each of them to be part of the trip. Through the kindness of local believers they were billeted in every city without cost and in the evenings they held meetings where they could enlarge on the vision of Prayer Canada and call more people to pray for the nation.

The plan was to visit with city mayors and provincial premiers, or their representatives, in every provincial capital and to communicate God's love for them. It was a daunting task but the Lord was with them from that first stop in Victoria and miraculously opened doors for them. Miracle after miracle excited them so much that they became the joyous, laughing, waving twelve that Arne had seen in his dream.

Arne did most of the talking at each intimidating visit and the team would pray quietly for the right words to be given to him. Each group of politicians probably expected this posse of Christians to make some demands or reprove them for some failing. So Arne's humble approach and request for forgiveness no doubt took them by surprise. Arne knew that they were ordinary people thrown into these powerful positions and that wisdom to govern does not automatically come with election success. It really is necessary for Christians to pray for those in authority.

After his presentation, Arne would ask, "Is there anything we can pray about?" At that point the Holy Spirit would arrange for some matter to be brought up that the team could pray about and often He spoke through them with words of knowledge.

Arne with the picture, Christ at Heart's Door © 1942, 1970 Warner Press, Inc., IN. Used with permission. Warner Sallman Artist.

Then Arne or one of the team would present gifts to the politicians: a copy of The Living Bible and a beautiful framed copy of the picture *Christ at Heart's Door* by Warner Sallman. There were no names in the written dedications on these gifts, just the name of the province. The Lord had told them: "You're not talking to a person; you're talking to a position."

Then, if there was an opening, Arne would ask them to provide a room in the governmental building where Christians could meet weekly to pray for leaders.

At some stage, they would walk around the various Parliament buildings and city halls seven times and quietly pray for the authorities' direction. There were many highlights of each of the different stops.

Chuck presenting the Bible to the RCMP superintendent in Regina

In Regina, a wonderful lady named Victoria McGuire arranged billets and transport, so that they were all able to attend their first appointment early the next morning, Thursday October 12 at 9:30 a.m., with Superintendent Cliff Morin of the RCMP. He spoke about vandalism and deteriorating standards of discipline and agreed that the "Christian concept" was the answer. The team prayed for protection and wise decision-making for all the RCMP members serving in the province. At Chuck's request, he was the one who presented the Bible to the superintendent. He recalled how the RCMP used to pick him up and send him home in a cab when he was drunk and he thanked them for looking after him so well.

Afterwards a couple of team members spent some time with the Staff Sergeant who accompanied the Superintendent, because God revealed his hunger. For two years he had been praying with his wife every night before bed: "Lord teach me to have wisdom to deal with people properly and teach me what it means to be a Christian." They were able to lead him in a prayer of commitment to Jesus.

Meanwhile the rest of the pilgrims were presenting the premier's Bible and picture to MLA Bill Allan who was very open and grateful for their prayer.

Later that day, Mayor Baker of Regina told them how he and another councillor in 1956 had brought in a daily prayer to open the council meetings. He said there was quite a tussle over it with several aldermen saying across the aisle, "What are you trying to turn this into—a Sunday School?"

Mayor Baker promised to make one of the board rooms available for a weekly prayer meeting. When presenting him with the Bible, Arne said, "I know things can change. God says we have not because we ask not. I want you to feel that God will answer every prayer you have in earnestness from your heart, believing that it's the best good for the people of this city and the people of this province."

The meetings in each city were all different but almost every time there was a gentle appreciative spirit and they were able to minister to those present. The officials ended every appointment with a "Thank you" or "I'm so glad you came." They were in no hurry to push the team out of their office.

Victoria McGuire, who would be leading the prayer group in the Regina city hall, hosted a meeting for the team that evening in her home and thirty-five people crowded in. John and Robert spoke and, with Harold, prayed for Victoria's son.

They traveled overnight to arrive in Winnipeg, Manitoba on Friday October 13 where they appeared for forty-five minutes on Willard and Betty Thiessen's TV show, *It's A New Day*, which had started two years before.

Then they met with a representative of the premier of Manitoba, as the premier was out of town, and later spent time with Mayor Steen. The mayor asked if they were going to meet with the lieutenant-governor of Manitoba.

"We'd like to," said Arne. "but our time is short. We only arrived at 7:30 this morning and we'll be leaving tomorrow at 8:25 a.m. We've already appeared on a local TV station this morning and we'll be sharing with a large meeting this evening."

"The Lieutenant-Governor is very much in favour," continued the mayor. "Very keen on prayer and prayer breakfasts. I think you would enjoying meeting him."

"Would you like to give him a ring and see if he's available this afternoon?" said Arne, not wanting to miss the opportunity.

Later the answer came. Mayor Steen reported, "He would like to see you at 3:15 this afternoon in his office on the second floor of the legislature building."

The Mayor also mentioned that he had pulled out his Bible the day before to look up 1Timothy 2, which Arne had quoted in his letter, "because I wanted to know why Paul had said you needed to pray for politicians."

"Do you agree with it?" asked Arne.

"Oh yes," laughed the mayor. "We need all the help we can get."

That evening, after their meeting with the Lieutenant-Governor, they shared with a large charismatic prayer group at their regular Friday night meeting. Sister Aquina, Pauline and Barbara sang and played. A beautiful time of ministry followed with healing and new life. The next day they boarded the train for Toronto.

Even the long hours spent on the train between stops were profitable. The team prayed with several people – some were healed, some were set free from different problems. There was a man on his way to Toronto for a serious operation who gave himself to the Lord and was healed: when he left the train he carried his own luggage. He had become an alcoholic in an attempt to kill the pain of a military injury and he had spent most of the time on the train in the bar. The men on the team would go down to sit with him in the bar and talk to him there. As a result of this healing, the conductor on the train was also saved.

In Toronto they started the day on Monday October 16 at 100 Huntley Street. They shared on this Ontario television program with David Mainse for about fifteen minutes and were able to use 100 Huntley Street as their headquarters for the day.

Pauline made the presentation to the Premier's representative in Toronto

The premier of Ontario was represented by Margaret Birch, the Provincial Secretary for Social Development. She had the room ready with enough chairs set out for all thirteen of them.

"I hope you won't mind if I don't get up," she said. "Yesterday I cracked two ribs. But I wasn't going to miss meeting the Prayer Canada team."

After introductions, Arne asked if he could pray for her. "Oh, yes," she said. So Arne walked over to her, put his hand on her head and prayed. He felt the Lord flowing through him and suddenly he was knocked off his feet and landed on his back. (That seemed to happen on this trip—when he prayed for someone, he was the one that went back.)

As he lay on his back, the minister leapt to her feet and started jumping up and down: "I don't have any pain!" she announced.

At that point, Pauline stepped out of her chair and came over. "If you will go home and pray for your epileptic son, he will be healed," she prophesied. Pauline was only in her twenties but already a prayer warrior with a prophetic gifting. The minister, a Pentecostal believer, did have an epileptic son. She was moved to tears by the love of the Lord.

Eventually every member of the team found that they had a valuable contribution to make, some individual connection with a person they were speaking with, or operating in one of the gifts of the Holy Spirit. They were all ambassadors in some way. The Lord regularly provided keys to open people's hearts.

Later both the mayor and his wife were very interested and were prayed for. The mayor said he would set aside a room for weekly prayer in City Hall. Then the pilgrimage continued by sleeper train for Montreal, changing there for Quebec City.

As they traveled in Quebec, two issues were of concern: language (only Robert could speak French) and the separatist movement (which this group from western Canada couldn't really understand). But what Robert observed more than anything was the spiritual hunger and openness. They had been a little anxious about the 160 French Bibles that they brought with them but in fact they could have given away 560. People would receive them gladly and say "I have a friend. Can he have one too?" Or "My daughter would like one also."

The evening before their official appointments in Quebec City, they were with a small charismatic prayer group and Robert was asked to say something. He told them what the Lord had told him—that Quebec was not to separate—and they were glad to hear it. "The Lord showed me a vision," he explained, "of a big boom chain around the outline of Canada." (This is the chain that holds floating logs together in the river). "There was one end of the chain going straight up into heaven and the Lord let me know that He wasn't going to let go of His end if we didn't let go of our end. I asked him where our end was and that's where He gave me a revelation of 2 Chronicles 7:14 being our end to the chain. We need to pray ..."

The next morning, although the Premier of Quebec had not confirmed that he would meet with them personally, the team made their way to the reception desk in the foyer of the high-rise building where the Legislature was held.

"Good morning," said Arne cheerfully. "We have an appointment to see the premier."

"I'm sorry," said the receptionist pleasantly. "That is not possible. The legislature is in session."

"Here is the letter notifying us to be here at 11 a.m. today," Arne persisted. "Would you send a note up to the premier that the Prayer Canada team is on the premises to meet their commitment and ask if he would spare a few minutes so we can speak with him?"

When she was reluctant to do that, Arne persisted: "Well, we've traveled three thousand miles to be here. We'll just sit here and pray until he comes or sends someone else in his place."

So she sent the message to the premier's office but the response came back that the premier was too busy. The team waited patiently. After a while the receptionist sent another message to the premier's office and was told that everybody there was tied up. Still the group stayed. She asked Robert in French how long the team planned to stay and he replied, "We will stay until the premier comes or appoints someone else in his place."

"We have a gift to present to him," added Arne.

The receptionist sent a third message to the premier's office and this time he sent his secretary to meet the group. Arne shared Prayer Canada's message with the secretary and gave her the Bible, telling her that they had brought Bibles to give to every premier.

The team then prayed for her and for the receptionist and for the government and Arne presented the secretary with the special picture of *Christ at Heart's Door* seeking entrance to the hearts of all people. Prayer and persistence again won the day.

The next appointment was 2:00 p.m. in City Hall to meet Mayor Pelletier.

There was high expectation for this meeting because of a dream God had given Arne three weeks earlier. In the dream he was in a beautiful, red-carpeted room with fancy chairs. He was sitting in one of the chairs donating blood. "Where is this place?" Arne asked. "That's the mayor's office in Quebec City," was the reply.

The dream was especially meaningful as he was often called on to donate his type AB blood which could be life-saving for certain blood types. Arne and Kathie had shared this remarkable dream at the Monday night prayer meeting that evening and the response was: "Arne, you will just have to offer to donate blood when you're in the mayor's office."

The morning after that prayer meeting, Arne had been surprised by a phone call from Mayor Pelletier of Quebec City. "I received your request to have you and your team meet me in my office," said the mayor and they made the arrangements. He said that he hadn't written because the Post Office was on strike, but he wanted Arne to know that he would be happy to meet them.

Arne was thrilled. But he didn't mention his dream at that point—the mayor thought he was a decent guy and Arne didn't want to upset this view. Instead he wrote him a letter saying that the Lord had told him in a dream to offer to donate blood. There was no reply. Arne wasn't sure what to make of that.

Now here they were outside the mayor's office at 2:00 p.m. The mayor and his assistant spotted them through the open door and the assistant came out to say, "It will be about five minutes, Mr. Bryan. And the mayor wants you to know that he has not forgotten about your offer to donate blood."

When the thirteen team members were ushered into the mayor's plush office, Arne saw that it was carpeted in red and furnished with ornate chairs, just like the dream. They were asked to sit down and one of the ladies sat in a particularly fancy chair.

"Oh, you can't sit there," said the mayor. "That chair is only for queens."

"Sir, might I remind you that she is a queen," said Arne. "The Lord says that His children are **kings** and priests before Him."

"You're right about that!" said the mayor and he allowed her to stay seated in the queen's chair.

"I have been anxious to meet you and hear what you have to say," continued the mayor. "I have arranged for all of you to go to the headquarters of the Red Cross here in Quebec City to meet the Superintendant and his wife, and they will arrange for a nurse there to take your blood. I trust that this will be acceptable."

Arne thanked him for the arrangements and then for the next fifteen minutes shared the key plans to set up Prayer Posts across Canada, starting with the capital cities. The mayor seemed impressed and permitted the team to pray with him.

They were delayed going to the Red Cross because their van had been towed but they handed out more French Bibles while they waited. At the Red Cross headquarters, Arne and Joan Hansen both donated blood. The superintendant looked after Arne personally and sat beside him to chat. "Did you know, Mr. Bryan," he said, "that the mayor has donated blood thirty-seven times?" Arne's offer to donate his blood probably touched the mayor's heart more than anything he could have mentioned.

The next morning they were forty-five minutes late for their train because of misreading the schedule. Missing that train would have upset the whole itinerary. When they got to the station the train was steaming and ready to go but still there and neither the conductor nor the trainmen knew why. Arne convinced the station agent to open up the baggage car for their luggage and so they caught the train and continued their journey.

There were other times when they had to wait in train stations but they used the time praying. On one of these occasions, Arne fell down to the ground under the power of the Holy Spirit. People came around them most concerned and wanted to call an ambulance. "No, no," the team insisted. "He's okay."

They were impressed by the overnight ferry crossing from North Sydney to Port aux Basques, Newfoundland. All vehicles had to be chained down because of the massive waves that often occur. The ferries were large ice breakers, looked like cruise ships and could carry twelve hundred passengers and 350 cars.

From Port aux Basques, it was a fourteen-hour bus ride to St. John's. Barbara played her guitar and sang most of the way. The other passengers applauded after every song and called for more.

"You're arriving just in time," said the bus driver as they approached St. John's. It was 9:00 p.m. on Friday October 20. "There's a Christian program on the radio. You should really get on there and tell people you're in town."-

"Folks, just give me a couple of minutes," he said to the other passengers when they arrived at the bus depot. "I've got to get these people on the radio. I'll be right back." He ran into the office, told them about the Prayer Canada team and asked the staff to connect by telephone to the radio station. By the time Arne and Harold Hansen joined him, they had two phones connected with the radio studio so that they could be on the Radio Hot Line.

It was at least 10:00 p.m. when Arne and Kathie arrived at the home of the local pastor who was hosting them.

"Do you know anybody in the government?" Arne asked the pastor, because they had no appointments arranged.

"No," he said but then added, "But my daughter works for the government."

Arne phoned her and explained why they were there. "I think I know somebody who would be happy to talk to you," she said. "He was just appointed Minister of Rural Affairs and Indian Development today and he's in a hotel here. This is his phone number."

The minister wasn't too put out to have a call so late and agreed to meet them on the steps of the Parliament Buildings the next morning, although it wasn't usually open on Saturdays.

By now it was 10:30 p.m. but Arne never gives up. "Do you know anybody at City Hall?" was his next question to the pastor they were staying with. The pastor looked up the Mayor's phone number but warned Arne that she wasn't very approachable.

"I'm so happy to be able to talk you," said Arne when the Mayor answered, "because the Lord sent us to talk to you."

"Oh," she said. "Well, I'm tied up. I have no time tomorrow. Saturday is busy.'

Arne just kept talking and after a while she said, "I guess I could cancel my two o'clock appointment ..." The Lord knew of course, when He chose Arne for this work, how persistent he could be and He gave them favour like this from time to time.

*Prayer Train Pilgrims in St John's NL –
(l to r) Harold, Robert, Chuck, Barbara, Mary Ann, Joan,
Sister Aquina, Tina, Linda, John, Pauline, Kathie, Arne*

So on Saturday October 21, they met first with the Minister, who was very interested and had a photographer present. They witnessed to the photographer especially and prayed for her as she had terminal cancer.

Then at their appointment with the Mayor of St. John's, Arne asked Linda to present the gifts. Linda had always felt intimidated by intellectual people but by this time she had witnessed enough miracles to take a deep breath and begin the presentation. When she mentioned that she was a nurse, the mayor was delighted. "So am I," she said and they had their connection. The mayor was happy for them to pray for her and her family.

Early the next morning they set off on the return bus drive and overnight ferry, sharing deeply with several other passengers.

They continued on by train, to arrive in Halifax, Nova Scotia, early afternoon on Monday October 23. That evening the team divided and went in three different directions. John was in the group that went to a Catholic charismatic group who were not sure how to proceed. "What should we be doing in this prayer meeting?" the lady in charge asked.

John gave her a word of knowledge: "You are limiting the Holy Spirit because you are afraid of what is outside that door. Give that fear to the Lord and God will touch."

As she repented of her fear, all of them ended up on the floor because the Holy Spirit had overpowered them with His presence.

The next morning they met a minister who was representing Premier John Buchanan and then the executive secretary of the mayor.

They rented a fifteen-seat passenger bus and drove on for Charlottetown, Prince Edward Island. The bus caused problems on the way and Harold supervised the repair of a broken spring when they got there. Arne phoned their host, a United Church pastor in Charlottetown, but he had gone to Moncton where his brother had just died and his wife knew nothing about the Prayer Canada team staying in the basement of the church. The day was saved by Sister Aquina who called friends at St Mary's Convent and arranged for them to stay there overnight. This was a retirement home for senior nuns and so they had to keep a low profile as men were not allowed.

They had to hurry off to the local community centre where they had a meeting scheduled. One of the ladies they prayed for there was healed and no longer needed a wheelchair.

When they returned to the convent by 10:00 p.m. as requested by Sister Ruth, the nun in charge, they were surprised to be led into a large meeting hall where twelve nuns waited to have the team pray for them. At that moment, the Lord spoke to Arne and said, "I want you to wash their feet." As Sister Ruth was setting down the basin and towels, she suddenly fell over backwards under the power of the Holy Spirit. In almost a trance, she said, "I was at the door when you came in today, and our regulations say that we are to wash the strangers' feet when they enter our building." The nuns had long since let this custom lapse.

After the nuns had allowed the team to wash their feet and pray for them, they each rose to receive a hug and fell down under the power of God—the most effective Holy Spirit meeting the team experienced on the trip.

Just as the meeting was ending, an elderly nun who was quite sick joined them. Arne prayed for her and told her to meet him the next morning at the front door at 8:00 a.m. "You're going to run with me around the building three times." The next morning it happened just as Arne had prophesied.

On Wednesday October 25, they had an informal meeting with Mayor Moran. He had no pins for their collection but gave them each a special printed dollar. Then Premier

Bennett Campbell received them very graciously. As a Roman Catholic, he was interested in prayer.

They were up at 4:30 a.m. on Thursday October 26 for the one-hour ferry ride to New Brunswick, munching delicious Nova Scotia apples.

Presentation to the Mayor of Fredericton NB

They had the afternoon and evening that day in Fredericton. They were beginning their talk in the board room with the premier's representative when the mayor joined them, having been told that was the arrangement. So they made the presentation to both of them and then the mayor walked them to City Hall and gave them a tour. He presented them with a special plate. They spent that night on board the train heading for Montreal and then Ottawa.

Presentation to secretary of Pierre Trudeau in Ottawa

The pilgrims arrived in Ottawa at noon on Friday October 27. They went straight to Confederation Building, close to Parliament Hill, where several MPs had offices, and one office was made available to them for phones calls, etc. That afternoon they met the mayor's representative and then went to Prime Minister Trudeau's office, where they shared with the prime minister's executive secretary. He was very moved by their approach and welcomed their prayer. He wept as the team formed a circle around him and prayed for him. He was an ordinary man in an extraordinary position and appreciated the spiritual support.

They were escorted through the Parliament buildings by a Christian security man who was on guard that day and they anointed every seat in Parliament and the Senate. They were encouraged to discover that there were fourteen active Bible studies on Parliament Hill.

They pulled out of Ottawa about midnight and had a relaxing trip to arrive in Edmonton early on the morning of Monday October 30. After warm fellowship over breakfast with supportive friends, they headed to the premier's office although they had no appointment, not even to see a representative of the premier, who was in Ottawa with all his staff. Using Arne's tactic of "keep on asking," they eventually saw the Director of Security who arranged a meeting with MLA Schiver from Lesser Slave Lake. He said he was a Muslim but was interested and concerned. They had a good time sharing. In the afternoon they had a meeting with the mayor's representative. There were twenty people altogether in the mayor's office.

Sadly the time was coming for the pilgrims to go their separate ways. Mary Ann flew out that day, while the rest of the team had a good evening rally. The next morning, Harold and Joan left for Golden and Pauline left for Penticton. The others spent the day in Edmonton and left with the feeling: Mission Complete.

They returned to Vancouver elated at what God had done for them. They had witnessed God at work, active through each of them. As they reported at the next Prayer Breakfast, the final miracle was that this bunch of thirteen varied individuals, mostly strangers at the outset, had not only survived twenty-one days constantly rubbing together like sandpaper but now they loved each other with God's supernatural love. Arne had been more than a visionary leader and general of crack troops; out of his soft heart, he had been a father and mentor to his team.

After meeting with premiers, mayors and the prime minister's representatives, they had all been made aware that Canada had many serious problems and that we have to pray. They had begun to understand the ferocious spiritual war being waged in individuals and over Canada.

As Chuck Giesbrecht said, "God taught me how to pray."

CHAPTER 8

1979:
PRAYER CANADA'S HEARTBEAT;
SURVIVING TROUBLES

During the next year, the regular heartbeat of Prayer Canada began to pulse nation-wide, the rhythm of meetings, special events and travel, repetitive but full of life.

After the Prayer Train Pilgrimage, God gave Arne another full-time assistant besides Kathie, although none of them was paid a salary. After her life-changing pilgrimage across the country, Linda Bowden knew in her heart that she was to be part of Prayer Canada.

Linda worked as Arne's assistant for about two years and grew in faith as she prayed for her financial support. Her father was one of her sponsors because he wanted her to learn about missionary work before committing herself overseas. Those years were a great preparation for her future life of missionary service in Thailand, depending on God rather than any human supply.

It was good timing. Arne and Kathie returned from the Prayer Train Pilgrimage to a busy ministry. While the team were away, volunteers had kept the prayer room open. They had run the regular meetings, prayed with visitors and dealt with prayer requests that came in by phone and mail. Now Arne had all the great contacts they had made on the trip to follow up and opportunities for prayer meetings in city halls and parliament buildings to seize.

Linda was part of everything that Prayer Canada did, helping to organize events and traveling with Arne and Kathie. Only about three years old in the Lord when she first met Arne, she saw him as a mentor, an encourager, and a great example of discipline and hard work. "I probably wouldn't be the person I am today without his investment in my life," she says.

"I'm just going to the prayer room to pray," she remembers saying one day. Arne looked at her. "You're angry," he said. "You're not going to pray. You're angry." He was right, of course. Still a young Christian, she needed to learn what was really going on.

On Sundays they prayed through the night with a dozen or so people. They fasted every Monday and the evening meeting involved usually forty or fifty people, with plenty of evidence of the Holy Spirit moving. Once when Linda arrived in the prayer room, Arne announced, "Okay, now Linda's going to pray for everybody." She had no warning, no time to prepare. She had been filled with the Holy Spirit for years and God had used her to touch people's lives supernaturally, but now Arne was teaching her to be always ready and forced her to rely on the Holy Spirit at all times.

"I would like to learn how to pray," thought Leoran Anhorn. He was looking at Arne's picture in the Vancouver Sun and reading an account of the recent train trip. It said that Arne was going to start another Prayer Canada prayer meeting, this time from 6 to 8 on Wednesday mornings, in the Upper Room. Leoran didn't know Arne or Prayer Canada but he decided to go along and has been praying for Canada early on Wednesdays ever since; in May 1980, he became a member of the Board of Directors of Prayer Canada.

Leoran's parents wanted him to be a pastor but he "didn't have the gift of the gab," as he says. However, prayer was something he could do and he embraced the vision of Prayer

Canada. Like Arne, he grew up in Alberta on a prairie farm but he went into the fishing industry and became a buyer for a fish company. His boat was a packer—he would go round the fishing boats, load their catch on his boat, weigh it and pay them for it, so that they could go on fishing.

One year Leoran Anhorn took the Prayer Canada board of directors and some family members for a sail on his "packer"

He says there were times in his career when he didn't know which way to go or what to do. Sometimes he flipped coins! "The thing is, *we* don't know," he says, "and a lot of politicians don't know either. They really need to rely on the Lord's help."

He once approached a minister in the Conservative government at a meeting in Abbotsford and introduced himself. "I'm from Prayer Canada," Leoran said. "We're praying for you." The minister was so thankful, basking in the idea that people were praying for him. That's what motivates Leoran and many others like him to pray faithfully week after week for all Canada's leaders, naming them individually before the Lord, whether they are local, municipal, provincial or federal politicians.

One Wednesday morning when the prayer meeting had been going about six months, one of the regulars (a bus driver) commented: "It would be easier for me to come on Thursdays."

"Wonderful," said Arne. "I appoint you to lead a prayer meeting on Thursday mornings!"

So the Thursday prayer meeting began, also from 6 to 8 a.m. Others joined him and both these prayer meetings still continue to the present day.

1979 was obviously going to be a busy year but that didn't stop Arne starting up new ventures. He didn't know the year would bring family tragedy and end in a crisis.

One day in January, Arne went over to Channel 10, the local TV station that was five blocks away, to get Prayer Canada meetings advertised during the free community announcements. He got talking to the station manager, who asked him if he was interested in one of their vacant spots for a TV program. This was an opportunity not to be missed – a free live community program, once a week!

After a two-second prayer, Arne boldly agreed to take a time slot. He just had to bring in three volunteers for three training sessions to run the cameras. Twenty-one days later, Prayer Canada would be on the air.

"What do you know about putting on a TV program?" was Kathie's alarmed reaction when he returned home.

"Oh, well," replied Arne. "We'll have music segments and interview important people."

"Well, you can look after it," she said. "I'm not going to be a part of it."

Planning got underway and Kathie changed her mind when Arne said that he needed her to be his Floor Manager.

"The Upper Room" broadcast on Channel 10 on Tuesday January 30, 1979 began at 10:00 p.m. with *Sweet Hour Of Prayer* playing in the background and the words "The Upper Room" on the screen. Arne could be seen sitting in a studio, smiling and saying, "A warm welcome and ***greeting*** from all of us here at Prayer Canada to you, in Surrey, New Westminster, Langley and Aldergrove, watching Channel 10 right now. This is a Christian non-denominational outreach to awaken Canada to Christ's call."

Arne introduced Kathie and his co-host for that week, John DeVries. He asked John a couple of questions about the drastic need for revival among Canadian Christians. John's answers and everything Arne said had to be timed to the last minute – a challenging discipline for both of them.

Arne continued, "What disturbing things are prevalent in every area of our nation's activities! Political, justice, education, health, unemployment, labour unrest. We pray **daily** for these areas of life. Will you?" He then led into 1Timothy 2:1-6, the mandate of Prayer Canada, which he read from The Living Bible.

Then came a section of announcements, including that there were five people waiting on the telephones for calls from viewers, details of the show schedule, information about the Upper Room and the prayer times both in the Upper Room and in Surrey City Hall, prayer groups in Keremeos and Williams Lake, and a planned telex national prayer chain for emergency prayer requests.

Arne asked his viewers to phone people who they knew were hurting so that they could turn on Channel 10 for the prayer time that was coming up. "We are going to pray for personal needs in just a few minutes, right **there** where you are in your living room, bedroom, kitchen or den, wherever." As always, Arne created excitement by suddenly turning the volume up on key words.

Then came an eight-minute talk by Arne on prayer. He quoted from Hebrews:

> For whatever God says to us is full of living power: it is sharper than the sharpest dagger, cutting swift and deep into our innermost thoughts and desires with all their parts, exposing us for what we really are. He

knows about everyone, everywhere. Everything about us is bare and wide open to the all-seeing eyes of our living God; nothing can be hidden from him to whom we must explain all that we have done. But Jesus the Son of God is our great High Priest who has gone to heaven itself to help us; therefore let us never stop trusting him. This High Priest of ours understands our weaknesses, since he had the same temptations we do, though he never once gave way to them and sinned. So let us come boldly to the very throne of God and stay there to receive his mercy and to find grace to help us in our times of need (Hebrews 4:12-16, TLB).

He added a personal comment: "These words the Lord gave me when I was baptized in a small Evangelical Free Church in Vancouver in 1948. These words have been a ***power force*** in my life ever since."

Arne introduced three young people, Rhonda, David and Paul, who sang scripture in song. After the song, Arne brought on his guest, Surrey Mayor Bill Vogel, and asked him if he believed in the power of prayer. Bill had four minutes to reply and after that they prayed together for Surrey, naming all the aldermen and women and school trustees.

With just a few minutes to go, John recapped the prayer requests that had been phoned in and then they prayed. Arne's biblical prayers, fervent yet intimate, always bless and challenge.

Arne concluded by saying, "God is answering prayer tonight just as He does whenever we call to Him." He urged them to speak God's Words in prayer and invited them to ask Him into their hearts—the call was very brief but clear. Finally, over *Sweet Hour of Prayer* in the background, a book recommendation (*Prayer the Mightiest Force in the World* by Frank Laubach) and an invitation to watch next Tuesday with their friends because "the Lord wants to ***help*** them."

With plenty of prayer, preparation, interesting guests and Arne's own personality, he continued these TV shows for sixteen years, half an hour every Tuesday at first, then a full hour on Sundays at 10 p.m. with the name "Sunday Night Live."

Arne wanted to build on the success of the Prayer Train Pilgrimage. The vision was to have a prayer meeting in every city hall across the nation and especially in capital cities. These prayer meetings could start anywhere—homes, churches, businesses—and then move into city halls and legislatures. He called them "Prayer Posts" where soldiers would come to receive their orders.

Arne knew how to open doors. He would write or phone people he knew, often through Full Gospel Businessmen connections, or people who had contacted Prayer Canada, and he would say "We're going to be coming your way on this date. Can we come and see you? Can you get some other people together who want to pray?" He would work out an itinerary, staying in people's homes, visiting people, linking people and challenging them.

"Why don't **you** start a Prayer Canada prayer meeting?" he'd ask, after presenting the Scriptures, even if there were only two or three people. Then he'd encourage and support them and show them how to get a list of the local authorities so they could pray for them by name.

There's no denying that Arne can be very strong and blunt but as Linda says, "It's the love of God in his heart that speaks and people hear that." She recalls how he would come and pat someone on the back and say "God's telling you to do this, that, or the other …" Then when the person protested with a loud "*Arne!*" he would say, "Well you'd better pray about it." Of course the Lord would confirm it in the person's heart.

In an echo of the days when cowboy Arne used to ride out over the range caring for livestock, Arne and Kathie and Linda drove around B.C. and also traveled all the way across the country that year, visiting prayer meetings and churches, and continued each year after that. They made contact with praying people and stirred up others to pray. They organized prayer for Canada's governments. Sometimes Arne was also able to spend time with his son in Creston, his sisters in the Okanagan and even his other relatives in Ontario.

One of the first journeys in B.C. included Salmon Arm, 100 Mile House and Williams Lake. Arne had just finished speaking at the Full Gospel Businessmen's lunch meeting in Williams Lake, in the Cariboo region, 540 km north east of Vancouver.

"We need to listen to what this man is saying about praying in City Hall," said a voice. It was the mayor, Tom Mason, attending for the first time and not yet saved. (He would later preach the gospel in India and the Philippines and write a book: *In My Father's Hand*.) Within a week, the local prayer meeting for Prayer Canada moved into the Council Chambers of Williams Lake City Hall. It has been there every Wednesday noon since then.

Perhaps Mayor Mason had been thinking about the wildly unruly Rodeo and Stampede which took place every Canada Day long weekend, together with a carnival with rides and games. They had to call in extra police from Quesnel and Kamloops to keep order. One year, when there were more than three hundred arrests for brawls and drunkenness, they had to use empty box cars for space to detain them all.

For three days before the next Stampede began, some of the Full Gospel businessmen, including the Prayer Canada leaders, marched around the Stampede grounds and prayed that the wine would be turned to water and that drunkenness would be eliminated. That year only a few arrests were made.

On these really long road trips, Arne always wanted to keep going. "Just press on!" he'd say when Kathie and Linda wanted to stop for a break. Sometimes they'd get into a town late at night and he'd want to go visit somebody. "Arne! We're not going. Enough's enough," Kathie and Linda would chorus.

"Well, if you want to just stay in the car you can but I'm going in," he'd say cheerfully and sure enough it would turn into another meeting.

They would drive through all kinds of weather and stay in a different city every night, in a motel or with prayer leaders. Staying in homes birthed great relationships with so many gracious people. Everywhere they went, Arne brought his urgent message: "God wasn't just making a suggestion when He said that we are to pray for our nation's leaders. It's a *command*!"

They also prayed individually for people in each meeting. Arne wanted to encourage prayer for everyone, first for those in authority, then for one another. This was easier in small meetings; in larger ones they formed prayer lines.

Arne would always ask Linda to say something in the meetings, some personal report of what the Lord was doing through Prayer Canada. She learned to be ready. On one occasion she was preparing to say something about an incident that had happened on the train trip but when she got up to speak she couldn't open her mouth.

"Linda's going to speak about the train trip," Arne was saying but Linda couldn't speak about anything.

She heard the Lord whisper, "I want you to share your testimony."

"But, Lord, this is for Prayer Canada," she answered. "I'm here to share what's going on."

She stood there silent. Arne put his arm around her, like a father, and said, "Well, she's having a little trouble getting her words together. Maybe we should do a praise and worship song while we're waiting."

Eventually she managed to share her testimony: Linda and her sister Gail who was two years younger had lived together in Vancouver for ten years, partying and having fun.

They were both nurses who could leave and take off for two or three months traveling and then find another job. But in 1973, first their older sister and then their parents in Ontario all became Christians and were filled with the Holy Spirit. Linda was angry and didn't want to hear about it.

A couple of years later Gail was rushed to Vancouver General Hospital with severe septicaemia that affected her lungs, liver, kidneys and then her brain, causing grand mal epileptic seizures for three or four days. The doctors weren't sure she would pull through.

Linda called her parents to come to Vancouver because Gail was dying—she had tubes everywhere and a respirator was keeping her alive—but warned them not to "preach." They didn't need to preach, though, because during that very confusing and scary time, the Holy Spirit drew Linda to God. She saw Oral Roberts on television saying, "If *you* out there think that you are unworthy, too unworthy to be saved, I want you to know there's hope." Linda had been angry because she had thought she was beyond God's love. Another time she wept at the song "Pass me not, oh gentle Saviour. Hear my humble cry…" Hers were desperate, almost suicidal tears that expressed the prayer in her heart.

About nine o'clock in the evening of October 9, 1975, the phone rang in Linda's apartment. It was Gail's neurologist explaining that they had decided to pull all the plugs. "We've done an ET and there's a lot of brain damage. Your sister's just never going to make it. We won't resuscitate her. She's out of our hands now."

Instead of telling her parents the news, Linda turned to her Dad and said, "I want to be baptized." What she meant was: *I want to get saved.*

Her father got out his Four Spiritual Laws and began diligently going through it. "The first spiritual law says … Now repeat after me … Spiritual law number two …" Linda felt something stirring in her belly like a fire. She thought she was going to throw up. "Law number three ..." All of a sudden Linda opened her mouth and out came a prayer language. She was singing at the top of her lungs. Her parents started to laugh–she hadn't even repeated the sinner's prayer yet!

"What about the phone call, Linda?" asked her father when they had quietened down.

"Oh, yes," she replied, suddenly sober. "I can handle this now. It was the doctor. They just pulled the plugs on Gail."

"Well, we'd better pray." So her father led them in prayer battle. Linda prayed in tongues. Two hours later her father got off his knees and said, "He's done it! We can go to bed."

At the hospital, Gail spent that night in a deep sleep, a coma. The next morning, she woke up, sat up and wanted to know where she was. Tests showed that everything that had been shutting down had been restored. They had feared extensive brain damage but the results were as if she had never had a single seizure.

When Linda finished telling the meeting this story of God's miraculous grace in her family's lives, there was a healing anointing and two or three people were healed that night.

Arne, Kathie and Linda took a small team with them for an itinerary back east which included the first annual residential Prayer and Fast Weekend in Sudbury, Ontario, August 30 to September 1, 1979. This was inspired by the successful Easter weekend meetings for prayer and fasting in March of the previous year. It became an annual event.

Arne had sent a letter to all premiers and cabinet members and to Ottawa, re-affirming Prayer Canada's commitment to pray for them all and asking for prayer topics for the weekend. The three days were planned with "spiritual meals" of prayer and worship over meal times. Arne taught on prayer but a large part of the ministry was in the form of testimonies and other sharing and praying for each other. Free periods were set aside for meditating on what had been said.

Afterwards, in Toronto with the rest of the B.C. team, Arne was asked to give Kathie a difficult phone message: Barry, her second son, had died.

When Kathie phoned home, she discovered that Barry had been pushing his little boy in the swing at a barbecue with friends when he just fell down dead. He was twenty-seven with two sons, Kyle (3) and Darrel (18 months). Kathie's family had already sorted out a flight for her to go home and she said to Arne, "I can go by myself. You stay here." She was experiencing a deep peace from the Lord and was able to let Arne continue the planned itinerary in Ontario with the rest of the team.

All her family met her at the airport and they went straight to Barry's home, where his young widow, Ingrid, put her arms around Kathie.

Little Kyle said, "Daddy was pushing me on the swing and now he's dead."

Perhaps he thought he'd killed him!

"Daddy's in heaven," Kathie said to comfort him.

"Oh?"

"Yes, he's with Jesus."

"Oh." That seemed to give him some understanding.

Kathie was amazed at the grace of the Lord that was carrying her through everything. At the service she said to a friend, "They're going to think I didn't even care for my son!"

After ten days, she flew back to Ontario to join Arne and the team who were in Ottawa by this time. They were staying at Linda Bowden's parents' place by a lake. Kathie looked out of a window and saw a double rainbow in the sky. She knew that one was for her first husband, who had died, and one was for Barry. The Lord said to her, "I will not require this of you again."

Back in 1965, Arne had trained to work in security at the Pacific Coliseum in Vancouver for the Billy Graham Crusade and other evangelistic events. Now in 1979 he received a phone call to ask if he would head up security at the Coliseum during the Pentecostal Assemblies of Canada World Convention. As usual, Arne said "Yes" and as head of security he was able to have Kathie and Linda attend the convention too.

Arne found out that a group of three or four pastors from Africa had not known that they would have to pay for their own food during the conference. Their accommodation was free but they were just not eating. When Arne found out about this, he took them out for a meal at a buffet with Kathie and Linda. The African pastors had never seen food in this quantity before. They all really connected. It wasn't just the food; it was a spiritual connection.

Arne made sure they didn't go hungry again. He even went in the kitchen at the conference and told them, "Chef, we need some rice here. You've got to put more rice on this menu." So Arne cared for them and they ate to their hearts' content.

These new friends loved the vision of Prayer Canada and invited Arne to bring a team to visit their own countries. Arne's generosity opened up Africa to Prayer Canada.

While they were preparing for Africa, the spiritual battle that was raging around Arne and Kathie in terms of finances reached a crisis. Arne was now eligible for his veteran's pension which helped a bit. Kathie worked at various crafts, sewing busily whenever Arne was away, filling boxes and boxes and selling them on charity stands in the shopping malls. But the rent on the Upper Room, miraculously supplied in one lump sum for the first year, now had to be paid every month.

"What if the money doesn't come in?" Kathie asked.

"Well, I guess we'll shut the door," Arne replied.

Every month Kathie wondered, "Is this the month we're

going to shut the door?" But it never was. They often had to pray in faith until the last moment, but the money was always there to pay the rent.

Now, however, they were about to lose their home. How could they keep advancing?

They had sold Kathie's house to the Alliance Church and invested the proceeds in a four-plex, where they lived in one unit and the other three were rented out. This was part of a business Arne had developed with another married couple. Arne was a one-third holder of a mortgage on the property and was due one-third of the profits of the company. His contribution was his work as an appraiser and house inspector. However, when the husband of the other couple died without a will, it became clear that instead of issuing signed shares in the company, he had just put the money in the bank. His partner's family then fought over the forty-two million dollar assets and insisted that nothing was owed to Arne. Arne was advised not to make any payments towards the mortgage until it was all settled, at which point he was taken to court because he was behind on the payments.

On the last day of the hearing, Kathie went with Arne to the court in Vancouver to get the final word. There was no recourse—they really were losing their home. Kathie prayed, "Lord, You are the righteous judge. I bow to You." At the same time, she was angry and took it out on Arne.

Returning home from Vancouver on the Skytrain, faced with having to leave their home and not having enough income to rent another place, Arne was silent while Kathie was stewing, filled with angry thoughts at the injustice of their situation.

All of a sudden Arne spoke. "What are we going to have for lunch?"

"What do you mean?" Kathie burst out. "You've got to get a *job*! *I've* got to get a job! And it's *crazy* to think of going to Africa! "

Back at home that afternoon, not feeling any better, she was helping a lady in one of the other four-plex units with some sewing.

"Kathie, I have a word for you," said the neighbour. "The enemy has been harassing you that it is a *crazy* thing to go a far off land." Kathie immediately remembered her words on the Skytrain, as her friend went on to assure her that the Lord would look after them and support them. The Lord always soothed her anxiety whenever it got too much for her.

The next day Kathie was scheduled to go to a prayer meeting in the home of a lady she didn't know well. But first she picked up her Bible and read Psalm 109:4 in the NIV. It was describing what God will do to those who harm His servant. Verse four hit her with Holy Spirit force: *"In return for my friendship they accuse me, but I am a man of prayer"* (Psalm 109:4, NIV). She began to cry. "God, they don't know what they're doing. Forgive them."

After this she found herself in a large wealthy home, telling the prayer group that she and Arne, the leaders of Prayer Canada, would soon have nowhere to live.

"Kathie," said the hostess. "I have a basement suite if you'd like."

That evening Kathie returned with Arne to view the eighteen-hundred square foot fully furnished suite and to talk to the woman's husband who was not a Christian. Arne asked him about the rent.

"Oh, don't worry about that till you get back from Africa," said the husband.

The Lord had guided them to this very generous family at just the time they needed another home. They moved into the huge basement suite (so huge they only used half of it) and were able to concentrate on spreading the work of Prayer Canada, even into Africa.

"...I have given you authority over all the power of the enemy..."
(Luke 10:19, TLB)

Arne & Kathie at Mission Fest, January 1989

CHAPTER 9

1980:
AFRICA AND BACK

Even though Arne and his team had visited all the provincial capitals on the train trip in 1978, there were two other capitals that they had not visited. For months Arne had been asking people if they knew anyone in Yellowknife, the capital of the Northwest Territories, or Whitehorse, capital of the Yukon. But no one did and praying brought no guidance. Then, round about 10 p.m. on Christmas Eve 1979, Arne clearly heard the Lord remind him about it.

"Lord," he said. "I don't have any contacts there."

God just seemed to press in, saying "You move and I'll move."

So Arne obediently booked the first available flight to Yellowknife, leaving January 10, 1980 with a return flight scheduled for January 13. "Now I need a contact," Arne told the Lord.

On December 31, Arne mentioned this situation to the other directors at a board meeting in a café. Right away, John Verseveldt said, "I know someone in Hay River." Hay River is on the south shore of Great Slave Lake and Yellowknife is on its northern shore. So Arne called John's friend and asked him if he knew anyone in Yellowknife who might be interested in praying for Canada.

"Oh, yes," he replied. "Claude Goebel, my insurance man. He is a Christian and I think he would be glad to hear from you. He lives in Yellowknife."

When Arne called him to introduce himself, Claude Goebel seemed delighted to hear from him. Arne said he would be there in a few days on January 10 and Claude offered to meet him at the airport and put him up in his own home. God had promised to move and He was moving.

The first evening in Yellowknife, Arne and Claude got on famously. The next morning Claude took Arne to his office, where he could use a spare desk and telephone to contact Christians on a list Claude drew up. Some of those were interested in praying for the authorities and Arne picked up some more names to call. One of those was Tagak Curley, an MLA from Rankin Inlet.

Tagak Curley, Inuit leader and at that time MLA for Rankin Inlet, NWT

The Lord had fulfilled His promise. Tagak Curley proved to be the link that Arne needed and he would became a great friend. They had a good chat. That evening Tagak took him to supper in Yellowknife's best hotel and introduced him to Bill and Ruth Dennis, who worked for the government. They were both committed Christians whom Tagak knew well.

After they shared with each other for a good while, Tagak told Arne he was appointing Bill and Ruth to head up Prayer Canada prayer meetings at the Legislature and at City Hall. This was only the first full day of Arne's visit and the Lord had already accomplished so much. Bill and Ruth Dennis were wonderful prayer warriors. They remained Prayer Canada's Prayer Leaders in Yellowknife for many years until they retired and returned to their home state of Louisiana.

It would be more than another year before Arne finally went to Whitehorse, Yukon.

On Tuesday February 12, 1980, Arne, Kathie and Linda set off on their first African adventure, an action-packed trip lasting forty-five days, with four other team members: Elsie, Maria, Ed Daly and Doreen Gowett. It was only seventeen months after the ground-breaking train trip across Canada.

They planned to spend three days in Israel on the way, including a meeting in the Canadian Embassy in Tel Aviv. However the first drama of the trip gave them an extra three days there. They arrived in Israel on the last flight allowed for the next six days, because there had been a serious problem with a traveler the day before.

Security was high. When they arrived, all their baggage was taken apart and searched, leaving the boxes and parcels unfit for reuse. Arne knew this was not right as they were carrying many books to give away during their African visits. He went to the authorities, told them that they had no way to find other boxes for their belongings and managed to convince them that they needed help. The inspectors who had torn apart their luggage were made to find suitable boxes and to rewrap their stuff. The team gave thanks to God.

Israel stirred their spirits. Guided by missionaries Grant and Barbara Livingston, the team was very moved to walk where Jesus walked. At one point, as they stood together praying in Capernaum, they felt the fragrance of Christ.

They went on to Africa. The purpose was to bring the vision of Prayer Canada to Kenya, Nigeria and Ghana, by visiting their capital cities and sharing God's love with their leaders. They wanted to let the authorities know that people were praying for them. They also took part in crusades in each country, enjoyed great fellowship with their hosts and went on a safari. Everywhere they went, Arne spoke in churches where the worship was fervent and Sunday services ran from 9:30 a.m. to 1:30 p.m. or even 3:00 p.m. They had at least ten days in each of the three countries.

They flew first to Kenya, where they presented a Bible to the mayor of Nairobi, had an appointment with the Secretary to the President and were interviewed for Kenya Radio. One night during the crusade in Nairobi, where they enjoyed wonderful praise with crowds of three hundred to five hundred people, the power went out because there was not enough water for the generators. So they managed with one flashlight reflecting off the ceiling during the teaching. The lights came on in time for the offering and altar call.

When the Prayer Canada team checked into the Kenyan airport to leave for Nigeria, Arne was handed a note telling him that he had to pay $550 in overweight charges. The baggage inspectors had weighed all the bags and charged extra for each one. Once again Arne knew this was not right and demanded to see their boss.

After some stalling, a man came over and said, "What can I do for you?"

Arne explained that they did not have the money to pay for overweight charges, as none of the other airlines had charged them extra and they had already given away a third of the books. His description of their missions trip made no difference. The man said, "I am sorry but I cannot waive the rules."

Arne simply responded, "Sir, I said that I want to talk to your boss."

The airport employee did not know who Arne was—he could have been an influential person so he brought his superior to speak with him. Once again Arne explained their situation.

"I'll see what I can do," said the second man. He went over to the luggage and crossed off all the charges that had been marked on each bag. "I trust that will help," he said.

Giving thanks to God again, they quickly boarded the plane. At that point the Lord spoke to Arne: "I want all of you to pray during the flight." It was a four-hour flight across the middle of Africa. "I want you to cut all the enemy's lines of communication between the north and south of Africa, and when you get to Nigeria, tell the people what you did. The enemy forces are in total confusion. Therefore bind, silence and paralyze their every action wherever you preach." Obeying this call to spiritual warfare, the group kept up steady prayer throughout the flight.

Landing in Lagos, Nigeria, they went through customs and then were caught up in a long line of travelers waiting to be checked and released. There had been a serious incident with someone trying to smuggle in arms. However their hosts included a well-known minister who, working with a friend in customs, finally got a message through about the seven Canadian missionaries. After an hour with little action, the seven were called forward through another exit, their passports examined and they were quickly cleared, thanking God again in their hearts.

What a joy to meet the group of Christians from the church waiting to greet them, eager to carry all the luggage to their waiting bus.

But their troubles were not over. The bus was soon stopped at an army roadblock and they were ordered to get out and unload all the baggage from the roof of the bus. They were unwillingly working on this when an army official arrived. After hearing their story, he apologized and told the soldiers the baggage was alright. "You load their bags back up on the van." Again they thanked the Lord.

Arne did not forget the last part of the Lord's instructions on the plane: "When you get to Nigeria, tell the people what you did." Their first meeting in Lagos was in the slums of that large city, among open gutters and broken sidewalks, but the church was spotless, well cared for and operated in beautiful order. Arne felt afterwards that it was one of the most Spirit-filled services that he had ever witnessed. There were thirty rows of thirty chairs, with maybe nine hundred people. There were no musical instruments but the acapella singing grew to a huge symphony of clapping hands and voices in harmony. After twenty-five minutes, the pastor rang a heavy bell several times to slow everyone down and calm the praise and worship.

Offering buckets were placed across the front of the church where there was a twenty-foot space between the stage and the congregation. Starting from the back rows, the people came to the front to place their offerings in the buckets. They had been advised the previous Sunday that the team from Prayer Canada would be there that day. Arne received a beautiful hat and jacket in that offering, which he still has. There were hundreds of children in the Sunday School, all wearing brightly coloured garments and looking clean and tidy.

When the Prayer Canada team was introduced as the speakers for the day, each team member shared their personal testimony, then Arne shared a message. He challenged the people to establish "Prayer Nigeria" to pray for their authorities according to 1 Timothy 2:1-4 and 2 Chronicles 7:14, so that their land would be healed. When he told the people how the Lord had guided them to pray and cut the enemy's lines of communication down the length of Africa, they were ecstatic about it. Prayers went up like a wall of fire against all the enemy forces.

Arne invited those who needed salvation or any kind of

healing or encouragement to come forward so the team could pray for them. As soon as he finished giving the invitation, the entire congregation arose and came forward like a tidal wave to fill that twenty-foot gap between the first row and the stage—an unforgettable sight.

The Lord showed him to divide the congregation into seven sections and each team member walked through the crowd praying for them. Their hearts went out to every one of those needy people, most of whom were already saved. It took about an hour to minister to them. Arne says, "The Lord wants us to remember that He has given the poor faith to believe in Him."

While they were in Lagos, the Prayer Canada team was advised to visit the Justice Minister, who was a Christian. The Minister of Justice greeted the team at the door of his spacious office in the Parliament buildings, furnished with plush, red carpets, and invited them to sit down. The team spoke with him for a while and then he got down on his knees before a carpet-covered bench, about eighteen inches high. He started to pray and the team joined the Minister in prayer, kneeling beside him, and praying for about half an hour. It was a wonderful feeling to know that the Minister of Justice in Nigeria was under God's direction.

Africa team (left to right) Arne, Kathie, Linda, Maria, Ed, Doreen, Elsie – Ibadan, Nigeria

The team were given Nigerian outfits – (left to right) Kathie, Arne, Maria, Elsie, Linda, Doreen, Ed, with two hosts

During their time in Nigeria, they drove from Lagos 128 kilometres northeast to Ibadon, for another crusade. At the Sunday Church service, there were Sunday School classes all over the church yard for young and old and even little tots. The team enjoyed going around and listening to what each teacher was saying. It was in Ibadon that each member of the team was presented with a colourful African costume.

Ghana: Kathie after the girls had braided her hair

Then it was on to Ghana, where they visited the Canadian Embassy in Accra and also taped another radio interview. They traveled from Accra to Kumasi for a few days to speak at a crusade and to meet with the King of the Ashanti Tribe.

That drive to Kumasi was about three hundred kilometres but, with very rough roads and a long detour, the journey took seven hours. Their driver stopped on the way at a very small village where they were invited for supper–a fascinating experience. The men of the village ran out to kill a chicken to prepare for the feast. While they waited, the five women in the team went into a shed across the way. At first all they could see were the whites of many children's eyes staring at them. They taught these children some songs, then gave them balloons that they had brought and were rewarded with the joy that lit up their faces. The children had probably never seen a white person before. The group was then invited into another hut where the dinner was ready. It was an elegant space, with doilies on the chairs. Their hands were washed for them using a basin and a jug of water.

Arriving in Kumasi, there was specific protocol for the meeting with this elder of the Ashanti tribe. They were taken to the palace, where the king was clothed in regal robes and seated on his very special chair on a raised dais at the other end of the room. The interpreter introduced them in the native language. They bowed and greeted him, the interpreter translating everything. After this formal greeting, the king took off his robes, stepped down from his throne and said in excellent English, "Thank you friends. Now we can have a visit." It turned out that he had studied at Oxford University in England.

Five days later, after the crusade, they returned to Accra by a shorter route but the last part was so rough "it shook our brains nearly out of our heads" as Linda said.

Wherever they were during this African trip, Kathie and Linda worked with the children, either in the church or on the streets. They had brought balloons and bubble gum with them. The children were so excited because they had never seen a balloon before. One evening meeting it was Kathie's turn to speak. The Lord had told her He wanted to bless the children, so she called all the children to line up at the front and some of the team helped her lay hands on them all. Then all the parents came forward and the rest of the team prayed for them. At one point Linda was praying for a cute little guy with a big grin and realized she had seen him before. "Haven't you been through this line already?" she said. "Five time, Missy," he grinned, "Five time."

Arne ministered powerfully during the whole trip. During those years, he often felt the Lord wanted him to do foot washing and one day he said to Kathie, "You know, I'm to wash the pastor's feet."

"Oh no, Arne, don't," Kathie pleaded. "Do you have to wash everyone's feet everywhere we go?" Kathie and Linda laugh now about how "encouraging" they always were but it's not a bad thing for a prophet to have someone who can bring him down to earth. Of course, if Arne has heard it from the Lord, nothing will stop him. He washed the feet of several of the pastors. They were always touched by the Lord and often broken to tears.

Soon after they returned from Africa the Bryans were able to rent an apartment in Guildford and move out of the loaned basement suite.

And then, at the age of 61, Arne died.

He was sitting beside Kathie in a Sunday morning service in an Abbotsford church (which, ironically, met in a funeral home). She sensed something was wrong and looked at him. There was no life in his eyes. She asked the lady next to them to call the pastor and felt for a pulse—there was none. The pastor stopped the service and everyone prayed for him. Arne sat motionless in that seat with no sign of life while they continued praying urgently for many long minutes.

Kathie remembered the double rainbow that God had shown her less than a year before, with His promise "I will not require this of you again." She said, "God, You promised!"

At that moment, she felt a faint pulse and Arne was back to life. God had restarted his heart. Evidently He hadn't finished with Arne yet. The head usher, John Matties, helped them take Arne outside and he sat on the porch while the service continued. Later John realized he should have called for an ambulance but no one had thought of it.

Instead, Kathie drove him to Royal Columbia Hospital in New Westminster and announced: "My husband's heart just stopped." That surprised the nurse, because Kathie's husband was walking up the hallway behind her. He was the seventh patient that morning to come from church with a heart problem.

The doctor was concerned that he could have picked up something in Africa but they found nothing wrong. After checking him out for three days, their report was that he really had been dead for those long minutes. His heart had gone slower and slower until it had just stopped but there was no explanation as to why it had started again. However, they wanted to insert a pacemaker. Arne said, "You can put one in if I can watch you!" So they set up a television screen for him to watch, as he only needed a local anesthetic, and Arne has been up to speed ever since. God still answers prayer.

"More interest is being shown in Prayer Canada across Canada this past year," noted the minutes of the second annual Prayer Canada board meeting on May 30, 1980.

Arne, Kathie and Linda had created this interest by traveling across Canada twice since the Prayer Train Pilgrimage, as well leading as the Africa trip. Arne and Kathie would continue their legendary trips every year after that, often one long trip in the spring or fall, traveling east by a southern route to Ontario or farther, and back home through places a bit farther north, as well as trips through B.C. or Alberta or by air to the Maritimes.

The Annual Three-Day Prayer and Fast was held that year at Springcrest Retreat Centre in Langley, B.C. Pastor Bob Birch of Burnaby Christian Fellowship was a guest speaker.

Arne was quoted in a long article in the *Vancouver Sun* where he explained Old Testament fasting as a discipline before battle. He described his own history with fasting, how he once fasted for ten days (a day for each province), and that he regularly fasted one day a week.

Then Arne lost his assistant. Linda felt very strongly that she should go back into nursing. The call was from the Lord but she argued with Him because it seemed a backward step; then she argued with Arne because she knew she had to obey the Lord.

It was a painful time for all of them because they loved each other so much. Arne and Kathie weren't sure that she was doing the right thing but within a year they were close again. They put her in touch with the Christian relief and development agency, World Concern, which needed nurses in Thailand to work in the Cambodian refugee camps there.

The Bryans and Linda remained firm friends whether Linda was nursing, in Canada and in Thailand, or ministering in churches in Eastern Canada, or long term missionary service teaching English in Thailand. Linda is thankful for all that she learned from working with Arne and Kathie and watching their example.

The Surrey television program was going well and Arne also pushed for programs in Nanaimo, B.C. and North Battleford, Saskatchewan.

Rod and Cathy Lindsay, prayer leaders in Nanaimo, had noticed that their local television station was advertising some available time slots, so Arne and Kathie went down there with Cathy Lindsay to discuss it. When the station manager realized it would be something like *100 Huntley Street*, he said "I don't think so."

Arne simply changed the subject. "I hear that you actually train people here to run cameras and so on?"

"Oh yes," he said. "We do."

"Cathy has three volunteers to train to run a camera. When could they come?"

"Let me see. Next Tuesday. We do it on Tuesday night."

"Cathy, could your people come and get training to run a camera on Tuesday night?"

"Oh, yes" she said. "I think we can arrange that."

"That's wonderful," Arne continued. "How long does it take to train them?"

"Only about three weeks."

"That's wonderful. Cathy, can you get ready for a program in three weeks?"

"Oh, yes."

"Sir, you said that you had a vacancy on … [Arne quoted the timing that the station manager had mentioned.] We'll be there and put on our first program." Arne got up to go. The station manager didn't stop him, didn't say no. He simply thanked them. The Nanaimo program ran for several years.

Much the same thing happened in North Battleford—only more quickly. The program was on the air within twenty-four hours of first meeting Howard, the Full Gospel Businessmen contact Arne had only just been referred to. Arne and Kathie went to Howard and Diane's home for supper, Howard made some phone calls and eleven men came that evening to hear Arne talk about starting a weekly noon prayer meeting in the city council chambers and maybe also a free program on their local television station. The television idea was new to them but one of the men, Jack, was interested to check it out. At 10:00 a.m. the next morning, they were down at the television station, where the station manager said they were eager to have some new programs and would even supply the cameramen.

"Well, the boys here are anxious to start a weekly Christian program," Arne said boldly. "Could we do the first segment from twelve to one p.m. today?"

"No problem," said the station manager. "We'll have the cameramen and the set ready. We'll call the program '*Prayer Canada Live*' and after this one it can be live in the evening."

The first show went off without a hitch. The three prayer warriors, Howard, Jack, and Arne, had a great time discussing and dealing with many issues. The hour passed quickly and they went to a restaurant for lunch.

"That's the mayor, sitting at the next table," Howard told Arne. He introduced Arne and Kathie to the mayor and Arne briefly inquired about a weekly prayer meeting in city hall, mentioning that their mission was to all of Canada. It wasn't appropriate to discuss further with him but the contact had been made—still within the same twenty-four-hour period.

At the Board Meeting on October 11, 1980, Arne reported on the first three full years of operation. In the Upper Room, there was the Monday evening "Prayer and Share" time, an all night of prayer first Friday of each month, the early morning prayer meetings every Wednesday and Thursday, and also Saturday morning with mostly men attending. In addition there was now a "School of Prayer" with teaching on prayer the third Saturday morning of each month.

There was the regular Tuesday evening television program in Surrey and the others in Nanaimo and North Battleford. The Prayer Breakfasts continued every month and the Three-Day Pray and Fast every year. Arne described the three prayer chains that had been set up to respond to all the prayer requests that came in daily. He outlined the long journeys they had taken to set up and encourage the home prayer posts, contact local government authorities and try to start prayer meetings in city halls. "So far," he said, "authorities have been most open to this approach and are very interested in Christians praying for them."

In fact there are numerous gracious letters on file from premiers, cabinet ministers and other government leaders, thanking Arne and Prayer Canada for their support and specifically for their prayer support.

"In the last two months since they've been having a Prayer Canada meeting in our city hall, our councillors have put through more business than in the previous two years. I've been mayor of the city for ten years and you can quote me," said Mayor Frank Ney of Nanaimo, B.C. during a Prayer Canada broadcast. He was one who really appreciated the prayer support.

Later, after the prayer meeting was started in the Vancouver City Hall, long-time Vancouver alderman and Marxist Harry Rankin said: "I don't really agree with all that stuff but, for some reason, everything has gone better ever since they've been there."

CHAPTER 10

1981 — 1983:
GREAT FRIENDSHIPS

Prayer Canada was newsworthy. On Tuesday January 13, 1981, the *Nanaimo Daily Free Press* ran a story about Arne as he visited the Monday noon prayer meeting in Nanaimo's council chambers, where they were joined by the mayor, who had just returned from Australia.

Arne was quoted giving the biblical mandate for Prayer Canada. Then he explained that he had never met anyone in authority who was not interested in having help to solve his problems. He also spoke about the significance of the Canadian flag, that the Canadian flag is the only one in the world which has a leaf. He talked about Revelations, chapter 22, verse 2, and the 'leaves used for medication to heal our nations' and explained how to Prayer Canada the red parts of the flag represent the healing blood of Jesus and the white parts represent the righteousness of Jesus."

In June of that year, when they were planning to fill a jet and fly a crowd to Ottawa for the third annual Three-Day Pray and Fast, Rhodanthe Lake wrote an eloquent article about Prayer Canada in the *Columbian* under the headline: *Prayer army travels on its knees.* She included one of Arne's regular sayings, quoting *My Utmost for His Highest* by Oswald Chambers: "Prayer does not fit us for the greater work. It *is* the greater work."

The article continued:

Far from being rejected, they've been openly received by all levels of government. "Who," asks Arne, "can argue with prayer?"

Prayer Canada considers itself the tip of the iceberg. It's the surface evidence of a mighty rumbling of an underground of prayer that is groaning in the hearts and on the lips of Christian Canadians.

Prayer is catching on. Prayer groups are in every community. Weekly lunch-hour sessions are happening in municipal and city halls in many provinces. The legislative buildings in Edmonton have regular noon-hour prayers presided over by the Minister of Health and Welfare. Victoria has given approval for a once-a-week room for prayer.

"God told me," says Arne Bryan, "that prayer is the entity I have chosen to bring my people into unity. (*Columbian*)

Everything seemed in place for progress toward the ambitious God-given goal.

In the spring of 1981, Arne finally made it to Whitehorse in the Yukon, the only capital still to be visited. The Lord didn't let him rest till he was up there, so he made enquiries and discovered that the father-in-law of Kirk Duncan, his pastor at Bible Fellowship, was the minister of a church in Whitehorse. As soon as he was invited, Arne flew up there.

Arne delighted in the midnight sun—he went to bed and it was light; he got up and it was light. In fact he hardly wanted to go to bed at all because there was so much to see, especially the magnificent Northern Lights, flashes of green, blue, even red and orange, streaking across the sky, declaring the glory of God.

Later that year, Arne led prayer meetings on Parliament Hill in Ottawa during the 1981 Three-Day Prayer and Fast. It was beautiful warm weather and he'd been told by an MP that the coolest place in Ottawa in summer is up on Parliament Hill, where the colder air comes up from the river. He led the Prayer and Fast team in marching around each of the three Parliament Buildings seven times, quietly in line praying. As they walked and prayed, they could see the television cameras on the corners of the buildings following them.

The second night they met under the trees. They had just finished communion together when an RCMP officer, resplendent in his red dress coat, walked over to them.

"Who's in charge of this group?" he asked.

"I am," said Arne.

"I want to talk with you," he said. Arne walked back to his car with him and the officer asked if he had permission to have a meeting on Parliament Hill.

"Well," said Arne. "Actually we don't have permission but I did write to Prime Minister Trudeau. Here's the letter that I wrote three months ago to request permission. We never heard from him but, you know, the post office is on strike. So I thought that was the hold up and we'd just proceed, because God didn't tell us not to." Actually he had heard the Lord say, *Just proceed. We're not held up by the post office strike or the prime minister.*

Then Arne told the officer, "Actually we proceed something like the way you people do: if you've got a disaster situation, you can call on the rest of the police from other cities. You can call on the army and navy and air force. Or you can even call across the line and get help from the U.S. Isn't that right?"

"I guess so."

"We operate something like that, only we can call on all the powers of heaven!"

At that point the officer phoned his superior, who joined him there with some others, so that Arne was surrounded by seven RCMP officers all in their red coats. The superintendent went over the same questions and Arne answered in the same way.

He didn't stop. He just kept talking to them for fifteen minutes—Kathie timed it—and the officers did not move in all that time. They just stood there almost at attention, never moving a muscle. Then he stopped talking. They didn't ask him to; he just quit. After a while the superintendent spoke up. "Now Mr Bryan, how long do you plan to be here?"

"We plan to be here for another day," said Arne and outlined their plans.

"Let me tell you this, Mr Bryan," said the senior officer. "We will be here and we'll see that nobody bothers you."

During 1981, Prayer Canada was in danger of being diverted from its goal. The prayer meetings focused on praying for the leadership of Canada at every level but they also prayed for the needs of the people who were there. Arne had always known he was in a spiritual battle but now he and Kathie were learning how to minister "deliverance" to those who were hindered by demons. This was so effective that people wanted to turn all the prayer meetings into deliverance meetings.

They sponsored a series of meetings in 1981 with Win Worley from Chicago, who taught on deliverance and ministered with quiet authority. He would pick someone out of the crowd and say, "Come up here. I want to talk to you." Then he would command the demon to leave in the name of Jesus and Christians who had struggled with problems for years found that they could now overcome them.

One man loudly refused to go to the front. He became disruptive–this was understood to be the demon manifesting itself. Arne, as the convener of the meetings and also a trained security man, began to move the man out of the meeting.

"Don't you handle me," yelled the man. "I'll do away with you!"

"If you do away with me," said Arne, "God will raise up **ten** people to take my place!" He was able to escort the man out.

About ten or twelve years later, at a meeting in a home in Prince George B.C., this same man approached Arne, though Arne didn't recognize him. He got down on his knees in front of Arne, with all the people watching, and apologized.

"We had one guy we were working on who threw a heavy old chair right across the room at me," remembers Arne. "I tell you when people get demon possessed, they have power like you wouldn't believe. A lot of people don't think the enemy is around but he's around, I tell you."

Arne and Kathie found deliverance very effective but controversial. The board discussed it at length during 1981. Arne and Kathie learned to instruct the person to fast on the day they were to be prayed for and also to tell their pastor what they were doing. That way personal deliverance ministry was separated from the regular meetings and it was clear whether the person was serious or not.

"I just felt the pain drifting away," was how a young lady named Iris described it. She had experienced both deliverance and healing from a back injury through Prayer Canada ministry in January of the previous year. It was John DeVries who had prayed for her back; later she married his older brother Abraham. She became a very effective deliverance worker herself and three years later she and her husband opened a prayer post in Sarnia, Ontario.

In 1983, Arne and Kathie set up three deliverance teams and handed the ministry all over to them. One team was led by John and Dolly Verseveldt. John was a board member of Prayer Canada from 1983 to June 1988.

After four-and-a-half years in the Upper Room at the Surrey Inn, Arne heard that the rent was about to be doubled.

"I'll find you a place," said the Lord. He wasn't telling them to stay in the Upper Room, so they wondered what would happen next.

A few days later, someone offered Arne two empty office rooms next to his, for only two hundred dollars per month. The Upper Room was already more than twice that. At the end of June 1982, Prayer Canada moved into the Roebuck Centre on 132nd Street.

At the end of the first year there, the person who had the other two offices moved out and offered them to Prayer Canada as well, for only a hundred dollars per month. Prayer Canada only needed two rooms, so they rented out the extra ones, which reduced their costs. The prayer centre stayed in the Roebuck Centre for about four years.

During 1982, Arne and Kathie travelled to Edmonton, Calgary, Red Deer, Regina, back to the Okanagan and Kootenay areas of B.C., as well as Vancouver Island. Arne always wrote up notes on each stop. So much was happening that he had to do it daily to keep up. If Kathie was driving, Arne wrote, read or slept.

They paid their own way on this trip and did not burden Prayer Canada with their expenses. It was wonderful when somebody blessed them with a donation to buy a 1974 yellow Chevrolet van that would save on motel costs. However there were times when Arne took on part-time work to meet personal finances. At a later date, as the finances began to come in, Arne was repaid for the Prayer Canada travel costs he had paid himself.

Of course the lasting advances came from divine appointments and hearts joined with those who were called to be intercessors. In October 1982, Arne flew to Toronto with Chuck Giesbrecht for several meetings and the Lord scheduled a significant connection with a businessman from South Africa, Ray Williams. Ray was also a pilot and on Friday

October 15 should have been flying a friend to the Full Gospel Businessmen's breakfast meeting the next day in Ottawa. However Ray felt he should pray about flying to Ottawa, although he had been offered the use of an aircraft, he loved to fly and the weather was not too bad. When he prayed, the Lord answered no, he should stay in Toronto.

That was why Ray was still in Toronto when he got the message that two men wanted to see him. Somebody among the Full Gospel Businessmen in B.C. had passed his name to Arne for when he was next in Toronto. Ray invited them to his own FGBM breakfast meeting in Toronto the next day although he noticed both Arne and Chuck smelled like smokers—and then it occurred to him it was probably because their cheap Jarvis Street motel room smelled of smoke.

At the breakfast meeting, Ray introduced them to the president of the chapter, who without hesitation looked at Arne and said, "Would you speak?" He invited Chuck to pray.

Arne got up to speak after the main speaker had finished and started to cry. He just stood looking at the people, moved to tears by what had seemed a terribly casual approach to God's business, as if it was just an ordinary matter. To Arne, God's business is passionate and serious. Filled with the Holy Ghost, he went on to share a hard-hitting word. This often happened. He'd have something prepared but get up and say something different from what he had planned.

What he said and the way he said it had a big impact on Ray Williams. The Lord told him to stay with these two men throughout the week. So he dropped everything and went to all their meetings with them—a busy schedule as usual.

On the Friday night, he drove Arne to the airport. Chuck had taken a flight home the day before. It had been a good week. After Arne and Ray said good bye to each other in the crowded airport, Arne walked a short distance, then put down his suitcase and came back. He threw his arms in the air and said in a loud voice, "Lord, put Your *mantle* upon Ray just now, in Jesus' name." Ray felt the power of God pass through him right down to the ground. Arne hugged him for the second time and left.

From that moment, standing among all the travelers at Toronto airport, Ray wasn't the same any more. He went up to the fourth floor parking lot and had the key in the ignition of his car when it occurred to him to go to the wall and look over to see what type of plane Arne was flying on. It was a DC10.

Ray spent a moment praying for Arne. There was a wind blowing through the parking lot and it was quite chilly and isolated. He had a feeling that there was someone on his right side. He turned and saw a woman, maybe in her late forties. Ray knew instantly that she was German, a Christian but not filled with the Holy Spirit.

"Sir, is that aeroplane going to Vancouver?" she asked in a heavy German accent, confirming the first word of knowledge.

"Yes, my dear."

"I have two children on board."

"Don't worry. That plane is going to arrive safely in Vancouver."

"What sort of plane is it?"

"It's a DC10."

"Oh!" she gasped. "That's the same as that one that crashed in Dallas!" She was in great fear, because there had been a lot of media coverage of a DC10 that had crashed on May 25, 1979, including a dramatic photograph just before impact. All DC10s had been grounded as a result, until the cause had been found and put right. But this lady was obviously still panicked.

"Don't worry, my dear," he assured her with authority. "That problem has been solved. I'm a pilot and I receive reports of these things and the causes of accidents. They know what it was and they have fixed the problem."

Then, surprising even himself, he raised his voice: "And

leave your husband alone! If he wants to watch television, leave him alone. And your children. Stop trying to control them and dominate them. Leave them to the Lord." Returning to his normal voice he offered, "Let me pray for you." He put his hand on her shoulder and prayed for her.

After he prayed the lady said, "Hallelujah! Thank you, Jesus!"

It wasn't too long before Ray and Mary Williams were hosting a Prayer Canada Prayer Post in their home in Toronto and co-ordinating five prayer meetings in the area.

The first time Arne visited the Toronto Prayer Post in 1983, he was carrying such an anointing that prophetic words came from him as he spoke or prayed with the individual people in the living room. Ray felt his life was changed by what Arne spoke to him that day.

Whenever Arne and Kathie traveled to Toronto after that, they stayed with Ray and Mary, who loved hosting them for their brief and busy visits. As they ministered together, there was always unity flowing in the Spirit.

They tried repeatedly to move the prayer meeting to City Hall but there were many rebuffs. Not disheartened, they continued, knowing that prayer knows no distance. Ray's group has been running for thirty years, with the exception of an eighteen-month sabbatical.

In the summer of 1987, Ray flew Arne and Kathie in his own six-seater Cessna plane to a Full Gospel Businessmen's breakfast in Montreal. He was happy to see Arne sleep soundly through most of the journey. "He had such trust," Ray comments. "He has been my spiritual Dad. It is a great joy to be able to pray. I thank the Lord for Arne."

Arne knew from the start that he had been given a big job. Intercession is not always exciting. It's one thing to start praying in the wake of a faith-building talk, but it takes enduring faith for small groups to persevere year after year in this invisible, unheralded task, knowing that it is scriptural, vital and effective.

Bert Lang's main problem as a prayer partner at the beginning was loneliness, because he was the only person present.

Arne had asked Bert to lead the Wednesday morning prayer meeting while he and Kathie were away on a trip in 1983 and Leoran Anhorn was also away. So Arne gave Bert the address and the key for the Prayer Canada offices at the Roebuck Center and Bert faithfully went there early every Wednesday for a couple of months and prayed alone for all the local and national government leaders.

Since that inauspicious start, Arne and Kathie have enjoyed decades of warm fellowship with Bert and Ruth Lang, and Bert has served on the board since 1991. Bert has a sly sense of humour. When asked if he is an early bird who likes going out to pray first thing in the morning, he pauses before quietly observing, "I don't mind sleeping in."

Ruth appreciates Arne's enthusiasm and optimism, but Bert's first thought is how consistent Arne has always been. "He's very much the same. He doesn't get too over excited or down. He's very steady all the time." He jokes that he has to respect Arne as an older man—eleven months older. But he goes on to say, "He's one of a kind. Very hardworking. He doesn't criticize or say anything to put you down. He's a good leader." And he adds with a quiet smile, "If you make a suggestion to do something, you're the one who's going to do it!"

Of course, Arne also invited Bert to the Surrey City Hall prayer meeting. Bert didn't go regularly at first because sometimes he was the only one there as well. After about three years, he persuaded a friend to go with him and they would go together almost every week—the sort of faithful intercessors who make a profound difference on the national stage. Over all these years, the group may be only three or up to a dozen people, including some City Hall staff. Like hundreds of prayer posts across the country, they have maintained a presence, steadfastly supporting those who make important decisions.

Like all Prayer Canada supporters, Bert is simply convinced of the importance of 1 Timothy 2:1-4. "You're familiar with the Scripture where it tells us to pray first of all for those in authority," he says. "It doesn't say anywhere explicitly in the Scriptures, as far as I know, to pray for other things. Don't pray specially for farmers. Don't pray for fishermen. Pray for everyone ... but it specifies praying for those in authority."

One day the previous year, Arne was in the Prayer Canada office with Joseph Baake, who traveled the world teaching on prayer and the Bible. Joseph looked at the map of Canada on the wall and said, "There should be a series of Prayer Centres like this across Canada." He put his finger on the map. "... And the first one should be *here*."

His finger was on the Crowsnest Highway just over the border in southwestern Alberta.

"I know someone who has some buildings there!" announced Arne.

In 1981 he had been approached at a Full Gospel Businessmen's meeting in Pincher Creek, Alberta, by Bill and Doreen White, who had asked for prayer. They were fairly new Christians, saved in 1979 in Hawaii at an Amway conference, and had recently failed in a large retail project. They had to close their stores and didn't know what to do with their buildings.

"The Lord has shown me that you're not thinking big enough for your buildings," said Arne as he prayed for them with his hand on Bill's shoulder.

What do you mean? Bill thought to himself. *We're practically losing everything we've got and you say we're not thinking big enough!* Doreen felt like punching Arne in the face.

When they talked afterwards and Arne heard that they had a foreclosure notice on one store in a rented building, he had a word of wisdom from the Lord.

"Look, Bill," he said urgently. "They're going to get in there and change the lock and take over everything you've got. We're going to go down there **tonight** with your van and my van and we're going to take all your stuff out of there, because they're going to do it **tonight**." And that's what they did. Sure enough, by the next morning the locks had been changed. They had cleared the place just in time.

However, Bill and Doreen also had three large buildings in Bellevue that they owned and didn't know what to do with. So now a year later, when Joseph Baake's finger pointed to the Crowsnest Highway, Arne knew he should phone Bill White.

"Would you consider using one of your buildings for a Prayer Centre?" he asked.

Bill agreed he would consider it. He was still under a lot of pressure but this didn't sound like a financial drain and he liked the idea of praying for government authorities. In the 1970s before he was a Christian, he had been the mayor of his home town of Bellevue and he wouldn't have said "No" to some prayer support. However, he made no commitment at that time, although Arne kept telling him he could do it.

Then one Saturday night in 1983, Arne and Kathie showed up at a Full Gospel Businessmen's meeting that Bill was hosting in a town near his home. Joseph Baake was there too. They had a great meeting with all of them sharing and then continued the fellowship at Bill's home in Bellevue. They talked till four in the morning when Arne and Kathie had to leave for B.C., all so interested in each other's affairs because they were all inter-related.

Stimulated by the night of rich conversation, Bill said to Doreen, "I can't go to sleep. I'm going fishing." But he soon gave up throwing his line out and sat on a log by the river to have a conversation with the Lord.

"I can understand about having Prayer Centres across

Canada, Lord. But Bellevue is a small place where people have left because without the mining there's nothing here. It's a ghost town."

"People said the same about Nazareth," answered the Lord, completely wiping out Bill's logic.

"Okay," Bill said. "I will open a Prayer Centre." And so began what he calls his covenant relationship with the Lord, without which we can do nothing for God.

The moment he said "Yes" to the Lord, he had a vision. There seemed to be an explosion, with black smoke and steam, and out of it people showed up, every one of them with different abilities that could help a Prayer Centre to function. He began corresponding with Arne and the board about opening an international Prayer Centre, trusting that the Lord would provide finances and people.

Soon after arriving home, Arne and Kathie visited John and Dolores Matties in Abbotsford to discuss a mission that they were helping organize. John was the head usher who had supported Arne the day he "died" a couple of years earlier in a church service in Abbotsford.

"Do you think the local TV station would be open to a Christian program?" said Arne. He wanted to see if they could start a Prayer Canada broadcast like the one he and Kathie had running in Surrey.

"I don't know," said John. "But we can drive over and find out." And that's what they did.

"Do you have room for a live program?" Arne asked the official at the Abbotsford television station. "Yes. We do." was the answer.

John had zero ambition to be on television but that was Arne's plan and Arne can be very persuasive. It was decided that John would gather some people to train on the camera and other equipment and then they could have a weekly half hour, live. By the time they were trained and ready to go, the time slot had been increased to a whole hour every Thursday evening.

John Matties was indeed a most unlikely television personality. Not a fluent reader, he also didn't know how to take notes, but he was ready to try anything for the Lord. His wife, Dolores, had laughed when they came back from the television station that first day, like Sarah at the promise that she would have a son. She thought the whole thing was impossible, didn't want anything to do with it and was quite annoyed with Arne for setting it up. But she wanted to make it work for her husband. So after a few weeks she began to sit in as John's co-host to fill in where he was having difficulty, especially when there was something to read. They both grew into very effective television hosts.

The hour was divided into three segments, separated with a two-minute song or music spot. They interviewed their invited guests (including politicians; missionaries; the Prayer Ghana president; David Mainse twice in 1986; and, even a prison inmate who had to have a guard with him), talking with them naturally about their life and what God was doing for them. Then they let people pray. They enjoyed people's testimonies, nudging them with gentle questions to share their lives. They didn't preach and they didn't do a lot of writing or preparation. "I couldn't do those things," says John. "It had to be led by the Holy Spirit."

These were live shows—whatever was said was broadcast. They approached each week in faith, praying: "Okay, Lord. This is Your program. We've got this person on the show, so it's up to You now to put it together."

The program was supposed to run for six weeks but they were kept on the air for eight-and-a-half years. When asked by highly qualified pastors how they did it, they would answer: "We can't give you any formula. We just go on there and the Lord works it out. You have to rely on the Holy Spirit to tell you what to do."

They had named the show "Real World" but after about a year the television station asked them to change the name because they thought it wasn't the real world. "The name stays," said John.

They had a prayer phone line at home and people phoned in after the show. "You know when I watched you," said a caller one day. "I could see that you couldn't really read well. The Lord spoke to me and said 'If I can use him, what's your excuse?' "

The Lord used even the thing that John couldn't do well, because he was willing.

Once a year they would spend a whole Saturday taping musicians and singers for the intermission music. Then they chose each week which item to use. They wanted each local church to be represented.

The program only came to an end because John went on night shift and the local churches couldn't continue it long term. John and Dolores would never have done it at all if Arne hadn't pushed them. "You can **do** this. You and the **Lord** are quite able." Arne is a motivator and an encourager who can get people to do the most amazing things.

Soon after the television program started, Arne was speaking at a 1983 Full Gospel Businessmen's meeting in Abbotsford. "The Mayor of Abbotsford has been waiting two years to have a prayer meeting in the City Hall," he said. "Who will answer the call and take this opportunity?" It was John Matties who came forward, volunteering to lead the city hall prayer meeting.

He and Arne went to see Mayor Ferguson on the Monday morning and he was still eager to have the meeting. John said he would be there to start the next Monday.

"No," said the mayor. "No, you won't. You come and bring a letter and we'll take it through the Council so nobody can put you out."

The prayer meeting is still continuing to this day, though now under different leadership.

Prayer Canada held the annual Prayer and Fast in Lethbridge, AB that year (1983). That was the sort of event around which Arne would build a trip so he and Kathie visited fifteen Prayer Centres on the way there and back. Soon they were off to Africa again.

CHAPTER 11

1984 — 1986:
GHANA; EXPO SIGN

Prayer Canada had received alarming reports that a serious two-year drought had caused a famine in Ghana. They asked the Lord what they could do to help and Arne made some enquiries. Their prayers were answered: the Canadian International Development Agency (CIDA) agreed to supply forty tons of powdered milk, and World Concern had agreed to pay half the freight charges to Ghana (which totalled eight thousand dollars) but only if Arne and Kathie would personally oversee the distribution to make sure it didn't fall into the wrong hands. Arne needed help on the ground and he knew just the person—Kwabena Darko, the most successful chicken farmer in Ghana.

Arne and Kathie spent nearly four weeks in Ghana in January and February of 1984. The powdered milk had been shipped three months previously. Arne and Kathie's job was to arrange for the shipment to be released so that it could be distributed to the people in need. The trucks of Darko Farms would help in the transportation.

Kwabena Darko was 16 when he became a Christian, after suffering four or five years of severe night-time demonic oppression. He went to a missionary meeting where the preacher read Psalm 91: "*He that dwelleth in the secret place of the Most High, shall abide under the shadow of the Almighty;*

and I will say of the Lord, He is my refuge, and my fortress, my God, in Him will I trust" (Psalm 91:1-2, KJV). Kwabena was the first to go forward. That night he told the Lord that he was trusting his Father in heaven to take care of him and slept soundly all that night. The troubles were gone.

Later, Kwabena studied at university in Israel to learn how to raise chickens, although all his amused friends protested that anybody could raise chickens. The Lord guided him how to breed one type of chicken for meat and another type for eggs. When he was the wealthy owner of Darko Farms, he and his wife Christiana generously helped anywhere they could, providing midday meals for his employees, sending a thousand hard-boiled eggs every week for Kumasi's prison inmates and feeding many other people.

Arne had met Kwabena three years before, during their first visit to Kumasi, Ghana. (Their friendship continued long after this visit. Kwabena and Christiana visited Canada in 1985, when Arne and Kathie took them to Vernon and Victoria and had meetings with them.) Arne is a man of many skills, but first he was a farmer. Ever curious, he was fascinated to observe how Kwabena ran his eight well-equipped poultry farms in Kumasi. They were all several miles apart to lessen the possibility of disease spreading. Each farm was fenced and the few special visitors allowed in had to walk through disinfectant to clean their shoes. Then they were given a special sterilized gown to wear before entering. The whole operation was equal in quality to anything in the developed world. When asked how he did it all, his answer was always, "By His grace!"

By His grace, Arne and Kathie obtained the release of the milk from the port. It took much paperwork and several visits to the steam ship offices in Tema (the main port) and to two government departments. It helped that the head of one department knew the Canadian High Commissioner to Ghana—they had taken air force training together in England. Arne prayed with the officials, which really pleased them. By the end of their trip, the milk was transported by the Darko trucks to a warehouse in Kumasi for distribution by SIM missionaries there.

The Canadian High Commissioner was very impressed with Arne and Kathie because they had invested so much time, effort and finances in bringing the forty tons of powdered milk to alleviate the famine in Ghana. He arranged an official dinner at his residence to honour them and the representatives of several other nations who were sending relief supplies to Ghana. Kathie was seated beside the representative from Spain, who sent medical supplies. Arne was seated beside the lady representative from Italy, who greatly helped in the relief work wherever possible.

As they were leaving this formal occasion, the High Commissioner (a Roman Catholic) pointed toward Arne and asked the lady from Italy, "Did you get him converted?"

"Well, no," she laughed. "He almost converted me!"

Arne would never miss a chance to share the gospel and one opportunity often led to another. One Saturday he walked across the road to watch men making mahogany window frames under a tree. They got talking and Arne took a photo. He gave each of them a Gospel of John, which they all opened up excitedly.

The men's regular work was in the local cocoa factory. A lady with them was a supervisor there and she was a Christian. She invited Arne and Kathie to speak at the next two Monday noon meetings at the factory. Arne and Kathie shared the message of salvation with about forty to fifty Christian workers who met regularly, plus some unsaved workers who had been invited, and several were saved. The assistant manager of the whole factory came to the second meeting and accepted the Lord as his Saviour.

There was also time to minister in churches, pastors' groups, schools, a Bible School, a Full Gospel Businessmen's group and a prison fellowship. They had an interview with a reporter from the Ghana Times, who accepted the Lord. No one was too high or too low for love and prayer, whether it was the Canadian High Commissioner or a pastor's houseboy.

They found people everywhere discouraged because of the difficulties in their country. Arne shared his heart burden: *"If my people...will pray ... I will heal the land"* (2 Chronicles 7:14, NIV) and the Christians responded by setting up "Prayer Ghana." Kathie also passed on to them a promise from the Lord: *"Tell the righteous it will be well with them, for they will enjoy the fruit of their deeds"* (Isaiah 3:10). (A few years later, Arne and Kathie began to hear good news of God's faithfulness to His word in Ghana, including a recovery in rainfall levels, which filled up the lake so that they had electricity and produced better crops.)

For one school visit, all the students were lined up outside in the schoolyard to greet them with a program of songs, drills and skits. However, Arne and Kathie were unsettled to notice that the children only had small slates for writing and the libraries were almost empty.

"We'll send you some **books**," promised Arne.

"How are we going to do that?" asked Kathie.

When they returned home they began work on a project to send educational books to Ghana. They discovered that there was a large warehouse in Toronto containing mostly schoolbooks. To get a reduced price, companies and schools would order one-tenth more books than they needed. The extra books were sent to this warehouse, where they were to be given to developing countries—a perfect solution for Prayer Canada. The following year they shipped a thirty-ton container and another in 1987, containing new schoolbooks, Bibles and other Christian books worth $396,000.

Arne's foot rests nonchalantly on the bumper of his new white VW Rabbit in a photograph in the *Nanaimo Daily Free Press* for Saturday July 21, 1984. Clearly visible, the license plate boldly reads: PRAYER.

The white Rabbit was a gift from the Lord. One day a lady from Abbotsford had walked into the Prayer Canada office in the Roebuck Centre and said to Arne, "I wonder if you could come to the auto place over here with me. And I want to see your car."

Arne showed her his rusty old green Chevrolet, which was at least ten years old, and she walked around it saying "Yes, yes" to herself. She had seen that very car in a dream and wanted to confirm it belonged to Arne. Then they went to the VW showroom on 104th Avenue, where she had already made arrangements for payment on a brand new VW Rabbit for Prayer Canada.

Arne and the white Rabbit
(Nanaimo Daily Free Press for Saturday, July 21, 1984)

"You can have a diesel or gas, whichever one you want," she said.

"Well," Arne said. "Kathie's been praying for a **white** car. So we'll have a white Rabbit."

She insisted that they get the best radio fitted so that they would have good reception when they were driving through the mountains. Arne and Kathie had a brand new diesel Rabbit for their long trips and all they had to do was pay the tax.

Arne was quoted during 1984 in three newspapers – the *Nanaimo Daily Free Press*, *The Aurora* of Labrador City NFL and the *Sonshine News* in Alberta. As he tells and retells the message of Prayer Canada, he always includes four foundations:

1. The now legendary stories of the Upper Room and miraculous train pilgrimage;
2. The challenge: the continuing call to Canadians to pray for the nation;
3. The command: Pray " ... *for all that are in authority; that we may lead a quiet and peaceable life in all godliness and honesty.*" (1 Timothy 2:2, KJV)
4. The guarantee: "*If my people ... shall humble themselves and pray ... and turn from their wicked ways, then will I hear from heaven ... and will heal their land.*" (2 Chronicles 7:14, KJV).

In those 1984 news stories, Arne reported about the seventh annual Three-Day Prayer and Fast, held in July in Toronto; about the legislatures in Victoria, Edmonton, Regina and Winnipeg all hosting prayer meetings; and about the regular Tuesday meetings in Vancouver City Hall and many others around the country. The one in Labrador City, for example, had started in 1979 and was still meeting on Saturdays at noon in the town hall. Also, over one hundred Prayer Posts had been established in homes and elsewhere—even some in prisons.

Arne said his goal was to set up a Prayer Post in the eight hundred cities in Canada with a population of five thousand or more. "The greatest task is not gaining approval from the authorities for holding weekly prayer meetings," he added, "but instead in stirring up Christians to go ahead and do it."

The mayors of Prince George, B.C. and Moose Jaw, SK were open to prayer meetings in their city halls but no Christians had yet stepped forward to lead them.

"We have the God-given privilege of deciding whether we want to obey God or not," enthused Arne, now sixty-five years old and at his prime in the spiritual battle for Canada. "I chose to say, 'Here am I, Lord Jesus, use me,' and travel the nation over, knowing in the end that every knee shall bow and every tongue confess that Jesus Christ is Lord. God's plan is not to compromise, and if we do—judgment. Let's get on with the job."

In 1984 the Prayer Canada headquarters moved again after three years at the Roebuck Centre, to the third floor of the Surrey Village Centre highrise opposite the Surrey Inn. This was very convenient, as Arne and Kathie had moved to the thirteenth floor of the same building the year before. Living "above the shop" worked well and the arrangement continued into their next location seven years later.

Kwabena & Christiana Darko visiting BC in 1985

Internationale Prayer Centre

The Internationale Prayer Centre, started in Bellevue, AB by Bill and Doreen White, was not mentioned in the 1984 news reports but it was up and running soon after that. (Arne wanted the spelling of the Internationale Prayer Centre to reflect the influence of Prayer Canada in other countries.) The Prayer Centre is in a 110' x 30' two-storey building, which also houses their apartment at the back. The Prayer Centre has five bedrooms upstairs and the prayer room in the basement, adorned with a dozen artistic murals of salvation Scriptures. As the Lord promised in Bill's vision, the costs and manpower for the Prayer Centre operation have been met over the years by many people. Bill and Doreen experienced the Lord's provision in many ways.

Arne kept in touch with affiliates in Africa, John DeVries was taking teams to the Philippines and there were visitors from other nations. The world map in the Prayer Canada prayer room showed about twenty groups in other countries including Australia, the Philippines, Thailand, India, Puerto Rico, Belgium and various parts of Africa, according to a 1986 article in the *Surrey/ North Delta Now*. (In 2014, there are 211 nations registered under Prayer Canada and they are working to establish Prayer Partners in each one. Arne is fuelled by a word the Lord spoke in his heart: "If our mission concept is less than the world, it's too small.")

The Internationale Prayer Centre hosted Wednesday night prayer meetings as well as several annual Three-Day Prayer and Fasts. Arne and Kathie regularly visited Bellevue on their cross-country trips and the Centre held various other events, with speakers coming to this little "Nazareth" in Alberta from all over the world.

In 1985, not long after he was ordained as a pastor, Bill White was invited to be part of the Board of Directors of Prayer Canada. During 1985 the Prayer Canada Board of Directors was Arne and Kathie Bryan, John Verseveldt, John DeVries, Tom Smith, Leoran Anhorn, Doug LaRoy, Joe Brown and Bill White. Various names had been added since the beginning and some had been called home. Later that year a vote of thanks was given to Dolphe Hoffman for "his long and effective assistance to Prayer Canada." He and Gloria remain firm friends with Arne and Kathie and Dolphe continues as an advisor to Prayer Canada.

162

For their 1985 trip across Canada, Arne and Kathie were joined by John and Dolores Matties from Abbotsford. They left on May 1 for sixty days, visiting fifty cities. The only province they didn't visit was Newfoundland.

"You can never frazzle Arne," says Dolores. "He's steadfast and, no matter what anybody says, it doesn't change one iota what he is doing or what he says or who he talks to."

They made a good team, traveling together in the old yellow van over huge distances, staying in people's homes wherever possible. They took turns sleeping in the van, so only one couple had to be accommodated in the hosts' house each night.

In Toronto they were hit with a thousand-dollar garage bill for fixing the timing chain on the van. They drove on to Moncton NB, wondering how the Lord would pay the bill. After a meeting in a church that met in the basement of his house, Ron Trites approached Arne hesitantly.

"I don't know..." he began. "My mother passed away two years ago and left me this money to give to somebody who needed it." He had been waiting for God to tell him who to give it to and now he believed it was for Arne. It was a thousand dollars.

In New Brunswick they met with the Speaker of the House and the Mayor of Fredericton. They also visited the French sector of Edmunston, NB, pleased that Prayer Canada material was being translated into French. During the Three-Day Prayer and Fast in Charlottetown, June 1 to 3, the Speaker of the House welcomed the group and commended their help in "upholding the Christian context in the P.E.I. legislature." On the way back they stayed with Bill and Doreen White, at the Internationale Prayer Centre in Bellevue.

In *The Leader* newspaper for Sunday July 21, 1985, Arne was quoted about the growing interest across Canada in praying for authorities. He described how a stop for lunch or coffee would often provide an opening to meeting local

Christians and how a meeting with a mayor would usually immediately lead to an opportunity to hold a weekly prayer meeting in their city hall.

Arne doesn't talk about failures and knows how to shrug off discouragements—he learned a thing or two during the dust bowl years in Alberta—but they happened. On November 16, 1985, Arne was given the following prophecy:

> God has given you a word a long time ago. You've had this word many times—you're going to get it again anyway. You've paid the price, you watched God set the foundations in place, you've gone through discouragements, heartaches and you came to a place where you just said, "It doesn't make any difference—God's in control." But it did hurt and it did cost you.
>
> But I want to tell you something: ... What you have seen up until now has just been a setting in place, a little tiny seed. Arne, you have not even begun to pick up the crop, the crop is not even sprouted, it has not even begun to come out of the ground, more than probably a quarter of an inch. And I want to tell you something: That crop is going to begin to come. It's growing in good soil. You are going to see the fruit of your labours come back to you over and over and over again, multiplied times again ... God is going to honour your faithfulness to the call and the work He has set before you.

In 1985 John Matties invited a young businessman named Marcus Unger to a Prayer Canada breakfast at the ABC restaurant in Abbotsford. Marcus had heard of Prayer Canada a few years before from Barb Dangerfield, the dynamic guitar-playing redhead who had been part of the Prayer Train Pilgrimage and was attending his church at the time.

He was happy to meet the famous Arne Bryan and pleasantly surprised when Arne wrote his name on a Prayer Partner card and told him he was now a prayer partner. "*That's* how easy it is to sign up to Prayer Canada?" he thought. He was impressed with Arne's tenacity, drive and forwardness.

John Matties kept inviting Marcus Unger to the prayer breakfasts and soon Marcus was playing the piano for them. In fall of 1985 Arne and Marcus went together to Calgary to establish a Prayer Post there and attend the Full Gospel Businessmen's Convention. They also met with Bill White and other Prayer Partners.

One strategic thing they discussed on the trip was signs. In Sarnia, ON, where Abraham and Iris DeVries had started a Prayer Post, a lady in the group made a banner of the Canadian flag with a picture of Jesus in the middle of the maple leaf. Arne thought they could have a photo of that banner made into a billboard on the freeway with the words "Jesus Is Lord Over Sarnia." So the city of Sarnia approved the first ever Prayer Canada sign—a large sign that was taken apart every four months and moved to a different part of the city. The rent for the sign, which started at $408 per month, increased every year but the Lord provided the finances. It was a clear message to the city and it inspired Arne, who was dreaming of signs proclaiming "Jesus Is Lord" at the approach to every town and city in Canada.

Marcus Unger had a sign painting business, Melodyland Signs. He had already been asked by James Wolf to paint a big "Jesus Is Lord" sign on the black roof of a machine shop on Huntingdon Road, near Abbotsford airport. Unsure which of six possible designs to use for the wording, he literally threw the samples face-down on the ground before the Lord. Then he picked one at random. He repeated the test four more times and every time the design he picked was the same one: "Jesus is *Lord*" with the word Lord on a slant.

That's the design he painted on the barn, where the planes coming in to land had a good view of it.

Whenever they met, Arne said to Marcus, "You have to make banners... You have to do signs..." He showed him pictures of the Sarnia sign. And he shared Isaiah 8:1 with him, from The Living Bible, where the Lord revealed the spiritual value of "Jesus Is *Lord*" signs:

> *"Make a large signboard and write on it the birth announcement of the son I am going to give you. Use capital letters! His name will be Maher-shalal-hash-baz, which means 'Your enemies will soon be destroyed'"* (Isaiah 8:1, TLB).

Arne says that "Jesus is *Lord*" on a sign means, "Your enemies will soon be destroyed."

Marcus thought: "God has given me this talent and I've already made one 'Jesus is *Lord*' sign. This is where my vision can meld with Arne's vision."

Early in 1986, after Arne had interviewed Marcus on his TV program, they were brainstorming together: "We need to put up a huge sign: 'Jesus Is *Lord* Over Canada'."

"It should be on the freeway so all the people driving up from Seattle can see it."

Arne had had the idea in a dream—he realized that there was no 'Welcome To Canada' sign for people crossing the border. He thought the best place would be by Highway 99 on the hill coming out of White Rock.

The City of Vancouver was planning to celebrate its centenary with a massive five-and-a-half month party for the world—Expo '86—with different countries sponsoring pavilions to showcase their national successes. Arne knew it would be an unparalleled opportunity for Prayer Canada and the gospel of Jesus Christ.

1986 was the year of the sign. Marcus made two 8' by 20' signs that would form a wide V shape with one arm angled to face the northbound traffic and the other to face the southbound traffic. One said "Jesus Is *Lord* – Welcome to Canada" while the other read "Jesus Is *Lord* Over Canada." At the bottom of both signs he painted I TIM. 2:1-4 and II CHRON. 7:14, then "Prayer Canada" with the phone number. Marcus reported at the board meeting on March 1 that the painting was complete.

Arne was working on permission from Mayor Ross, who was encouraging Surrey to do something special for Expo. Arne's project didn't fit the regulations but he made a case for it: "If we want something special then we've got to make special arrangements." The mayor said he liked the idea and gave verbal permission, though he didn't put it through the council.

That was enough for Arne and he began to look for a suitable field beside the road. He walked up and down the back roads asking farmers if they would allow the sign to be built on their property. Nine of them said "No" but the tenth said "Yes" without hesitation, because he had watched Arne on the Prayer Canada TV show *Sunday Night Live*. By now it was April.

Completed Expo sign,
pictured in The Province, August 15, 1986

They needed strong construction materials to display such a big sign and Arne asked for donations from a couple of companies. The property owner let Arne and his crew of volunteers through the locked gate onto the field and they cleared the ground and dug the holes (three feet deep). They set donated six-inch galvanized stove pipes in the holes and braced them. Then a concrete company came and poured donated concrete. The team drilled holes in the pipes to bolt the huge signs on securely. The whole structure had to be high enough to be visible and strong enough to withstand the wind.

And the conviction and faith of Prayer Canada had to be strong enough to withstand the winds of controversy that were about to swirl. The whole sign was up in May. Almost immediately the calls started coming in to City Hall. "Get that sign down now! It bothers me. I have to go by it every week and it bothers me!"

The calls were referred to the mayor and he said, "No. It's approved and it stays until the end of Expo."

Other people wrote to the mayor thanking him and the Council for allowing the signs and the property owner reported that he heard only compliments. But in July a notice from the Permits and License Department warned the property owner that the billboard was illegal, because of size, location and third party advertising, and must be removed. (Prayer Canada's signs were not in the minds of those who had originally drafted the bylaw about advertising on private property alongside highways.) Arne made a phone call and was told no removal order had been made.

In August a postcard sent to Prayer Canada imaginatively charged that the sign contravened legislation about truth in advertising. (The sender claimed that religion was a business involved in sales). Referring to the statement "Jesus is Lord," the writer said: "Your statement is untestable and also unprovable, so it is a false statement. Thus you can be prosecuted under the act and may be found guilty of a criminal offence and liable to a fine of up to $25,000 or one year imprisonment." They prayed for the person who sent the card.

One of the many newspaper articles about the signs said: "Bryan may indeed have friends in high places. He's counting on Mayor Don Ross to save his motorway messages. 'He's got my blessing,' said Ross. 'I personally think the 'Jesus Is *Lord*' sign is inoffensive.'"

Damaged Expo sign, September, 1986

One morning the sign was found badly damaged. Clearly people were still seriously riled by it. Undeterred, Arne said the destruction only made the point that Prayer Canada was needed more than ever. "The reason they get mad when they see that sign is because they're convicted of who they are," he said in *The Province* on September 12. "Jesus is Lord and they know they're serving Satan." The eye-catching headline was: *Devil Made 'Em Do It.*

Marcus fixed the sign and it stayed up for the rest of Expo. Publicity about the damage only benefited Prayer Canada. Also Marcus painted small 2' by 3' cardboard signs that individuals could buy for twenty-five dollars.

Prayer Canada supported the spectacular Christian "Pavilion of Promise" at Expo, where visitors walked through three mirrored theatres and were immersed in a high-tech presentation of "The Scroll," a contemporary musical telling the story of God's communication with humanity and humanity's response to God. Outside in a three-hundred-seat amphitheatre, visitors were entertained with live music and theatrical performances. Hundreds of Christian volunteers had a once-in-a-lifetime experience and many people were saved.

When 100 Huntley Street asked for financial support for the Pavilion of Promise in the lead up to Expo, Prayer Canada regretted that they had no funds to donate. Arne prayed about it. "Well you know how to put on a breakfast," the Lord reminded him. So Prayer Canada hosted a Prayer Breakfast in April in a downtown hotel, with Christian broadcaster Phil Gaglardi (the first B.C. Minister of Highways) as the speaker. They had a good turnout and raised $4200.

During Expo, Arne was often on site, taking part in the Chapel service at the end of performances and meeting people. Out of that came the promise of a Prayer Post director in Halifax, NS.

Expo came to an end mid-October and at the November 10 Surrey council meeting it was reiterated that the sign did not conform to the municipality's sign bylaw. The council had not enforced the bylaw during Expo but now Mayor Don Ross agreed that the sign had to be removed. The legal branch of Surrey City Hall tried to get in touch with Arne about taking it down but Arne and Kathie were away on holiday. The city workmen asked the owner of the land to let them through the locked gate so they could take the sign down but he said firmly, "You've got to get hold of Arne. It's his sign." Finally they obtained the legal authority to cut the lock on the gate and move in there without his permission. They used heavy machinery to cut the pipes and removed the signs.

When Arne returned from holiday he approached the mayor about it, shocked that the sign had not only been taken down but had vanished. In fact the issue went on for more than a year but neither the signs nor the six-thousand dollar compensation Arne billed the city for was forthcoming.

1986 was also the year that Arne tried to find a wife for Marcus Unger. "Okay, Marcus, you're twenty-nine and it's time you found a wife," he had said during the Calgary trip the year before. "So what kind of wife do you want?" And he held out a piece of paper headed "Ten Things About a Wife."

"God will bring her, Arne," said Marcus. "When it's the right time, He'll bring her to me."

In early 1986, Marcus was at a Prayer Canada breakfast at the Green Room in south Surrey and asked Arne if he knew anyone who could give him a ride back to Abbotsford. Arne turned to a nurse named Cathy who was sitting at the same table. "Okay," she said. "I don't have to work till three this afternoon."

As they chatted during the drive they seemed to have a lot in common.

"Do you like classical music?" he asked casually. She just pushed in the tape that was in her machine ready to play— the Hallelujah Chorus from *Handel's Messiah*.

When they reached his home, he said, "This is my Mom." Cathy greeted her brightly with "Hi, Mom!" immediately hitting the right tone for his family.

Marcus invited her to a classical concert the following Saturday and Cathy said "Yes." He invited her to a prayer meeting and Cathy said "Yes."

One day after many evenings together, the realization suddenly hit him how perfectly God was putting their lives together. He remembered a discussion with God in a dream and the five things he had told God he needed in his life companion: she had to be musical, have an evangelistic heart, love children, fit into his family, and pray. Cathy was perfect! He jammed on the brakes in the middle of the street and said, "I'm not joking. Will you marry me?" And Cathy said "Yes!"

All this happened while Arne was away on a three-week trip. "I knew it! I knew it!" Arne claimed when Marcus shared his good news. "Okay, let me see the ring. You don't have a *ring*? Doesn't count!" ("That's Arne," says Cathy. "Black and white.") A week later, when they had the ring, Arne agreed to marry them the next year.

During 1986, the Board of Prayer Canada started some productive initiatives. John Versveldt suggested that some people hesitated to get involved with Prayer Canada because they weren't sure how to pray. As a result the Lord showed Kathie the layout for a Prayer Manual, so that each group could follow a common format and purpose.

The first few pages contain the goal of Prayer Canada, the command (1 Timothy 2:1-5), the guarantee (2 Chronicles 7:14), a letter of guidance from Arne, a list of governmental addresses (so Prayer Partners could write to tell authorities they were praying for them), a list of Scriptures on the value of praying for government authorities, all four verses of O Canada and a page of Prayer Meeting Directives.

The bulk of the little book contains names: federal cabinet ministers, Supreme Court judges, premiers and cabinet members of each province and territory, plus the leaders of the United States and Israel, Canadian ambassadors and other world leaders. Each Prayer Post could add the names of their local authorities.

The board also decided to invest in more regular phone calls with Prayer Partners, fostering closer ties and giving a flow of Prayer Post reports for the newsletter, which would also contain instruction on prayer.

Board member John DeVries and Fred Vance traveled on behalf of Prayer Canada to Rankin Inlet in the Northwest Territories, at the invitation of Tagak Curley, to visit the Prayer Post led by Bill and Ruth Dennis.

In early September, Arne and Kathie drove to Winnipeg

and back. They gave out the small "Jesus Is *Lord*" signs to each contact and were involved in some television presentations.

In November, Arne and Marcus went to Missions Fest in Calgary, where Marcus was kept busy painting signs. Big highway signs were the ideal but involved a lot of expense and negotiations over city permissions. So Marcus prepared a lot of small 18" by 30" signs saying "Jesus Is *Lord* Over..." and Arne would ask people where they were from. "Leduc? Okay. Calgary... Edmonton... Marcus will paint you a sign for ten dollars." When he quoted the verse in Isaiah 8 and explained "Jesus Is *Lord*" meant their enemies would soon be destroyed, people said, "Oh, yeah. I'll have one." The signs were small enough for people to hang in a window or display in their store or business place, a silent witness, a constant prophetic prayer. Twenty such signs went to cities all over Alberta to declare that Jesus is Lord. Since Arne and Marcus teamed up, hundreds of these signs have been delivered or mailed across Canada.

Arne by the prayer board,
pictured in Surrey / North Delta Now, August 27, 1986

Some nagging concerns were revealed in minutes of board meetings. For a couple of years, the minutes had noted:

"Income less than this month last year" and "Donations to date are low." Letters about the finances were sent to Prayer Partners.

The November 1986 minutes ended: "Important Note for ALL Board Members: pray for the Holy Spirit's direction in the matter of the viable continuance of Prayer Canada. Come prepared to make your prayerful and thoughtful contribution to this vital matter."

By March of the following year, the figures were more encouraging.

Arne ended 1986 suffering from a dangerous tropical disease. Kathie phoned from Puerto Rico, where they were spending Christmas with Brenda and her family, asking John DeVries to get as many people praying for Arne as he could. The disease was dengue fever, which causes pounding headaches, raging fever, a bubbling rash, and excruciating muscle and joint pain, and may lead to other potentially fatal complications. His temperature was so high they took him to the hospital. A couple of days later he also developed viral pneumonia.

Kathie nursed him in the hospital during the day. She walked him to the shower and then pushed him in a chair to brush his teeth but when she gave him the toothbrush he looked at her puzzled, as if to say, "What's that for?" It was an anxious time for Kathie.

They had to come home on a later flight and Arne used a wheelchair at the airport but they thanked God for answering the prayers of many.

But there would be more fights to come.

CHAPTER 12

1987 — 1989:
A NOTORIOUS PRAYER FIGHT;
THE OLD HOME

On Wednesday March 11, 1987, the inaugural meeting of the Prayer Canada prayer meeting in Victoria, B.C. was held in Room 322 of the legislature building. Twenty-five or thirty people attended, including several Socred MLAs.

Arne had spoken at a Full Gospel Businessmen's luncheon in Victoria a year or so before. "Is anybody here interested in praying?" he had asked and Ray Jansen had put up his hand. Arne had come straight over to him and took his business card. Ray thought he would probably just be put on a mailing list but as soon as he got back to his office after the lunch, Arne was there.

"God's calling you to **pray**!" said Arne, sticking his finger in Ray's chest. Arne, the commando, was on a recruiting mission for people who would obey the Lord with no reservations.

A Prayer Canada prayer meeting had started back in 1978 in the Legislature after the Prayer Train Pilgrimage but had closed two-and-a-half years later for some construction, although prayer partners continued praying elsewhere. After the 1986 election, Prayer Canada applied and was given permission to meet for prayer in Room 322 of the Legislature and Ray Jansen was the one who ended up leading the revived prayer meetings in March 1987.

He didn't know what he was getting into. There was unusual interest in this prayer meeting, with news reporters attending and writing down everything that was said, because Premier Bill Vander Zalm was known to be a devout Catholic and a supporter of Prayer Canada. Of course the Christians were only there to pray, so they prayed for the reporters.

Stan Biggs wrote in *Christian Info* a few weeks later: "Prayer Canada has remained non-denominational, simple in purpose and enjoys the respect and support of governments at all levels in every part of Canada." But the newspapers made out that it was controversial.

Ray tried to answer questions politely and accurately, but the resulting stories had a cynical, mocking tone, as if Christians praying for a Socred government was highly amusing. "The government needs all the help it can get" was a common theme, as was the dilemma that an MLA might face if he visited the prayer room and "heard a directive that doesn't jibe with a memo from the premier." Humourist Eric Nicol wrote: "Until now the legislature's only contact with calling on the Lord for assistance has been that of opening parliament with a prayer. That formality disposed of, the members have felt free to spend the rest of the session uninhibited by conscience. Politics is the art of the possible; religion, the doctrine of the eternal"—thereby unintentionally making a good case for Prayer Canada.

The fourth meeting fell on April Fool's Day, bringing to mind Psalm 14: "The fool says in his heart..." and this time the reporters had a real "religious circus" to write about. It even reached the pages of *Maclean's* in the issue for April 13, 1987 under the headline: *An unholy prayer fight*. The first three Prayer Canada meetings in the B.C. legislature building had attracted so much media attention that other religious groups thought they should be allowed to pray too and protest groups took advantage of the public stage.

Ray Jansen arrived at that fourth meeting to find the small room bursting at the seams with over a hundred people there, including a film crew and reporters with camera, notebooks, tape recorders and cynical grins. There were Buddhists, Quakers, people loudly protesting about uranium mining in the north, a self-declared bishop of the "Gnostic Church," a new age guru, witches screeching and praying in tongues, and chanting Sufis (mystic Muslims). Arguments broke out. Competing prayers and shouted insults filled the room.

Ray went to ask the sergeant-at-arms if he would clear the room but he said, "I don't think we can, because it is an open meeting. Parliament is public grounds and they have a right to be here. I think you should just continue until the hour is up and then we can do something." Ray led the Prayer Canada group to pray in tongues through the whole time, either out loud or quietly. One strummed his guitar and a few sang through it all. Ray was secretly hoping God would send fire down from heaven, like on Mount Carmel. It was a wild introduction to spiritual warfare. As Stan Biggs put it in *Christian Info*:

> Several left confidently, having in their minds put an end to 'this fundamentalist organization with its foot in the door of the Legislature through its influence and connection with the Premier.' They had demanded that the government must 'close the doors to Rom 322 and the bigoted myopia of PC's attempt to use the people's Legislative Buildings to control and influence the course of government policy'. The Christians also left confidently knowing that their conflict was not with flesh and blood, but principalities and powers and that God would, in the face of repentance, humility and trust, do His work His way.

(Seven months later, newspaper reports horrifyingly illustrated the spiritual evil that swirled around this event. The new age guru was the victim of a grisly murder in London, England, stabbed in the heart by a "disciple" of his and left with his decapitated head resting on his lap.)

The day after the ambush in Room 322, Ray discussed it with MLA John Reynolds, the minister responsible for the legislature. Realizing that the prayer meeting had become more of a problem than a blessing and that prayer transcends geography, he moved the Victoria Prayer Post out of the legislature. But the press interest continued, even to the point of calling Ray while he was with a client at work. Reporters were trying to get a quick quote on controversial issues that had no quick answers and ended up saying that Ray wouldn't answer. He regretted taking the call but he had to be available to his clients.

"Well, you're a **commando**! You can go through it!" That was Arne's encouragement for Ray, when he was feeling a bit bruised from this battle. "Arne had little sympathy for complaining or excuses," says Ray now. "He just won't hear them and you know he's right."

Ray knows that Arne gets a call from God or a word or an open door and he just keeps going until the door gets slammed in his face and then he keeps on going anyway. "There's no rhinoceros with a hide like Arne's!" he continues. "Criticism he doesn't hear. He's got his mission and he's too busy being on the mission to be concerned about the details of other things."

But then Ray goes on to talk about Arne's compassion and care for people. "Well, let's pray about that," is Arne's first reaction to a tale of trouble or worry. He wants to hear what God says about it and pray the problem through, so that you can get back to your call and purpose in God—a constant example in hearing the voice of God and acting on it immediately.

Arne was in Victoria himself, a few days after the notorious prayer meeting, for the provincial prayer service at the Church of Our Lord on Sunday April 5. This was in response to a proclamation to pray by the Lieutenant-Governor of B.C., the Honourable Robert Gordon Rogers. Arne brought a powerful exhortation to the crowd of three hundred people. There was also praise, intercessory prayer, commissioning of the pastors of Victoria and rededication of God's people.

As an article in *Christian Info* said:

> There was a gentle awareness that the Hand of God moves in response to intimate, secret prayer, a diligent seeking of His Kingdom before all things, and a loving obedience to the One who has placed His church as a standard between the forces of light and darkness.

The first trip Arne and Kathie had taken with John and Dolores Matties in 1985 was so good that the four of them traveled together on other trips, both long and short. One quick trip they took to Edmonton, later in April 1987, included a spontaneous and adventurous diversion. A couple of prayer partners in Edmonton asked Arne and John to go along for company as they drove their half-ton pickups loaded with recipe books for a promotion in Yellowknife. Kathy and Dolores were happy to stay in Edmonton.

Within an hour, Arne was asked to drive as his driver was getting sleepy. It was usually a five- to six-hour trip but the weather did not co-operate. A few inches of snow and many miles of almost sheer ice made conditions treacherous, coupled with near blizzard conditions half the time. There was a touchy ferry ride too, battering its way across the mouth of the Mackenzie River, but they made it to Yellowknife and a few days later returned safely to Edmonton.

In May, John Matties was asked to join the board.

On all Arne's journeys, he was as eager as ever to reach the unsaved. He could walk into a place and walk out with a salvation under his arm, just because he was bold enough to ask. A lady on a ferry, for instance, going to Vancouver for a visit, overheard Arne sharing with an engineer and leading him to the Lord. She introduced herself afterwards, eager to hear more.

Arne's other trips in 1987 included visits in May to Washington State and Victoria B.C., and then up to the Yukon, visiting Whitehorse (where he spoke on the radio), Haines Junction and Burwash Landing. Arne and Kathie always had very blessed meetings in a little First Nations church in Haines Junction YK. They stayed with the pastor, John Brown and his wife Sadie. John was also known as Nulata, his Tutchone name. He was from the Wolf clan and helped preserve the knowledge of his native language, providing the old names of places in his area, as well as where the trails were. When he died, a eulogy was offered for him in the Legislature to remember his thirty years of service in the Pentecostal church and his expertise as a wilderness guide, hunter, fisher, trapper, musician and dog sled musher. He was a man of many talents.

Arne was always interested in Cinnamon Junction YK, a little place with a café, service station and airstrip. Many private pilots from Whitehorse liked to fly in to feast on special cinnamon buns—about ten inches square and three inches high.

On one of his trips to the Yukon, Arne was sharing some verses in Isaiah 42 ending with verse eight: "...*I will not share my praise with carved idols*" (Isaiah 42:8, TLB). It was only when he finished reading the passage out, with the last words hanging in the quiet church, that Arne realized they were meeting in a Catholic church with carved idols all around them. "I think the Lord had me not notice them so that I would read it," says Arne.

On June 1, Arne and Kathie set off on a three-week trip to Toronto for which they remarkably had no plans. The original plan for Ray Williams to fly Arne to twelve Maritime towns for meetings had to be cancelled at the last minute. Arne and Kathie's tickets to Ontario were already bought so they decided to go anyway and trust the Lord for guidance.

They set off believing the prophetic word that the Lord had given them: "I have planned this trip before the foundations of the earth—in every situation find My peace. It will be there—even in the hard places—look for it, for My peace will be there."

Arne worked the phones from the day they arrived to set up meetings and appointments so they were able to do something meaningful every day. They stayed in several different homes, Ray Williams lent them his car when needed and everywhere there was warm fellowship. They ministered or met key people in Mississauga (where a careless driver caused damage to Ray's car but no injuries), Brantford, Port Colbourne, Toronto, Montreal (flying in Ray's twin engine Cessna), Cambridge, Sunridge, Welland, Oakville and Milton.

On Saturday June 20, near the end of the trip, there was a memorable luncheon in Brantford. As Kathie said in her report: "Only fourteen arrived but all were in unity. Iris and Abram (DeVries) were there from Sarnia, the Seplys and Jim Cooper from Port Colbourne, several from Toronto. The Lord blessed with His presence and all were ministered to. They kicked us out of that room at 4:30, so we went into the restaurant and continued fellowshipping until 7:30 p.m."

Arne was as outspoken as ever as he ministered across the country, forceful despite his high silken voice, disturbing but lovable. Wherever he went, he made sure his listeners heard two scriptures in particular: 1 Timothy 2:1-4 and 2 Chronicles 7:14.

During the summer of 1987, Arne was expelled from a Surrey prayer meeting, twice!

Don Fults, a Christian realtor who, thanks to Arne's persistence, eventually became a vital member of the team, was initially offended by Arne. The first time they met, Arne was selling memberships to the Social Credit Party and

Don at the time didn't think ministers should be involved in politics. However he did go along to a couple of Prayer Canada breakfasts.

Arne visited a prayer meeting that Don had started with a friend and talked about the fire of the Holy Spirit. Don suspected he was trying to take over. He didn't really know Arne, so he put him out of the prayer meeting.

Arne & Don Fults

A couple of weeks later, Arne came again and in his hand was a certificate with Don's name on it telling him that he was the head of the Whalley Prayer Post for Prayer Canada. "We don't need a Whalley Prayer Post for Prayer Canada," declared Don and sent him away again.

Undeterred, Arne went a third time and somehow things were different. (He thinks the Holy Spirit had been at work.) "I need help," Arne said. "I'm leaving tomorrow for a six-week trip across Canada and I need someone to look after the Prayer Canada office."

"Does it have a phone in it?" Don asked. "Can you run a real estate business out of it?"

Don Fults himself volunteered to spend the next six weeks in the office and he also asked someone he knew, Imelda Cyr, if she would be a secretary for Arne.

The next morning Don and Imelda were in the Prayer Canada office having a time of prayer together at eight o'clock. "Oh Lord, let us be of use," they prayed. "Let us be of some use to You here, Lord." At that point the phone rang and a voice pleaded, "Help! Help! I'm a witch!"

Not knowing what do, they told her to come to the office. They prayed for her and trusted God together—a memorable introduction to Prayer Canada.

After the six weeks of answering the phone there, plus attending to his own business, Don moved out but continued his involvement, attending the 6 a.m. prayer meetings regularly. And at some point it dawned on him that Arne was the man who had been dangerously sick with dengue fever in Puerto Rico, the man that his church had been praying for the previous December.

In spite of their bad start, Arne and Don found they could work together with great blessing. Who could find fault with Arne's go-getter spirit, fun-loving nature and fiery heart for the Lord? One day they were walking along together and the forty-three-year-old Don said, "Hold on, Arne. Don't walk so fast!"

"Well, Don," Arne called over his shoulder, already several paces ahead, "I'm sixty-nine. I don't know how much time I've got *left*!"

By the next January, Don Fults was hosting the Whalley Prayer Post.

The next September in 1988, with Prayer Canada near its tenth year, Arne celebrated his seventieth birthday. In April of that year the board were concerned that the numerous trips might be over-taxing him and Kathie. The action decided on was: "They should earnestly be convinced that any particular trip is in the Lord's will." The board also prayed for a mini-motor home for them.

Maybe Arne had reminded them of the vision he had back in 1977 of the giant suit of armour with a diminutive Arne dangling inside, and the Lord's words: "If you stay within me, I will enable you to take great strides across the land." Arne knew the Lord was still striding across the land and so Arne would continue the exhilarating ride.

Arne was tickled to pose with this suit of armour in a Florida bed & breakfast where they stayed

However, it seems that there was extra spiritual struggle during 1988. An Intercessory Prayer Group, meeting in the Prayer Canada Prayer Room on a Wednesday night in April 1988, wrote a report about how the Lord had led them to pray:

"Satan has launched a powerful detailed attack on Prayer Canada specifically to **destroy** the prayer cells or the foundation on which Prayer Canada has been built. ... This is a long-term very well planned offensive strategy. Simply, the devil is using different strategies in the different prayer groups to cause them through *feelings* of ineffectiveness to *disband. DON'T GIVE UP* !! Seek the face of the Lord and ask Him for a strategy to counter-attack the attack of the devil."

They came against the attacks with Scripture and believing prayer.

The board made sure Prayer Posts had more support and more teaching so that they would be sure their prayers were effective.

It was, as usual, a busy travel year for Arne and Kathie. They were not slowing down. In March they traveled on Vancouver Island with Marcus and Cathy Unger. Marcus took his accordion, to play in meetings if there was no piano, and Cathy sang. Arne would give his testimony and raise up a Prayer Post and then they would pray. There were many small meetings in homes, where the people knew how to pray and Arne was a spark to light the fire.

Arne and Kathie went to Spring Conventions at two Bible Colleges—Three Hills, AB, and Briarcrest, SK. In the first half of May they went north to Whitehorse and Burwash Landing, YK and Dawson City, B.C.

Then May 20 to 31, they hosted Tagak Curley the former NWT cabinet minister, whom Arne had first met in January 1980 when the Prayer Post had started in Yellowknife. Tagak was the guest speaker at the Prayer Breakfast in Surrey on May 21, and also spoke at churches and FGBM luncheons. Arne took him to Lillooet and Williams Lake, B.C.

In July and August 1988, Arne and Kathie drove through Alberta, Saskatchewan, Manitoba and back, visiting Prayer Posts and ministering at the Three-Day Prayer and Fast in North Battleford. Early in this thirty-one-day trip they stopped in Delia, where Arne had grown up, to visit an old friend, Marguerite Friedly. Back in 1939, when Arne and his parents had left Delia, Marguerite's father had taken over their old farm. They were a Christian family. Marguerite had been a pretty sixteen-year-old at the time and, of course, had liked the dashing twenty-one-year-old Arne a lot.

Over the years she and her husband had prayed for Arne and supported Prayer Canada, and Arne and Kathie had visited them in Delia. Now she was hoping he would help her with a history project she was working on. Would he confirm that he was the baby in an old photograph she had in the museum? It turned out it was Arne's baby picture.

Then she asked him if he would do something else for her. She begged him to baptize her. She had not wanted to be baptized in church because she had a problem with one leg and one arm and by this time was on oxygen.

"Yes, I'd be happy to!" said Arne. "We can baptize you in your bathtub."

She was a little lady so it was not difficult. They had a very happy baptismal service and it meant a lot to her and her husband.

Arne and Kathie drove on, continuing the southern route for the outward trip and coming back through communities further north, as they usually did. In Verigan, SK, Arne had an opportunity to speak to Premier Grant Devine. New prayer partners came on board in Fort McLeod, Brandon, Portage, Medicine Hat, Lethbridge, AB and Castlegar, B.C.—altogether a normally productive trip. A note in the minutes says: "A new awareness of the Christian's responsibilities seems to be filtering into Christians' lives."

On the way back, when they drove into Saskatoon, they had a message from the RCMP that the Friedlys wanted them to call.

"Arne," said Marguerite's husband when Arne called, "My wife passed away yesterday. She wanted you to perform the funeral."

"We can *do* it!" said Arne. They had one day in their schedule where nothing had been arranged yet. About three weeks after Marguerite's baptism, Arne was able to conduct her funeral. It was very significant and moving for Arne to be able to minister a baptism and a funeral for his old friend near his first home.

The Lord often used Arne and Kathie as pastors to the people they stayed with. They prayed for a motor home for a long time but eventually the Lord said, "Fifty per cent of your ministry is in the homes where you stay." They were always ready to wash their hosts' feet if the Lord told them to do it. It was usually after they came back home after a meeting, maybe at eleven o'clock at night, that the Lord would say, "Arne, I want you to wash their feet."

The Lord would use that simple, maybe foolish, act to reveal the fault lines in the lives of these hard-working people. It was heartrending to see the struggles some families were going through. Often there were tears, and forgiveness was asked and given, until they were melded together like solid rock and ready to go on serving the Lord who loved them so much.

The final big trip that year was to the Maritimes. They stayed the first night with Rod Trites in Moncton, NB and that night they did some praying and planning. Rod said he couldn't go with them because he was anxious to acquire a good garbage truck to look after his large four-hundred-home mobile park.

"Rod you have to come with us," insisted Arne. "The Lord says, if you look after His business, He will look after yours."

The next morning the three of them set off to cover the Maritimes, first taking the ferry to Prince Edward Island. By noon they were entering Charlottetown and almost the first thing Rod noticed was a large sign on a telephone pole: "Quality garbage truck for sale." That excited him. He had to phone immediately and soon he was standing right in front of the vehicle he needed. It was in good shape and the price was ten thousand dollars less than he thought he would have to pay. After another phone call to his son back home to come over and get the truck, Rod was rejoicing and eager to continue the Lord's business. They all knew the Lord had arranged it.

The whole trip, eighteen days across PEI, Nova Scotia, Newfoundland and New Brunswick, was one of the most Spirit-directed and worthwhile trips they had been on. Fifteen Prayer Posts were started in the Maritimes and also two in Montreal.

A note in the minutes: "Our God is able if we will pray and then act as He directs."

In August 1988, Don Fults joined the board of directors. At that first meeting, he spoke about how important it is to learn to know the voice of Holy Spirit. It is still his opinion now as chairman of the board: "You really have to have a glimpse into the Lord's mind. You can't just sit there and say 'Well, I think this...' because it just doesn't work."

The board found that God does not tell one person one thing and another something opposite. If they don't have one hundred percent unity, they don't move. But it depends on each board member speaking up. Don remembers one of his early board meetings when he kept quiet about a proposal although there was a "no" in his spirit. He was new and hesitated to speak up. That resolution was passed but it turned out to be wrong.

"You know I felt at that time that I shouldn't have said yes," another new board member said to Don.

"I felt that too," Don replied.

"Well, why didn't you say so? I would have backed you up."

"Well, why didn't you say? I would have backed you up!"

They learned what Arne had known for a long time: Listen to God and be bold. That's what made it possible for Arne to speak God's word for others and help them to hear God for themselves, like when Don said to him, "I'm thinking of getting out of real estate." It was at a time when interest rates were making it difficult for realtors.

"Well, Don," Arne said thoughtfully. "There's success and there's persistence."

That was all he needed to say. Don is still in real estate—a vehicle for ministry.

Arne's ability to hear God almost gave Don a heart attack one day when they were just getting used to each other. Don was driving him somewhere in the old yellow van and they were talking about a trip Arne was about to take with a visiting prophetic minister involving one-night stops all the way as usual.

"You know Arne," Don said. "You should make two night stops with him instead of one night. It takes people one night to get used to the way a man talks. And so the second night they'd get the message but the first night..."

Arne suddenly slapped Don on the knee while he was driving and yelled, "Out of the very **mouth** of God himself!"

"What did I do?" asked the shocked Don. "What's wrong?"

"No, no," said Arne in a more normal voice. "That's just the very truth!"

Asked to describe Arne now, Don says: "You know Jeremiah? Not too far off his character. God gave him a vision, he grabbed onto it and he's never let go and he's never varied from that. He's never wanted to start a church—he starts prayer meetings in City Halls and in Council Chambers and in legislatures and in parliament buildings all across Canada, from Labrador to Yukon Territory."

He adds: "Arne and Kathie made some big sacrifices in their lives together. Their lives became Prayer Canada. Like Jeremiah's life became the servant of God."

"You got an extra bowl of soup?" Don's voice would say on the phone during his single years. Or he'd just arrive unexpected at lunch time and Kathie would create a meal out of nothing for him. Kathie, her gift of hospitality and her deep freeze made innumerable people welcome over the years.

Don says, "Kathie was a sweetheart and a sweet spirit." Then he adds, "But you knew they both were tough too. Spiritually tough. God trained them for the job."

A couple of years later, Arne asked Don to be chairman of the board, succeeding Ron Ward. Arne remained the president and leader of Prayer Canada but this separation of duties allowed him to contribute freely at the board meetings.

Arne and Kathie did appreciate company on their travels. That is how it happened that four of them were involved in a dangerous accident in February 1989. Arne and Kathie were on their way home in the snow after a trip to Mission Fest in Calgary with John and Dolores Matties, and were only about ten minutes along the #1 Highway, after a stop in Hope, B.C. for some tea and a check with the RCMP as to which road was safe to travel on. They knew there were blizzard warnings out.

John was driving when the snow really closed in. In white-out conditions, John slowed down to about thirty kilometres per hour but the driver behind did not slow down. He slammed into them three times, pushing the Rabbit off the road, and then drove on. As they careened down a six-foot slope off the highway towards a big tree, John turned the steering wheel to miss it and circled back to the edge of the highway.

"Everybody okay?" asked John. "Arne, are you alright? *Arne!*" Arne's seat had broken and the impact had knocked him unconscious. Dolores was hurt—it turned out to be a broken wrist and ribs. John's seat broke also and he landed on Kathie's rib cage so she couldn't get out. They were alone in a snow blizzard in a small white car.

But they were not alone for long. A pick-up truck stopped. Two elderly ladies and a man got out and laid a blanket over Arne. They parked the truck so the wind wouldn't come in through the broken windows. They laid hands on Arne and prayed. They stayed until help came and then they were gone. Nobody had been driving on that highway because of the blizzard. Where had they come from? Afterwards the Prayer Canada travelers called them "our three angels." They never did find the blanket afterwards.

After fifteen or twenty minutes, Arne seemed to recover. Two ambulances came and put Arne and Dolores in one, John and Kathie in the other.

"Does she talk English?" they asked Arne about Dolores.

"Yes," he answered. "She's just praying in tongues."

Dolores started witnessing to the ambulance men, telling them they'd better get their lives together. She was thinking, "What if it happened to them, and they didn't make it?" Again at the hospital they had to ask if she spoke English. All of them were thanking Jesus for their safety, rejoicing and finding everything hilarious. The Rabbit was a write-off, later replaced by another one, red this time, and the Lord was good.

Undeterred, John and Dolores accompanied Arne and Kathie on other short trips and long tours. "One thing about Arne, you can never frazzle him," says Dolores. "He's steadfast and no matter what anybody says it doesn't change one iota what he is doing or what he says or who he talks to." They often observed that God had already set up an appointment for them and Arne's boldness just rang the door bell.

"Well, we don't know anybody here," said Arne when they arrived in Kamloops B.C. one time, "but we're going to have a prayer meeting here."

They walked into a random store in the mall and asked if there were any Christians there.

"No, but there's a Christian guy working a couple of stores down there." Praise God, the sales clerk knew a Christian who had made himself known to people around. They found him in a clothing store and he was so interested in the conversation that they were still talking when the mall was being locked up.

"Why don't you guys come for supper?" he said.

His wife was surprised but soon discovered that she knew John and Dolores and had even been in their home once; when they were living in Penticton they had hosted her youth group.

Another time, some years later while driving in northern Ontario, the four of them came to a town called Hearst, also known as the Moose Capital of Canada. Hearst was 85% francophone because many early settlers had come from Quebec. They stopped at a phone booth for Arne to call someone, when a lady came running up to the car.

"Arne!" she panted. "I knew it was you because of the bald head. Please pray for me—my husband and I need prayer."

In its twelfth year, Prayer Canada had achieved so much and spread far and wide around Canada. The strategies God had given to Arne to build this prayer blessing for the country were working. He just had to keep doing the same and more. God had more blessing for them and would take care of them through more difficulties.

**"..I have set my face like flint to do his will
and I know that I will triumph."
(Isaiah 50:7, TLB).**

*Arne & Kathie 2008 with flowers for their birthdays
from Surrey Mayor, Diane Watts*

CHAPTER 13

1990 — 1994:
TRAVELS, A NEW HOME AND MORE TRAGEDY

Arne enjoyed traveling with Harry Rusk. In March 1990 they were up in the Yukon, staying with a couple who were weighed down with many troubles. After Arne turned the light out at about midnight, it was extremely quiet for a few minutes.

Then suddenly Arne said, "Harry, you've got to take Gladys on that cruise through the Panama **Canal**!" He had suggested this many times before, almost nagging, but Harry again kept silent because he and Gladys were not married.

Arne suddenly clicked the light back on as if he had just understood Harry's hesitation. "I don't mean **now**, you know! After you marry her... You're going to **marry** her, aren't you?"

"We've been talking about it," Harry confessed.

"You've been **resisting** it for the last year!" was Arne's accusation and they both broke out laughing.

The next morning their hosts asked what had been so funny in the night. "You were laughing," they said. "And we were laughing because you were laughing!" It had cheered their spirits.

Arne finds joy everywhere. Anyone who greets him with "Hi Arne. How are you?" always gets the cheerful answer, "I'm **blessed**!"

As Harry Rusk says, "There are no dull moments with Arne!" His joy is infectious. "He's always positive, always uplifting and he truly lives the Scripture: *'Encourage each other and build each other up...'* (1 Thessalonians 5:11, NIV). He always has a kind word to say about everyone. I've never heard him put anyone down."

Harry and Gladys Rusk leading worship in Edmonton City Hall

Harry met Arne in 1980 or 1981 when Arne spoke at the large church in Edmonton where Harry was training to be a pastor. Harry was very touched and spiritually lifted by Arne's talk but someone advised him not to get too friendly with him—"He's dangerous." That warning spurred Harry to find out for himself, and he and Arne became lifelong friends. In September 1990 they became more than friends when Arne performed a beautiful wedding ceremony for Harry and Gladys in a park in New Westminster.

That year Arne and Kathie traveled to Rankin Inlet for their first visit to the Arctic. Arne had been asked to perform the marriage service for Tagak and Sally Curley on April 28, 1990. After the happy wedding day, he also spoke in two church services. They stayed in the Bible School started by Kayy Gordon from Vancouver's Glad Tidings Church. The temperature was -18° and they enjoyed skidooing on the ice.

While Arne was away, John DeVries fulfilled some speaking engagements for him in Alberta. John had been an active supporter of Arne and Prayer Canada from the first year, trusting Arne's revelation and admiring his tenacity. He was one of the Prayer Train Pilgrims in 1978 and occasionally travelled with Arne at other times. John also pastored an independent Pentecostal Church and had a significant missionary outreach in the Philippines.

Arne valued John as a faith-filled intercessor and also a gifted Bible teacher. He was the one who was asked to draw up guidelines for Prayer Post leaders, for selecting new board members and for people who traveled and ministered on behalf of Prayer Canada.

Then in 1990 Arne and Kathie were thrilled when John made a dramatic and generous proposal. He would build a three-storey house on 109th Avenue in Surrey that would be a permanent rent-free facility for Prayer Canada. The basement would house the Prayer Canada offices and prayer room, the main floor would be a spacious two-bedroom apartment for Arne and Kathie, and the upper floor would be for John's use. The setting was delightfully rural, down a quiet little spur road and backing on to a creek, but close to main roads through Surrey. Having the office and prayer room just downstairs would be ideal.

Construction began on the Prayer Canada house as Arne and Kathie traveled (Montreal and the Maritimes in June) and continued with their regular commitments (prayer breakfasts in Kamloops, Edmonton, Lillouet and Abbotsford, as well as locally). Ron Ward, who had joined the board the year before, had been in India and seen the establishment of Prayer India—another exciting international development. New board member Lindsay Morris travelled in B.C. and Alberta with his job and called on Prayer Partners en route. He was blessed with the fellowship and the following year visited Prayer Partners in Montreal, QC and Welland, ON.

In May and June of 1991, Arne and Kathie drove all the way to Ottawa and back, with good meetings in Salmon Arm, B.C., Calgary, AB, Moose Jaw, SK, Brandon, MB and Thunder Bay, ON.

As usual the Lord arranged surprises. Driving through Ontario, they stayed in a motel in Sault Ste. Marie where they had no active contacts, but the motel owners turned out to be Christians who invited them for dinner and then arranged an event. Two days later in Parry Sound, a lady overheard Arne making a phone call and she introduced herself—she was on Prayer Canada's mailing list. She invited them for lunch and was possibly going to start a Prayer Post.

Their meeting in London was cancelled, so they were able to visit and stay with some of Arne's Ontario relatives. Altogether twenty relatives visited, all calling Arne by his childhood nickname "Doc." In Exeter, Arne was interviewed for the newspaper. In Brantford, Linda Bowden arranged a meeting—about thirty people who had been fasting all day for it. After stops in Port Colborne and Welland, they went on to stay with Ray and Mary Williams in Toronto for three days before going on to Peterborough, Brockville and then to Ottawa for a few days.

(l to r) Cam's wife Sharon, Scott, Shane, Sherri Ann, Shana Lynn, Arne

The return trip included a television interview and possibly a new television program in Brandon. They arrived in Regina at 9:00 p.m. but there was no accommodation, so at midnight they had to drive on to Moose Jaw. The next day they went on to Medicine Hat then spent a weekend with Bill and Doreen White at the Internationale Prayer Centre in Bellevue and enjoyed an overnight visit with Arne's son, Cameron, and his four grandchildren, Shana Lynn, Scott, Sherri Ann and Shane, in Creston. They then traveled through Nelson and Castlegar to Oliver to visit Arne's 80-year-old sister Hilda before arriving home. It was a typically varied and successful trip.

On the drive into Ottawa during that trip in 1991, Arne and Kathie had a surprise meeting with their friends Al and Elaine Jones who lived in Etobicoke. Arne and Kathie had met them first in Toronto. Then when Al and Elaine had to come west in 1989, they had invited Arne and Kathie to join them for several days together in Campbell River. They all got on really well, so well that their conversation was peppered with affectionate insults that sounded as if they loathed one other.

"Arne, just get another car!" Al would say as he watched Arne squeezing himself into his little Rabbit. "Al, write a cheque!" was Arne's comeback.

Arne and Kathie had been driving down the 401 towards Ottawa during that long trip in 1991 when they became aware of Al and Elaine driving beside them and flagging them over. (The little red VW with "Jesus Is *Lord*" on the back couldn't be missed.) They were both going to Ottawa, so they arranged to meet in a park there, where they had a good talk. Then Arne said, "Let's have a word of prayer before we go"—both couples had other things to attend to.

"No!" objected Al. "I don't want a 'word of prayer.' What I do want is a word from the Lord. I have a need even my wife is not familiar with. You get a word from the Lord tonight and I'll buy you breakfast in the morning."

That night the Lord woke Arne up for an hour and a half and gave him both a word and a dream. Over breakfast he prophesied with tears, looking out of the window of the restaurant and seeing it again—an overpass with a drive-through underneath—as if he was still dreaming.

"It was a beautiful time," says Al. "A unique time of fellowship."

Whenever Arne and Kathie were in the area on ministry, Al and Elaine insisted they stay with them, although they don't work with Prayer Canada. "Arne's always ready to put his shoes on and go," says Al. "But we sometimes got two or three days with them."

Al likes to quote a friend's comment: "It's amazing how the voice of God sounds just like Arne!" Their lasting friendship is founded not on Prayer Canada but on mutual prayer support. Arne and Kathie appreciate being able to pray things through with them and Al knows Arne can hear a word from the Lord for him if anyone can. At least three times in particular, Al called and said, "Arne, I want you to pray about this." Arne would pray and hear an answer from the Lord that didn't make sense to him. But Al would respond: "That's exactly what I needed!"

Al cherishes the friendship to this day. He can mimic Arne's lively voice perfectly and enjoys confusing people on the phone. "You can always expect him to say 'I'm blessed!' and he blesses others. He's always ready. We visited many homes where there were Prayer Posts and, when we left, Arne and everybody there was blessed. He never left a home the way he went into it—he made a difference on behalf of Jesus. He loves the Lord beyond words. His dedication is incredible. Aggressive dedication."

One time in Niagara Falls they went to a special restaurant that happened to be in a casino. They joked about it and took a photo. They went to pay the cashier. "Well, praise the Lord," enthused Arne. "That's the right price... so I'll **pay**!" Then he went on, "Honey, have you asked Jesus to come into your heart?" He led the cashier to the Lord as people behind waited to pay for their meal. The Spirit of God touched her and she had a real born again experience. Arne can be both funny and godly at the same time.

Good friends: Arne & Kathie, Al & Elaine Jones

Kathie and Elaine also got on really well. One time they wanted to go to a garage sale the next morning but Arne wanted to sleep in. Al agreed Arne could sleep in as long as he got a word from the Lord. The Lord blessed them with a really necessary personal word.

Even today, Al and Arne call each other about once a month to stay up to date. "I've always respected Arne and Kathie for the way they have devoted their lives to Prayer Canada," Al says. "And they've endured spiritual confrontation. Satan hates Arne with a passion! But, as he says, he's blessed."

At last, in September 1991, even before it was completely finished, Arne and Kathie moved into their beautiful new home. God assured Arne that this would be his home to stay— no more moves. At age 73 that was good news.

After dark that first night, Arne went into the bathroom and saw a kind of glow from the opaque window. He stepped into the bathtub to get a better view and saw two huge golden trumpets. The Lord told him that they could stay in this home as long as the two trumpets were there. They have been visible in the window every night after dark since then.

He was delighted by the little stream of fresh water that flows along at the back of the property. He traced it to its source, about half a mile across the road and into Hawthorne Park. There he found a small swampy area where water bubbles up continually, flowing as a little rivulet of water into a small depression. It eventually reaches their place as a stream at the bottom of a small ravine. When heavy rains come, it sometimes swells to eight or nine feet wide and two feet deep. In a very dry season it's reduced to a trickle of clear fresh water, six or eight inches wide and an inch or two deep—but Arne has never seen it dry up.

It's understandable that the former inspector of river crossings for Canadian Bechtel would be interested in his own mini-river but there's more to it. That ceaseless flow of fresh water speaks to Arne of God's unstoppable love. Arne knows that, when God calls us to do something for Him, He always provides whatever supply we need.

Prayer Board in the Prayer Canada office
—Linda Bowden points to where she works in Thailand

In addition to big journeys and big events, Arne and Kathie's lives were filled with all the regular faithful commitments—Monday evening prayer, Tuesday noon prayer at City Hall, Wednesday and Thursday morning prayer, monthly Prayer Breakfasts.

The monthly newsletter became the quarterly twelve-page *Prayer Post Courier* and, with better computer help, the production was less labour-intensive. Kathie was now producing it and cheerful volunteers helped with labelling and mailing. A vital communication tool, it is filled with Arne's voice, inspirational teaching, encouraging news from Prayer Posts and fascinating letters from prayer partners all over the world. Reading it is like having a good time of fellowship.

Arne & co-host Don Fults interview guests on Sunday Night Live

Arne still hosted the television program *Sunday Night Live*, a full hour on Sundays at 10 p.m. Don Fults was now his co-host. Arne started on local television in 1979 and continued until 1994.

Arne and Kathie took frequent short trips as well as long hauls, often with companions. During 1991, for example, they went to Powell River in March with Gerry and Pat Pelland, and to the Yukon in April with Nick Klassen. In 1992, they traveled to Quesnel in February (John Unghy drove them in his truck and a Prayer Post was organized at City Hall there), and to Prince Rupert in April with Fred Manke.

Arne and Harry Rusk flew to the Yukon but the local pastor who was scheduled to pick them up and drive them around was nowhere to be found. They got a ride from the airport to a local mall and prayed. After a few minutes of wandering in the mall, Harry met a First Nations lady he knew from Ross River, Mrs Grady, who was shopping with her teenaged daughter.

"No problem!" she exclaimed, when Harry explained their predicament. "We'll be your taxi." So with the four of them sitting comfortably in the wide cab of her three-quarter ton truck, they set off—Whitehorse, Haines Junction, Carmacks, Ross River, Faro, Mayo and Dawson City—encouraging the Prayer Posts and praising God for Holy Spirit-directed friends. "You really filled us with the Word of God," they said, "and we needed that."

Later that year with Don and Margaret Fults, they visited John and Siony DeVries in Post Falls, Idaho, then returned via Radium, to visit with Wayne and Linda Frater, and Vernon.

At the end of July 1992, Arne and Kathie set off for a thirty-six day trip to Ontario, with stops in Creston to spend time with Arne's four grandchildren, in Bellevue for a Three-Day Prayer and Fast, and at Briarcrest Bible College where they met some African students. They turned back in Brockville, Ontario and returned home by Yellowstone Park in the States.

In Arne's journal of the trip, he mentions by name all the people they fellowshipped with and all the people who hosted them, old friends and new, and he includes details that interested him, like what they ate and what crops they saw growing beside the road.

There were usually three Prayer and Fasts each year in different parts of the country and Arne used to lead all of them. However, Ray Jansen took on the organization of the local

Prayer and Fasts in 1987, first in Victoria and then in Whistler, where Leoran Anhorn made his chalet available for them. Currently they are held at Dogwood Bible Camp in Hope, B.C.

The first time Ray and Brenda attended a Prayer and Fast was in Abbotsford in 1986. Ray was amazed to see how God used the gifts of word of knowledge, prophecy and deliverance within a group of people to minister to others: "It really showed me, when the gifts of the Holy Spirit are in function, that ministry is just sweet and beautiful and there is real effective change." It hooked him on letting the Holy Spirit be the leader and to this day that's how he runs the Prayer and Fasts, following Arne's example.

Usually between thirty and sixty people attend for the three days. They start with praise and worship to come into harmony and then the first meeting is all about getting to know each other. That is followed by a time of cleansing, repenting before the Lord and unloading hindrances from the past and distractions of the present. After that they pray for each province, premier and cabinet member by name, then for different countries and each country's leader, and then for the body of Christ throughout the whole world and whatever global issues are current at the time. The Holy Spirit leads in specific directions within this general framework. They let the Holy Spirit pray through them, learning as they go along.

Arne usually gives a report and Ray speaks a little about prayer: "We are in conversation with God and God is coming down to dwell in us and to speak through us." When an issue comes up during prayer, someone may bring some teaching on it, seemingly planned by God. Occasionally the meeting has to be nudged back on track. Arne always encourages people to maintain focus and not to be distracted from the direction the Lord is leading.

There is a nucleus of about fifteen people who find the Prayer and Fast times so refreshing they wouldn't miss them. "It's like being on a world tour, only you don't get worn out!"

In May 1993, Arne and Kathie toured in the Yukon, and Marcus and Cathy Unger took a month off to go with them. They travelled in Marcus's business van which had no side windows in the back. Marcus painted "Jesus Is *Lord*" signs wherever they went, about forty of them altogether.

Travelling north on the ferry from Prince Rupert was as breathtaking as an expensive cruise. They disembarked on a Sunday morning in Haines, Alaska, USA. Arne hadn't planned a meeting and didn't know anyone there but, after stopping for breakfast, they found a note on their vehicle: "Please join us for Church service." (Marcus' van had to belong to Christians, with Jesus Is *Lord* and Prayer Canada signs on it.) They went and found that the Church was experiencing a movement of the Holy Spirit. Arne had an opportunity to share the vision of Prayer Canada and the people loved it. They immediately put up the sign that Marcus painted and started a Prayer Post— another international Prayer Post.

Arne always planned his trips but still listened to God all the way. "Oh, I feel like I'm supposed to stop here," he would say from time to time during their travels. They established Prayer Posts wherever possible, even if it was only two people in a small First Nations community.

Yukon was surprising to Marcus and Cathy. They watched spring bloom while they traveled. One day, there was snow and bare trees; the next, blue sky and green leaves. Their journey took them to Whitehorse and then all the way up to Dawson City, along the Top of the World Highway. They were impressed by a hill in Dawson City: the top of that hill was the southernmost point where you can watch the sun go around without setting.

While they were in a small church there, a couple walked in with their seven children. "The Lord told us to be here this Sunday morning," they said, "because God wants to give us a message."

The family lived in Coffee Creek, a hundred miles up the Yukon River, and they could only afford to travel to town once a year, because it took a barrel of fuel in their boat to come down the river and three barrels to get back home up the river. The husband had delivered all their babies up there. "How could you do that?" asked Cathy, a nurse.

"Well, God showed me. There was nobody else."

The family knew this was the Sunday they had to be there and it was exactly the Sunday that Arne was there. The Lord gave Arne a powerful word for them—you could tell by the look on their faces. When they returned to their totally isolated spot, they took a sign with them: 'Jesus Is *Lord* Over Coffee Creek.'

Arne and his team didn't take the ferry for their return trip to allow them to visit numerous small places. One photo shows a public phone way up a pole with a ladder propped up to reach it. The phone is at the perfect height when the snow is deep!

In Faro, which was once a bustling mining town but at that time was more like a ghost town, they drove down the main street and saw a lady walking along.

"Hello," said Arne boldly. "I'm looking for ...[He mentioned the name of a contact]."

"Hello. I'm the mayor of this town."

"Good! I would like to have a Prayer Post here to pray for you and the council."

"Come on in, then. Let's talk about it."

As usual when they visited the Yukon, they had outreach meetings in the First Nations villages of Burwash Landing, staying with a lady named Lena Johnson who bought a "Jesus Is *Lord*" sign and nailed it on the back of her log cabin. For over twenty years it has warned spiritual enemies that they will soon be destroyed.

In Watson Lake, near the B.C. border, they visited the famous Signpost Forest which began in 1942, while US Army engineers were working on the Alaska Highway. One of the soldiers had been so homesick for his hometown of Danville, Illinois, that he put up a sign pointing home with the distance in miles. Others did the same for their hometowns and, more than ten thousand signs later, visitors are still adding to it today. Arne added a "Jesus Is *Lord*" sign.

Marcus and Cathy learned so much from the Bryans on this and other trips, the sort of things you only learn watching God's servants in action.

"They taught us about how the Holy Spirit moves in a person's life. Once a lady couldn't get set free from some bondage in her life. The cat walked in as Arne prayed and you could <u>see</u> the demon jump over to the cat. The cat ran up the wall ... up the curtain ... this cat went crazy! So we got hold of the cat after that and prayed and got rid of the demon out of the cat, because the demon didn't belong in the cat either. The lady was calm afterwards and so was the cat."

Arne and Kathie taught them about how to treat people and how to minister to people with love and honour. "Also how to honour guests that come to your home. Don't just ship them off to the back room.

"Arne and Kathie's lives have been so intertwined. I honestly believe he has lived as long as he has because of her tenacity, holding on to God's word, the promise that He gave her through a rainbow saying He would never require her again to go through the death of her husband. Every time that Arne went through a serious health problem, she said, 'No you promised me.' I think that's why Arne's living as long as he is!

"Kathie has been the love of his life. They loved each other. And they were in spiritual agreement."

Arne and Kathie's days were also filled with joys and agonies of family life.

"These boys need a dad," Kathie's daughter-in-law Ingrid said, having asked Kathie to come over one day.

"No they don't," said Kathie bluntly. "They've got grand-pas and uncles. But you need a husband." Ingrid had been lonesome since Barry died. "Let's pray about it."

Within six months Ingrid was happily married. She and her husband had a daughter, Angela, who has always loved having Arne and Kathie as a third set of grandparents.

Kathie's oldest child Brian and his wife Judy live in Victoria on Vancouver Island.

Kathie's oldest daughter, Brenda, lives in Florida. She has four children—Melanie, Miles, Marlon and Marcel—but her husband left her and things were often difficult. However, Arne and Kathie visited her every winter for eighteen years, thanks to the generosity of a friend.

Kathie's fourth child, Beryl, was working in Banff, Alberta in 1985-6 when she had an unplanned pregnancy. Kathie always went down to Florida for the birth of Brenda's babies and now she needed to be in Banff with her unmarried middle daughter for her baby. But she also wanted to be with her youngest, Barb, who was about to get married. "Lord, how are you going to work this out?" she prayed.

"Mom, what do you think if I come home?" said Beryl on the phone one day.

"Thank you, Lord," Kathie prayed. "Problem solved."

Beryl's son Jordan was born in July 1986, on the day of Barb's bridal shower, which he attended in his little basket. Barb had a beautiful wedding and Beryl became a wonderful mother to Jordan. Arne and Kathie loved looking after him when Beryl had to be at work, and he soon had a little cousin, Kurt, to play with.

Sadly, Barb's husband was diagnosed with a brain tumour in 1989 and he was unconscious on pain medication when Jordan wanted to go and see him in the hospital in 1992. Arne and Kathie took him for the visit and he had many questions.

"Uncle Rob's finished his life on earth," explained Barb gently. "So he's going to heaven." They talked together about how beautiful heaven was.

"Oh, can I go there now too?" asked little Jordan.

After Rob died, Beryl and Barb were very close, supporting each other, taking camping trips together. Kurt often went to his other grandparents but Beryl lived only half a mile from Arne and Kathie and so Jordan was really happy to be with them. He always wanted to sleep on the floor beside Arne, so they threw a quilt down there for him to snuggle up in.

In June 1993, Jordan was again with Arne and Kathie. Beryl had brought him over the night before. Arne and Kathie were hosting the Prayer Canada board and spouses for a dinner and they were all sitting round the table before the meal, talking about difficult experiences. "Well, I've had enough," said Kathie light-heartedly. "I don't want any more problems. Finished."

Jordan, nearly seven, was playing with Ray and Brenda Jansen's children in another room. (Ray had become a board member the previous June.) Jordan came in and asked, "Grandma, can I sleep over again tonight?"

"We'll have to ask your mom," replied Kathie.

When he phoned home there was no answer and Kathie thought Beryl was probably on her way. Jordan phoned again in a little while, but again there was no answer. By about five o'clock, Kathie was concerned. "I'm going over to see what's wrong," she said.

She saw Beryl's car there. She banged on the door. No answer. She had a key so she went in and hollered. No answer. She knocked on the bedroom door, went in and saw Beryl lying motionless in bed. She touched her and screamed so long and loud that she couldn't understand why people didn't rush in to see what was wrong. Beryl had died in her sleep. The bed was undisturbed so at least there had been no distress.

Arne was there as soon as he could be. (It was their night to be on television but Don Fults and Bill White said "We'll look after your TV program. Just go.") Kathie's prayer partner came quickly from White Rock too. The police also had to come.

Kathie didn't experience the same grace from God that He gave her when Barry had died, fifteen years before. This time she experienced pain and turmoil.

"I have to tell Jordan," she said as Arne drove her home. They prayed that the Lord would give her the right things to say. They took him in the bedroom and sat down.

"Jordan," she began. "Your mum's gone to heaven." He was not quite seven but he knew what this meant because his Uncle Rob had gone to heaven.

He thought about it and asked, "Now where will I live?" All his questions were around security and those were questions that could be answered.

"Well, you can stay right here with grandma and grandpa."

"Where will I sleep?"

"You can have that room right there."

"Now I don't have a mum or a dad."

"Yes. But you've got grandma and grandpa and you've got aunts and uncles."

God was covering him. Barb had lost her father when she was about the same age, so she came and slept there that night with Jordan.

"I don't feel like crying or anything all the time," he said.

"No, you won't have to cry all the time," said Barb. "Sometimes you might get angry ." But he didn't go through those stages. God just covered him.

After the family had gathered, it came up that when Jordan was a baby, Beryl had asked her brother Brian, "If anything ever happened to me, would you take Jordan?" It made perfect sense: Brenda's husband had left her and she lived in Florida with her four children, Barb had a child and was working, and Arne and Kathie would have loved to have him but they were traveling so much. Brian and his wife

Judy couldn't have children and they were delighted at the prospect of taking Jordan in.

Brian went over to Jordan. "Jordan, do you know what we're talking about?"

"Yes."

"Is that okay with you?"

"Yeah."

Brian and Judy took turns telling him his bedtime story while they stayed there the next few weeks. By the time they all went back to their home in Victoria, he was running to Judy as he would to his mom.

There was an urgency to find out Beryl's cause of death because both Barry and Beryl had died suddenly. Six months later they got the report. There was a genetic problem in their father's family—something that grows like a callous in the heart and causes severe arrhythmia. That was the cause of Beryl's death. It had been years since Barry's death so they couldn't prove it had been the same condition but they hadn't proven any other cause of death either, so it was a likely assumption. Kathy's mother-in-law and another sister-in-law might have died of the same condition.

When Barry's son, Darrel, was about to be married, the doctor sent him for an MRI and discovered that he had the same condition so he was fitted with a defibrillator to protect him. Now everyone in the family gets an MRI and Kathie's sister-in-law and her son have defibrillators.

Arne and Kathie persevered with the work of the Lord. In August 1993, they drove all the way from B.C. to Quebec with Bill and Doreen White. In Winnipeg, Arne was featured on the television program "It's a New Day," which generated a number of inquiries to the office.

That year John Matties came off the Prayer Canada board. He was not retiring—he and Dolores were getting too busy! In September, Marcus Unger took John's place on the board.

Arne liked to keep reminding the authorities they were supported in prayer. In November 1993, 295 letters were sent out to all MPs in Ottawa, enclosing the current copy of the *Prayer Post Courier*. Don suggested putting a prompt in the next Courier that all Christians should write to their MPs telling them they are praying for them and then watch for the results.

Prayer Canada Board 1993: (left to right) back – Don Fults, Arne, Kathie, Marcus Unger, Bob Wright, Bill White, Ron Pilkey; front – Leoran Anhorn, Ray Jansen and Bert Lang

Grateful for B.C.'s proclamation of May 1 as Prayer Day (eight years later to be extended to a Prayer Week), Arne was planning to write to the prime minister at the beginning of 1994 requesting a National Day of Prayer, to be held annually on the Sunday before Canada Day.

A press report, probably in 1994, notes that there were more than 125 Prayer Posts across Canada and a mailing list of over 3,000 people.

Around this time, Arne was contacted by Lynnette Fruson, who had been blessed during a visit to the Upper Room in their very first year of operation. At the time she had not been able to be involved with Prayer Canada but years later, after moving to Kelowna, she began to ask around for a Prayer Canada group. "Oh, there was one once," she was told.

She phoned City Hall. "Oh yes we had a room for Prayer Canada but no one came so we cancelled the room booking."

She tried the contacts that Arne gave her and found Lawrence Walrod, who was one of the original prayer partners. So the Kelowna Prayer Post began again and Arne met with them several times to encourage them. They met in homes until 2000, when the mayor said they could meet in the foyer of City Hall—a good, but not a peaceful spot. The next mayor arranged for them to have a room—but they were always moved around. Eventually a new receptionist said, "Oh that's no problem. Nobody uses the board room at noon. I'll go and put a notice on the door right now." It has been a perfect prayer room ever since.

Phil Johnson took over the leadership from Lynnette a few years ago.

"Arne's a neat guy," Lynnette says. "So passionate. I admire him and Kathie so much. What a blessing in my life. Great encourager."

Arne and Kathie were invited to represent Canada at the All Nations Prayer Convocation in Israel, organized by the Jerusalem House Of Prayer For All Nations, September 5 to 15, 1994. They took a team of fifteen, including Bill and Doreen White from Bellevue, and stayed at the Mount Zion Hotel in Jerusalem where most of the prayer meetings were held. They were all thrilled to be in this special land.

Representatives from 140 nations came together to pray, a beautiful and spiritually profound assembly. Arne and Kathie met with three pastors from Ghana who were involved with Prayer Ghana. A pastor from Estonia came to Bill and Doreen's room every night to wash his shirt because he only had one. Arne gave him five shirts immediately and Bill and Doreen kept in touch with him afterwards and sent him more white shirts.

CHAPTER 14

1995 — 2003:
STICK TO THE MANDATE

Following the plan of operation given by the Lord from the beginning, six Prayer Breakfasts were held during 1995 in addition to the regular Surrey ones—in Edmonton, Slave Lake, Kamloops, Chilliwack and two in Campbell River.

Ray Jansen traveled in B.C., Alberta and Saskatchewan with the Full Gospel Businessmen's Fellowship, and met with Prayer Canada prayer partners when possible. In September, Arne and Kathie went to Montreal as a prayer team with Bill and Doreen White.

"I have received untold blessings during my term of office both from your prayers and our gatherings together," wrote Lindsay Morris as he resigned from the board in September 1995. He had been a board member for five years. "One night at a Full Gospel banquet," he recalled, "Arne called for commandos and before I knew it, I had volunteered. That was the first time that I had even heard of this group but the Lord propelled me into joining up and, as difficult as it is not to criticize our governments sometimes, I have certainly grown in that area. Arne has been a tremendous inspiration and will be a friend and brother forever. Kathie's commitment to Arne's calling has been God-inspired and a blessing to all of us." Linday's was just one voice among thousands, grateful for the blessing of working with Arne and Kathie.

Just as much in love as the day they married, Arne and Kathie celebrated their twenty-fifth wedding anniversary in July 1996. It was clear that Kathie was Arne's eternal sweetheart. She was also his armour bearer and fellow commando in the prayer battle for Canada, both of them prepared by God and put together by God to fulfil His purposes.

Arne loves to give a little something to his visitors. It's a way of blessing them. He once gave Don Fults a blue stone to remind him of the Rock of his salvation and later a red coloured stone to remind him of the blood of Jesus that cleanses from all sin. Don later shared at a board meeting in August 1996 that he had kept these two stones on his desk at work and had had many opportunities to share what they meant with clients and salesmen.

Not many prayer movements continue vibrant and muscular for two decades. Prayer Canada was now approaching that longevity, and its leader was undeniably aging. But a feisty rancher, with natural optimism and a call from God, does not preside over a declining work; he keeps reviving it. Arne and Kathie didn't think of retiring. There was work to be done, the vision was still there and they loved serving the Lord alongside all the valiant Prayer Partners around the country.

Board member Leoran Anhorn says that once in a while Arne will get a call from somebody complaining, "I was the only one in the prayer group!"

"Well, thank the Lord for that!" is Arne's response. "Just like Jeremiah, you know. Just keep on **praying**, because the Lord answered Jeremiah's prayers. You and the Lord make an unbeatable team."

"I believe Prayer Canada is getting better all the time," Leoran continues. "It's never been big groups of people. There are some benefits of being small too, because you're all praying. Sometimes in big group one person will take the lead but this way everybody gets a chance. Everybody's a leader. Everyone's in unity."

Marcus Unger notices that the effect of Prayer Canada is more widespread than appears on the surface. "Arne is always promoting prayer, because as he says: *'The king's heart is in the hand of the Lord'* (Proverbs 21:1, KJV). And now, because of the faithfulness of Arne and of the prayer groups across the country, you hear churches more and more saying: 'We're going to pray for so and so in the government.' Arne has taught individuals who are dedicated to pray for Canada and they've gone back to their churches and given the message to their pastors and on and on."

Various people were able to visit Prayer Posts on behalf of Prayer Canada during their own travels. These welcome offers spurred discussion among the board members: How could they be sure that the various traveling representatives were accurately communicating the vision that God gave to Arne? The trips were not just to encourage prayer in general but to impart the vision that prayer will change the nation. This was when John DeVries was asked to write guidelines for those going out under the name of Prayer Canada, even though in 1998 he had moved to live in Post Falls, Idaho.

Paul & Anna Mae McPhail, prayer partners in Chatham ON.
Paul is also the current Secretary of Independent
Assemblies of God International

Arne takes every opportunity to serve God. In 1997 he became the acting B.C. Regional Secretary for the Independent

Assemblies of God International—the organization of about 750 independent churches across Canada that provides his ministerial accreditation. It is a central body through which the member churches can share information, help each other and hold a convention every year in a different part of the country. He was confirmed as the B.C. Regional Secretary in 1998, the year that he turned 80, and he served for about three years.

"There's no president in IAOGI, only secretaries," says Arne. "Jesus is the president."

In 1999, a Prayer Post started in Creston where Arne's son Cam lives. That story began at the end of a Prayer and Fast in Victoria in 1992 when a young lady named Lynda came up to Arne. She wanted to apologize that she had no money to put in the offering. "But," she continued. "God said to me: Give yourself, offer yourself."

"Well," responded Arne. "What can you do? Do you have secretarial gifts?"

Lynda had to say "No." She had to say "No" to all Arne's list of possible useful gifts.

"Well," he said. "If the Lord is calling you to come, I would welcome you to come and live with us for a time. Just be with us for a few days in Surrey and we'll see what the Lord will do."

Lynda came over to Surrey and stayed with Arne and Kathie in their Prayer Canada house for a few days in the summer, joining in with all that was going on and worshiping the Lord on her autoharp in the prayer room downstairs.

Her few days in Surrey started a series of God-connections that led her to visit and then work in Israel, where she met and married Russ Kroeker. In 1999 Russ and Lynda returned to Canada. They settled in Creston and Lynda wanted to start a Prayer Canada Prayer Post there with a friend of the mayor. The Mayor of Creston was really moved that people wanted to pray for her and she suggested a prayer breakfast at the Recreation Centre with the Chief of Police and the head of the Recreation Centre as special guests.

Back in Surrey, Arne thought he would ask the local Prayer Canada representative to attend this Creston prayer breakfast, instead of going himself. Then he received a phone call from someone in Creston that changed his mind: "Arne, don't come to the prayer breakfast. You mustn't come. They're moving too fast here."

Arne's response was, "I've been waiting a long time for a prayer post in Creston. I'm with whoever is *moving*." He decided that "the head commando and his lieutenant" should go personally to deal with the enemy forces there.

Towards the end of that Creston prayer breakfast, Arne prophesied over the Mayor. He ended by bending over and kissing her on the head, lovingly like a father. "Thank you, that's just what I needed," she said, surprised but accepting.

Arne got talking to a group of police officers. He always likes to tell them he's praying for them and none of them ever says "No, don't do that" or "That isn't a good idea." They always say, "Oh, thank you. Thank you."

He told them the story about the RCMP officers in their red dress coats on Parliament Hill surrounding and quizzing him in 1981 when the postal strike had delayed their permission to meet there, including his statement: "If you've got a disaster situation, you can call on the rest of the police from other cities. You can call on the army and navy and air force. Or you can even call across the line and get help from the US. We operate a bit like that," Arne had said. "But we can call on all the powers of heaven!"

After Arne had finished his story, with laughter all round, the Creston Chief of Police said, "That's the kind of power I'm interested in."

The next day was a Sunday. Arne shared in the Pentecostal Church's evening service and his son Cam was there. After

Arne had spoken about Prayer Canada, God told him to go down and prophesy over a teenaged boy in the congregation. He looked like a nice young man but Arne had to say what the Lord gave him:

"God says your name is **Vicious**! I've never had this as a word for anyone before but that's what He says. Vicious. Your name is Vicious!"

It was as if fireworks had exploded in the congregation. They clapped and cheered! Later it was explained that this young man, Andy Gabruck, was not vicious to people—he was vicious in the spiritual realm. He had been chosen as the valedictorian of the graduating class of 1999 at Prince Charles High School but when the principal heard that Andy was planning to talk about what God had done for him, he warned the teenager against it. Andy insisted. He stood up to his principal. In the end the principal said, "Well, just follow your heart." When Andy gave his moving speech at the high school graduation, the whole class got up and threw their hats. He gave glory to God. That nice young man really was vicious in the Spirit and Arne's apt word solidified his courage and boldness. He is now a pastor in Kelowna.

The Prayer Post in Creston is still going strong, as Russ Kroeker says, "Every Saturday at ten o'clock." He adds, "And we go until we're done, sometimes three or four in the afternoon."

It was sometime after 1999 that the Mayor of Charlottetown, PEI, pulled a framed picture off the wall behind his chair—a beautiful original pencil drawing of Charlottetown City Hall—and gave it to Arne and Kathie. It is much admired in its honoured place in the Prayer Canada prayer room, a memento of the generous appreciation felt by many of Canada's elected governing officials. The Charlottetown City Hall hosted a Prayer Post for fifteen years, under the diligent leadership of Darrell and Carol Stairs.

Mayor of Charlottetown giving picture to Arne

One night in Charlottetown the Lord spoke to Arne in a dream: "I want you to get an earthen vessel and fill it with dirt." He and Kathie had just held a meeting in a church there and Arne knew what he had to do. The next day he went to a pottery place and picked up a nice big pot. It weighed about fifty pounds with the soil in. He brought it to the church and set it up on the stage.

"You know," he said to the pastor when he showed him the pot. "we came from dirt." He picked up some dirt and gave the pastor the message that the Lord had entrusted to him in the dream. "This is where we came from. Whenever you feel you're pretty important, come over here and pick up a handful of dirt and remember, 'This is where I came from.' Don't get so proud or arrogant because God just made you from the **earth** itself."

They had to set off to the next place, leaving the pastor and his wife with an important word from the Lord.

On a warm Sunday evening in August 2000, Arne was preaching at a meeting in a First Nations community near Vernon, B.C., when he stopped what he was saying and walked over to pray for a young man who was helping with the new church. Neither knew each other but Arne prophesied over him with a word of knowledge affirming the project he had just completed and speaking of increase, because of the calling that he would walk into. "God's given you a national mantle and he's going to put you into a national place."

When Arne learned the story behind this young man, he was most interested. The young man was Rob Parker, pastor of Community Baptist Church in Vernon, and the project he had just completed was *Link Canada*: Rob had led a team of intercessors who had completed a seventy-three-day prayer walk from Calgary to Ottawa, asking God to raise up the level of prayer in the nation and calling the Church to repent so that God could heal the land.

As they walked, God had led them to pray for the government in each province they went through, in line with 1 Timothy 2:1-2. When Rob spoke in churches along the way, he began to ask the leaders, "How often do you pray for our political leaders?" Then in Ottawa, as they prayed around several embassies on July 1, the Lord said to him, "There is no Embassy of Prayer here for Me. I want there to be a House of Prayer within walking distance of Parliament, where people can come and learn about prayer and pray for the government." That was the call that Rob and his wife Fran were carrying.

Rob, in turn, learned more about Arne and was deeply moved to realize that it was the pioneer of Prayer Canada who had prayed for him and had imparted something to him. He had to laugh at how he had felt pleased with his own achievement, when here was a man in his eighties who knew so many things and who had ploughed the ground for all these years. He recognized God at work.

Over the next couple of years, Arne kept in touch with Rob and Fran to explore where their visions meshed together. The Prayer Canada board began to discuss whether Rob Parker could be the one to take a leadership position if Arne were to step down in the future. In February 2002, Rob came to meet with the board in Surrey. He and Fran were keen to support

Prayer Canada through their church and wondered what else God would do.

In the fall of 2001 and in January 2002, Arne and Kathie, accompanied by Don and Margaret Fults drove to Idaho to John DeVries' church in Post Falls. They made various other stops during those trips, including Creston, where Arne's grandson Scott was in the meeting, and also Vernon to see Rob and Fran Parker. Arne preached there, sharing God's call to pray for the government at all levels, educating people about its importance and of course refreshing them with encouragement.

However, Arne reported to the board that he had had a dream about dry bones and thought they should wait to see some flesh on the bones, in the form of Prayer Canada Prayer Posts in the Vernon area. They waited.

During this same period the board were also praying about a promising new way of raising finances. Metasoft was a company that would help them to apply for grants from different charitable foundations using the Internet to make the contacts. The Better Business Bureau had given it a good report. Arne presented the idea to the board in September 2000; he and Leoran visited the offices in Vancouver and Ray Jansen had an Internet tour of the company. They all reported that the intentions of the company were sincere and businesslike.

They registered in November and Ray began sending proposals to foundations to discuss grants. They planned to allocate the donated money to pay a salary to their current secretary, cover the newsletter expenses, update the website and perhaps invest in some new office equipment.

During 2001, more than fifty proposals were sent out but no grants were forthcoming. It was disappointing. The agreement made with the company stipulated that the registration fee would be refunded if no money had been raised within a specified time and eventually in December, after some anxious months, the refund was received.

Through the many years of financing Prayer Canada, Arne and the Board of Directors have had to maintain businesslike wisdom while moving in obedient faith—a two-pronged approached familiar to Christian non-profit organizations. They pray believing that God Himself will provide all that they need, because they only want to do what He is blessing, but they also take action.

In October 2001, after the Metasoft project had failed and while they were waiting for the refund, Don challenged each board member to ask God to reveal His plan for Prayer Canada. "How are we to finance His work?" In September 2003, after Arne had outlined another difficult financial situation, Marcus prayed for ample money to meet all the needs; the minutes record: "All members called it *done*." In September 2009, in response to a letter from Arne to the board asking for donations, they decided: "Whatever God asks you to do, do it and He will pay for it."

Arne knew they also had to communicate with the field, keeping Prayer Partners and others alerted to financial needs. With deep gratitude they received some large donations and legacies, and were equally thankful for the faithful, often sacrificial, gifts from Prayer Partners and supporters all over the country. Always concerned to operate without extravagance, if money is not on hand for a particular expenditure, the project is put on hold. The extensive travels of Arne and Kathie paid for themselves plus some extra, as does each issue of *The Courier*. Even so, the finances sometimes dip into the red before the donations come in. Every Prayer Breakfast, every Banquet, every issue of the *Courier*, every Prayer and Fast, every other meeting and event is in part a fundraiser.

A frequent need was for secretarial help—it was more than Kathie could do—but there was rarely enough money to pay a proper salary. In May 2003, Pat Argent, who would become the new secretary, explored some fundraising options but found that it was not possible to augment a wage that way. Office equipment is also essential but expensive. Sometimes the directors themselves undertook to cover a proportion.

Financing the work is a perpetual spiritual and practical challenge but the Lord always provides. He has proved His faithfulness through all the years of Prayer Canada. His servants depend on Him and thank Him. Prayer Canada is His work from start to finish.

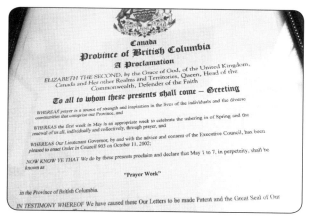

Proclamation of Prayer Week in British Columbia

September 2002 marked twenty-five years since God had told Arne to pray for the government authorities of Canada. How was the vision coming along? An article that year in *The Valley Sentinel* in Valemount, BC, a small community in the stunningly beautiful Rockies just west of Jasper, mentioned prayer posts in two hundred cities and forty-one government buildings.

Arne (described in the article as "84 years of age … energetic and appears to have no intentions of slowing down") is quoted: "Today you can be a prayer warrior to direct and guide the authorities. You don't need to be a councillor or a mayor."

The Mayor of Valemount said: "Prayer is always positive. No one goes and prays that trouble or bad things will happen. They have never asked us for anything, advised us or suggested anything. The only thing they have asked us is if there are issues to pray for. I view it as a positive action. We give them a great deal of credit–they faithfully give one hour a week because they care about their community. I think it's really special that they are dedicating their own time to pray that mayor and council are honest, just and moral."

And what happened about the other big issue of these years—the possibility of Rob Parker augmenting the leadership of Prayer Canada? Eventually the board members could see that the mandate God had given Rob and Fran was different from Prayer Canada's and that the two callings had to be pursued separately but in fellowship. God was providing two complementary and rich routes to blessing for Canada's authorities. Arne was called to raise up local weekly prayer posts in homes, city halls, provincial legislatures and in Parliament, an army of faithful Prayer Canada commandos. Rob and Fran were called to go to Ottawa and create an Embassy of Prayer that would saturate the government in prayer at the federal level and also train teams of intercessors from churches across the country.

National House of Prayer in Ottawa

In 2003, the Lord showed Rob and Fran the building at 17 Myrand Avenue that would become the National House of

Prayer in Ottawa. Originally an annex to a Roman Catholic Church, housing retired nuns and at one time the Chinese Embassy, it now became an elegant and spacious Prayer Embassy just a few minutes' walk from Parliament.

Rob and Fran were sent out from B.C. to Ottawa by some big name ministries but Rob believes the significant anointing to equip them for national prayer had already happened in his office in a meeting of six people some years before. Anointing often precedes appointment. It was late summer of maybe 2001. Arne, Kathie and Don Fults met with Rob and Fran to pray, together with Ray Bale, a local pastor, still wondering if God would join them together, an awe-filled anticipation in the air. That time is remembered as a significant impartation from Arne to the younger couple as he anointed them with oil, a blessing from the pioneer.

The night after that time of prayer, Arne had a dream in which he felt as if he was having a heart attack and was going to die. He shared it in Rob's church that morning while assuring everyone that he was fit and strong. A few minutes later he gave them an awful shock by falling face forward off the platform. He got up and was fine, if a little shaken. The power of God had been at work. Perhaps it was a sign that an impartation had been released from him to the Parkers.

Arne of course was pleased at the success of the National House of Prayer and has kept in touch with Rob and Fran, letting them know he is praying for them. As Fran says: "Arne is a good encourager. He's like a dad. Hard worker. Dedicated to making sure he fulfilled whatever God told him to do. And God hasn't told him to stop. So he's going to keep going."

The board of Prayer Canada considered other names for leadership after that but none worked out. Of course the fact that the position pays no salary made the role less attractive. But Arne did not worry; God promised that He was preparing someone for the job.

"Arne," said Don Fults at the board meeting in March 2003. "I'm concerned that this schedule for your spring trip is pushing too hard." This trip with John and Dolores Matties was a heavy schedule with lots of meetings on both sides of the IAOGI National Convention in southern Quebec.

"But the trip's a week shorter this year," Kathie pointed out. "Five weeks instead of six. And it's easier on both of us, because there's some down time. That's better than staying more than one night in a place."

"And we are seeing increasing concern to pray for those in authority," enthused Arne. "Osoyoos is very interested to start a group and Keremeos." He didn't want to change his schedule. When the trip took place, April 15 to May 22, it was called the President's Tour. Arne spoke at thirty-four places, put over 6,500 miles on the road and had many good reports.

Arne and Kathie and the board were giving a few of Arne's responsibilities to others to spread the load. Kathie did more of the driving on their trips. They also looked for key people who could be overseers of regions. Sylvia Nelson, for instance, a retired teacher, emailed from Regina, SK, saying the Lord had spoken to her to tell her to join Prayer Canada and visit all the communities in Saskatchewan. She organized four meetings in Regina for them during their tour. She was appointed Overseer of Saskatchewan. Others were approached to be Overseers for Manitoba, northern Alberta and Prince Edward Island. A few years later, Ron Short was named Regional Director for South Eastern BC.

In 2003 Arne and Kathie were invited to teach at a Bible Conference in the Arctic. Since their 1990 visit to Rankin Inlet for Tagak and Sally Curley's wedding, a lot had changed in the north, both politically and spiritually.

Politically, Rankin Inlet was no longer in the Northwest Territories. It was now part of Nunavut, a new territory created on April 1, 1999—an entirely new governmental unit of Canada and one that Tagak Curley had been a prominent part of negotiating. He had been an MLA of the Northwest Territories until 1987, and in 2004 would become an MLA again, for Nunavut.

Nunavut was described as "...both the least populous and the largest in area of the provinces and territories of Canada. One of the most remote, sparsely settled regions in the world, it has a population of 31,906, spread over an area the size of Western Europe." (Wikipedia)

Spiritually, the Holy Spirit had begun to move in the churches in a new way. This sweet move of the Holy Spirit first came to widespread notice after a powerful sound like a mighty, rushing wind had been recorded at an afternoon youth service in Pond Inlet. This was about one month before the creation of the Territory of Nunavut. The forty or so people who were praying fervently at the end of the meeting were taken completely by surprise. They turned down the volume on the sound system, thinking there was a fault, but the noise only grew louder, like thunder, filling the church. People fell down under the power of the Holy Spirit with no one touching them. The building began to shake.

Later that day, when they played back the tape of the meeting, the people praised God as they realized what a powerful visitation had come to them.

In fact a swell of prayer, repentance, deliverance and praise had been growing for some time in many communities and continued after this dramatic event, all across the north, transforming lives in undeniable ways. Several times a year, Christians travel long distances for Bible Conferences and enjoy several days of teaching, worship and prayer. Arne and Kathie were invited to one organized by the Arctic Bible Conference Group in Baker Lake in September 2003, although at that time people from the south were not normally encouraged to come up there.

The July before the conference, Arne and Kathie were in Seattle to celebrate the eightieth birthdays of Jim and Marie

Watts and were surprised to be greeted at the door by Lynda Kroeker from Creston. They had no idea that Lynda and her husband Russ had been married by Jim Watts, nor that Russ, an audiovisual expert, was doing the video recording of the celebration.

"Do you know about this Bible Conference that's going to be held in the Arctic in September?" he asked them.

"No."

"I think you're supposed to go," he said. "The Lord's showing me you're supposed to go."

"Okay!" Then Russ muttered, "What does it cost to get up there?"

"Well it's very expensive. About $3500."

"If the Lord pays my way, I'll go." That was the closest Russ could get to obedient faith.

Through the summer Arne wondered what the Lord would do for them. He called a couple of times. "Well, we're waiting on God," was the response. So he left it.

Then, just three or four days before they were leaving for the Arctic, he called again.

"Hi, Russ. God was talking to me about you last night in a dream. He told me to call you this morning and say, 'You pay and I'll *repay*.' That's all He gave me."

"I know what that word means," Russ said.

Arne had no way of knowing about the sleepless night Russ and Lynda had just had. The Lord had woken Lynda with a deep feeling of grief that they were about to miss God. God said to her, "The budget restrictions that you have placed on going to the north don't please Me and I want you to tell your husband to lift the budget restrictions."

Lynda went back upstairs and said to Russ, "God told me to say to you 'Lift the restrictions on the budget'." Immediately Russ's hands went up, lying there in bed. "I repent, Lord. I lift all restrictions off." That freed God to move. It had to be spectacular moving, because tickets to fly to the Arctic have to be booked months in advance and only if you have permission to go.

With recommendations from his pastor and from Arne, Russ made contact with the pastors in the Arctic and permission was given for him to come. In fact, the pastors in Baker Lake were thrilled when they heard Russ was skilled at video-taping meetings.

"We've been praying," they said. "The Lord showed us someone was going to come and do video. He told us that this man is to stay with the chief videographer in Nunavut." Knowing that white people from the south sleep on beds with legs, they had already bought and flown in a suitable bed a month previously.

Armed with their permission and encouraged by their prophetic faith, Russ used all the money he had available to buy the tickets. The airline was having a one-day sale, just that day, so he got both tickets for a total of $3500.

The baggage was another issue—they were taking in effect a whole television studio packed into suitcases, far in excess of what two passengers were allowed. They traveled in a series of planes, each smaller than the previous with tighter baggage restrictions. It became increasingly impossible but God made a way every time. (After the conference, when they were leaving Baker Lake with the same mountain of suitcases, they were asked, "How did you get here?" Russ and Lynda recounted the story of their miracle journey. "Well if we brought it here, then we have to get you back," was the response and they waived all the restrictions.)

There were fifteen hundred people at the Bible Conference, all hungry for Bible teaching. Arne taught, Kathie and Lynda prayed and Russ recorded everything so that the teaching could be taken back to their remote communities and shown on their cable systems. At the end of the conference, God showed His glory to the people through a sign which caused a holy hush to fall on the people—gold flakes appeared in open Bibles, spraying onto clothing and cascading onto the floor. It was recorded on the DVDs and witnessed by Arne, Kathie, Russ and Lynda, who kept the flakes carefully in their Bibles for years.

And what about God's promise to repay what Russ had paid? The first instalment was a shiny copper penny that Lynda picked up on the path as they walked to the arena for the meet-ings one day—"a symbol of unexpected resources." They were then given something towards their travel expenses before they left and asked back for the next conference, all expenses paid. In the next four years they visited the Arctic fifteen times, in-cluding a "three day" side trip to Waken Bay which turned into five weeks because Russ was so invaluable to them. He neither expects nor asks for payment for his work but they provided everything he needed and gave him enough cash for their ex-penses for the next several months. God kept His promise.

He is still keeping His promise for the future of Prayer Canada.

What makes God smile? Arne, who has a fresh, enquiring approach to Scripture and is always open to hear from the Lord, wrote notes on that question in his journal on Thursday, 27, November 2003:

> The smile of God is the goal of your life: *"May the Lord's face radiate with joy because of you..."*(Numbers 6:2, TLB*).*
>
> Obedience unlocks understanding. *"Look down in love upon me and teach me all your laws..."*(Psalm 119:135, TLB).
>
> Partial obedience is disobedience. Will you serve God's purpose in your generation? *"For the eyes of the Lord search back and forth across the whole earth, looking for people whose hearts are perfect toward him, so that he can show his great power in helping them..." (2 Chronicles 16:9a, TLB).*

CHAPTER 15

2004 — 2012:
SPREAD THE LOAD

Arne is not afraid of taking Prayer Canada in new directions if it is the Lord's leading.

"The Lord wants us to pray for the marketplace. For the businesses and business people in commerce. God is interested in His people prospering in every way." This was John Grady, President of Executive Security Ltd. and also President of the Christian Chamber of Commerce, speaking at a Prayer Canada Prayer Breakfast at the beginning of 2004. He quoted 3 John verse 2: "*Above all things I wish that thou mayest prosper and be in good health, even as thy soul prospereth*" (3 John 2 KJV).

His eloquent presentation made Arne realize that Prayer Canada should enlarge the goal that had motivated their work for decades: "To establish Prayer Posts in Homes, Churches, City Halls, Legislative Buildings." That year they added "Marketplace" to that list in the Prayer Manual, and also on the back page of the *Courier*, on their letterhead and in their advertisements.

The first Marketplace Prayer Post began in April under the leadership of Don Fults in the Scottsdale Square Business Centre, Surrey, B.C., where the owner, Rod Adams, offered the boardroom for the Thursday noon meeting. As always they prayed for wisdom for those in authority, so that people can live in peace and godliness, but they also prayed for wisdom for local businesses to do well, so that the area around could prosper.

In the same year, a "Christian businessman" came to Arne and Don with what turned out to be a fraudulent proposal, although it sounded like a wonderfully generous blessing at the beginning. The developer wanted to donate the top floor of a forty-floor tower to Prayer Canada and the tower itself would be named "Prayer Canada." There would be no cost to Prayer Canada because their charitable tax standing would be a help to the developer.

However the full presentation he made to the board revealed a very different picture. Prayer Canada would have the option of purchasing the top floor at a cost of nearly two million dollars. They were being enticed to invest, and call on their supporters to invest large sums of money for a non-guaranteed return of maybe five percent to go towards the cost of the fortieth floor and for the name of Prayer Canada to be displayed in neon lights on the tower. In addition, the capital would have to be raised in two weeks but the buildings were still at the conceptual stage and there were no legally binding limits set on investments and costs.

The board agreed with the conclusion of John DeVries who wrote a letter summarizing the situation: "Prayer Canada is a prayer focusing charitable organization. Our people would be approached to invest 'unsecured' finances into a project that might be highly successful or fail. We as a charitable organization would be enticing prayer minded elderly people to place their finances into an unsecured 'risk capital' venture. I believe this is totally outside of our prayer mandate."

Prayer Canada escaped the tantalizing but deceptive image of its name in neon lights high over the city. Regrettably, some people, without discussing with the board and without a lawyer to safeguard their investment, did give the contractor large sums of money for which they received no return.

Arne and Kathie were pleased to visit Rob and Fran Parker at the National House of Prayer in 2004 while traveling during May through Ottawa with John and Dolores.

In Toronto during that trip, two young teenagers were transfixed as Arne was talking to people at a barbecue after a morning service. Other kids were off playing and called to them to join in but one of the boys just said "No" and both of them stood there listening.

Arne was excited to see this interest and talked with them. "You boys are **commandos**!" he announced and they jumped at the idea. Then he prayed with them and the idea of a brigade of young people praying for Canada was born. They would be called "Commandos."

Later in Creston, Arne called up a girl for prayer and she also was thrilled to be a Commando. He could see that this was not just for boys. And again in Tumbler Ridge in northeastern B.C. another half dozen youth were signed up.

The idea was to keep in touch with the Commandos by email and teach them to pray for the authorities. But Arne found he didn't have the time. Marcus Unger was eager, having worked with youth when he was younger, but his business didn't allow him the time either.

2004 was also the year Arne had a near-devastating accident in the Ford Windstar van that they had bought new in 1998. He was nearing home along 104th Avenue and slowed a little near 141st Street, looking for an address. Just at that moment, a vehicle rammed into him from behind at an angle. Arne was knocked into the side of an eighteen-wheeler going by on his right at about sixty kilometres per hour. It was such a shock that he turned the wheel left and bounced across the median in front of the approaching cars. As he sailed across the road, still holding onto the wheel and the advancing cars no more than two hundred feet away, he thought *Oh Lord, they're going to think I'm crazy!* But he reached the other side and crashed into a big cedar tree, bashing in the front of the van, as well as the back and the side.

A man came along and said, "I thought you'd never get out alive!" The door had to be pried open before he could get out but he stepped out on his own.

The medics took half an hour to lay him carefully on the stretcher, not sure what broken bones there might be, and took him to Royal Columbian Hospital in New Westminster instead of the Surrey Hospital, suspecting serious injuries. But Arne was tougher than that. After checking both Arne and his pacemaker, he was sent home that night. His body was bruised and whiplashed and he needed treatment for two years but he didn't let that slow him down.

Arne took Bert Lang with him to meet the man who had rear-ended him. Bert took notes and wrote down the driver's admission of guilt, which he read in court after the driver changed his story. The verdict went Arne's way. The van, however, was a write-off and they had to get a new one.

In 2006, Arne had a phone call from Surrey Mayor Diane Watts. Some local Muslims were asking why Prayer Canada was the only group allowed to pray in the council chamber of City Hall and she asked if Arne would go in and talk the problem over with her.

This was the original Prayer Post that had been meeting weekly in Surrey City Hall since January 1978. They began in the board room of the old city hall in Cloverdale and then moved into the council chamber of the new city hall on 56 Avenue near King George Boulevard. But its peaceful operation was interrupted when a reporter from the *Now* newspaper showed the leader of the Muslims in Surrey an article Prayer Canada had published in the *Courier*. Its headline was *Can a Muslim Make a Good Canadian?* because it was commenting on a piece in an American newspaper, *Can a Muslim Make a*

Good American? It was not intended to be offensive but it raised this question about who should be allowed to pray in the council chamber. ("The only reason we are there," says Arne, "is because Prayer Canada was the only group of people who **asked** to pray in City Hall.")

Arne prayed about it and took directors Leoran Anhorn and Bert Lang with him. It was difficult to imagine how this situation could be solved—they certainly did not want to embarrass Mayor Watts—but they knew they had to pray in City Hall.

Arne with Mayor Dianne Watts of Surrey, BC

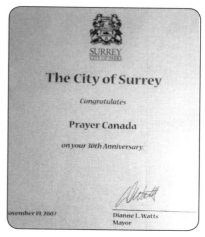

Congratulations from the City of Surrey, November, 2007

After a friendly greeting, the Mayor asked if they would mind changing the location of the prayer meeting from the council chambers to the board room. That was a wise change that Prayer Canada was happy to make.

Arne once again stayed at the National House of Prayer in 2006 when he was invited to attend TheCRY, a moving prayer event on Parliament Hill for a big crowd from across Canada, led by a passionate group of young adults who just wanted to pray for Canada. For the whole of that twelve-hour meeting, he sat under an umbrella—it was a scorchingly hot day—and the Parkers made sure he had food and water. The new generation of prayer warriors were blessed to see a man of his age caring so deeply. TheCRY was repeated in different cities over the next few years and Arne also attended one in Vancouver.

Arne and Kathie with Prime Minister Stephen Harper

He stayed at the NHOP again in 2007 and attended the National Prayer Breakfast in the ballroom of the West Block of the Parliament Buildings. It was amazingly the first time he had ever been to this annual non-political event that has been organized by a group of Christian MPs since 1964. He relished the opportunity to mingle and introduce himself to people, telling them what he does and handing out his card. He worked the room. He hadn't been warned that networking and promoting was not encouraged but, being Arne with his winning personality, his manner was accepted. He was even acknowledged by name from the podium during the MC's welcome: "I met a man here named Arne Bryan..." He praised Arne for the work he was doing at nearly ninety—an almost unprecedented honour, in front of the Speaker of the House, the leader of the opposition and ministry leaders, a sweet pat on the back from the Lord for His faithful servant.

After thirty years of Prayer Canada, many of the early Prayer Partners had gone and their places were taken by younger folks who themselves are aging. Where would our country be without their prayers?

Bill & Doreen White's 50th Anniversary

Bill and Doreen White, of the Internationale Prayer Centre in Bellevue went across Canada several times to visit Prayer Posts, sometimes with Arne and Kathie sometimes without, and they attended every Mission Fest in Edmonton. For fifteen years they visited a number of Bible colleges in western Canada and as far as Manitoba, going to their summer opening conferences and graduation conferences and giving seminar talks.

Bill and Doreen were blessed to be a blessing to others. It's no wonder they got on so well with Arne and Kathie. Doreen has gone now and Bill is eighty-six years old but he still prays every day for the local mayors and loves to go 'hunting' if the road isn't frozen.

He has an 8' by 10' trailer covered in various Scripture verses that he calls the "Godmobile." The back door lifts up to reveal a little counter and then it goes over the roof displaying the question: "ARE YOU GOING TO HEAVEN?" Since 2007 he has parked on the highway and at parades, meeting people, handing out special tracts and answering questions. People see the signs and stop out of curiosity. The Godmobile and the tracts do the persuading for him; he can just ask them questions.

That area is his backyard, where he was born and raised, and he tells people about the mine that you can see from the road, where 269 men died in an explosion. Then he points at the sign and asks what they think about Jesus. Those who don't want to talk take pictures. So the Scriptures will feature in their holiday photos.

Bill says of Arne: "I don't know of a person I'd rather listen to, or talk to, or have pray for me. He lifts you up."

In January 2008, Arne wrote to all the prayer partners: "We bless you for dependability to keep the doors open for prayer in your city. This is absolutely essential." And he quoted, *"Run up and down through every street in Jerusalem,"* says the LORD. *"Search high and low and see if you can find even one person who is fair and honest...If you find just one, I'll not destroy the city "* (Jeremiah 5:1, TLB).

He continued, like a coach at half-time: "We don't know how many days we will have to keep a consistent spiritual protection for our cities and the authorities there. The enemy is always trying to send in the arrows to defeat the work you are doing in your city but praise God you are the victor. You and the Lord make an unbeatable team!"

That year, the Spring Trip across Canada was undertaken by Ron and Bonnie Short of Cranbrook, leaving in April for forty-two days. Arne set up an itinerary for them through to Nova Scotia and back. Ron had been appointed the Regional Director for South Eastern B.C., after he spoke at the Prayer Breakfast in Surrey the previous September and had felt called to take a number of responsibilities off Arne's plate. Meanwhile Arne and Kathie flew to Florida for their grandson's wedding.

Arne and Kathie made one really long trip in 2009—to Beijing, China. They were invited by the Chinese government to an International World Conference for Seniors, to view what the Chinese government was doing for seniors specifically at a one-thousand-acre area set aside for that purpose on the edge of Beijing.

"Do you have room for some more at the Seniors Conference?" the co-ordinator in B.C. emailed to China at Arne's request. The answer came back: "Yes. You can invite some more." So Arne and Kathie invited five more couples, all committed Christians, making the Canadian contingent the largest amongst the ninety-nine nations represented.

Before setting off, they were instructed not to talk about Jesus or the Bible. Arne ordered a thousand tracts and divided them among the twelve team members. The written word could do the talking. During the journey and the six days in China, they gave out all those tracts plus a quantity of Prayer Canada material and led sixteen people to the Lord. Arne talked to the stewardesses on the Chinese plane and gave out material. Everyone wanted it. At the hotel people came running from all over to get the information.

Arne in China, October, 2009

Every day the delegates were taken by bus to wonderful historic sites around Beijing. Day One was the Great Wall. Arne couldn't walk farther than the first level but he had a good view of the thousands of people enjoying the impressive structure. The Lord said to him, "You know, this wall has no value for what it was originally intended. It's just a tourist attraction. That's something like the government. They thought they were going to rule the world with communism but they had to bow to democracy in order to become wealthy with world trade."

They were shown everything at the beautiful seniors' centre, the swimming pools and hot tubs, billiard room, reading room, etc. Only the first unit had been built at that time but already ten thousand seniors lived there.

At the last of the four lavish banquets that were laid on for them, Arne was sitting beside the governor of Beijing, who asked him to say a few words at the beginning. Arne needed no persuading. He stood up, the governor stood beside him and Arne started to pray, all translated of course. He prayed for China and for Beijing and for the large group at the banquet, about 225 people. Then he put his hand on the governor's head (about Arne's shoulder height) and prayed for him. He looked very nervous so Arne said, "Sir, this will mightily bless you!" The governor stood like a statue while Arne prayed. After the prayer, the crowd clapped for several minutes.

In 2009 and 2010, the travelling was done by their pastor's wife, Margaret Mubanda, and a good friend, Janet Burgess (now Weldeghebriel). In May 2009 they flew to Moncton where Arne's friend loaned them his car, and they drove to Saint John, St. Stephens (where they were interviewed on the "Open Mic" radio show), Fredericton and back to Moncton, then on to Charlottetown, PEI and Halifax NS, ending up in Moncton again.

Not only was Arne skilled in knowing who he could trust to do this work but he also planned every step of the way for them. They didn't have to worry about where to sleep or what to eat and they enjoyed many kindnesses all the way. In home meetings and in churches, they were received as envoys of Prayer Canada. Their words had power and the Holy Spirit came amongst them.

Margaret (r) and Janet in Prince Rupert

Margaret and Janet set off again in September, driving through Hope north through the interior of B.C. to Terrace and Prince Rupert, taking about eighteen meetings en route. Wherever they went people were waiting for them, already gathered. The most beautiful meeting was in Kitimat.

The next year they drove to Calgary and Edmonton and often had three meetings in a day. Wherever they went people were committed to prayer. "The elderly people were the most encouraging," says Margaret, "because they take prayer passionately. They don't just talk about it; they pray. We may not see it but the prayers of these people have done a tremendous work for Canada ... for communities."

The next year, during a holiday that turned into a Prayer Canada trip in May 2011, Arne and Kathie themselves visited Kitimat, B.C., off Highway 16 near Terrace, and found that the prayer meeting was in the fire hall next to city hall, just as Margaret and Janet had described it. But the three flights of steep stairs were a problem for Arne, so someone went looking for an elevator.

"We've got no elevator," said the fire fighters, "but we've got something better!"

They strapped Arne in their rescue chair and hustled him up the three flights of stairs with no problem, very happy to have a real person to practise with. "When the prayer meeting's over, let us know and we'll bring you back down," they said.

Arne, of course, was delighted with the experience.

In March 2011 another big test of faith came. Twenty years after moving into the Prayer Canada house and hearing the Lord's promise that they would not have to leave it, Arne and Kathie were told that the house was going to be sold. It would be put on the market in May. John DeVries had to sell it because of his own financial situation in the very difficult economic climate at that time.

Arne prayed and heard the Lord say, "I had it built for Prayer Canada. You've occupied it for twenty-one years. All you have to do is pay for it now." That settled it for Arne. It would remain the Prayer Canada office and prayer room as well as their home.

Arne contacted all the board members on the Saturday, giving them the details and urging them to ask God for His wisdom. Mostly the reaction was, "It's Prayer Canada's property. It was built for Prayer Canada." They all agreed to come together on the next Tuesday evening.

Some real estate friends valued the house at about $700,000 and so that's what Arne was believing for. He believed that Prayer Canada would receive enough money to buy the house. The Lord showed him the property all tied up in a huge plastic bag.

When the board met they were all in agreement, all united in faith. There were four thousand people on the mailing list but, because Arne no longer had the strength to be the promoter of a big fundraising project, they discussed hiring a firm to do it for them. All the money and pledges would be handled through a lawyer and supporters were assured that, if the project didn't go through, their money would be returned to them.

The board knew the need was urgent, as Surrey is the fastest growing city in Canada with a strong real estate market. But it would have to be God—Prayer Canada had always operated on low budgets, "on the edge all the time," as Kathie said. She had moved house a lot of times in her life and just wanted to know if she should begin packing again. This was a huge issue but God had always looked after her without fail and she knew He wouldn't fail them this time. She trusted in God's promise and resisted even planning how to pack up.

In fact an investor bought the property in October and Arne had to adapt to a new reality. The new owner agreed to let Prayer Canada and the Bryans remain as tenants. It just meant they would now have to pay full market price for the rent instead of the nominal rent they had been blessed with previously.

As the Lord had said, "I had it built for Prayer Canada. You've occupied it. Now pay for it." Clearly His plan was not for a large investment in property but a settled home for the ministry.

The *Prayer Post Courier* continued to be a conversation between Prayer Canada and the prayer partners across the country. In the Spring 2011 issue, the Grand Forks BC Prayer Post reported being encouraged by two brief interactions with city hall personnel. One Monday as they gathered to pray, the Mayor was showing some people around city hall.

"Would you like us to meet in another room?" offered the Prayer Post leader.

"Oh, no. We want you in there," answered the Mayor. Then he turned to his guest and explained, "They pray for us every week in the chambers."

Two Mondays later, again some people were in the chambers but the leader said, "We must be out of the chambers before twelve because a group comes in on Monday to pray for us."

A heading on another page of that issue read: "Prayer Canada has a new directive!" After discussion in a board meeting, Marcus Unger had submitted a short article encouraging prayer partners to continue praying faithfully in council chambers (which usually, as it did in Grand Forks, garnered appreciation from the Mayor and Councillors) but also to attend public council meetings and to pray quietly during council business.

"You have already done your spiritual warfare in the closet," he wrote. "Now is the time to observe how the Lord answers your prayers."

That struck a chord with Blanche Johnson, Prayer Post Leader in Meadow Lake, SK where they had not been given permission to pray in City Hall; they now realised they could attend council meetings and pray.

The Courier always starts with an inspiring article by Arne or an excerpt from a good book. There is often more Bible teaching under the heading "John's Corner," submitted by John DeVries, and news articles by various people.

A 2013 issue includes a letter from Irene Cheese, Prayer Post Leader in Campbell River, B.C., full of thanks to God for many blessings. Then she adds: "To think I was ready to call it quits a few months ago when I thought God was calling me to lay it down. Then I realized, after much prayer, that it was all enemy opposition, which meant I was doing something right that the enemy didn't like. That's not the time to back off, but press forward with God's strength and grace." She is 81 years young and her friend is also 81. The two ladies are a powerful team as they pray at City Hall every week.

In 2011, Ray and Brenda Jansen from Victoria had to go to Regina for the National Convention of the Full Gospel Businessmen's Fellowship and opted to drive instead of flying (although it was November) so that they could visit Prayer Posts on the way there and back.

The tour lasted twenty-six days, taking the southern route eastwards, as Arne usually did, through the southern Okanagan, Kootenays, the Internationale Prayer Centre in Bellevue to Regina. They returned via North Battleford, Edmonton, Red Deer and Vernon. They delivered prayer manuals and signs: 'Jesus is *Lord* over Keremeos' and 'Jesus is *Lord* over Swift Current.' They met a candidate running for councillor in Trail, B.C. and a new MLA in Yorkton, SK, and appeared on community TV in Yorkton, on Bishop Yaroslaw Sereda's show.

Everywhere they shared the message of Prayer Canada and enjoyed instant fellowship with people they had not known before. They saw a great desire for God's presence and were very moved by hearts surrendered to Jesus. Sometimes the person Arne had arranged for them to see had never even met Arne or heard of Prayer Canada. But they always warmed to the idea after a simple explanation of 1 Timothy 2:1-4 as a command not a suggestion and a few minutes praying, blessing the local mayor and councillors, asking for godly wisdom to make good decisions and to rule righteously.

At an evening meeting in a church, Ray turned it into a prayer meeting. He divided people up into small groups and encouraged them to pray: "Don't pray out of your head but let the Holy Spirit lead. And when you're done, we'll have a report to see what the Holy Spirit was praying about in your group." The people were blessed that a prayer meeting could be exciting. They said "We should have this more often. Come back again."

"No," they answered. "You do it."

"Arne never offers a clinic or a conference on prayer," says Brenda. "He will say: 'You want to know how to pray? Let's

pray!' (Brenda claps her hands for emphasis just like Arne does.) 'Let's get into it and the Holy Spirit will teach you. Let's have a hands-on experience on how to pray.' "

"Arne fears God more than men without a doubt," adds Ray. "And he always leads to a trust in God."

"He's never two-faced," continues Brenda, "What you hear in prayer is what he'll walk out in his everyday life."

In October 2012, Arne and Kathie set off on a cruise to Mexico, but by the second day, they had both suffered injuries. Before they were even out of Vancouver Harbour, while folding Arne's wheelchair so that they could move over to the other side of the ship to see Stanley Park as they sailed by, Kathie managed to slice two-thirds of the way through the little finger on her right hand—there was a lot of blood! "I'd worked in hospitals for years," she laughs. "You'd think I'd know how to fold up a wheelchair!"

Her finger was beautifully sewn up by the ship's doctor with no loss of feeling and little scarring as a result. The captain sent her a plate of home-made chocolates afterwards. She was disappointed that she couldn't go swimming but intended to enjoy the hot tub.

They were in the hot tub on the second day when Kathie got her bandage wet and went down to the medical room to get it re-bandaged. Meanwhile Arne got out of the hot tub, headed to the showers and slipped on the tiles, falling right down on his back. There was no carpet between the hot tub and the showers like there was in other places around the pool. When Kathie returned with her fresh bandage, there was a crowd around Arne. It was another nasty shock and Arne is still having treatment for his back. But, being Arne and Kathie, they decided that they were going to have a good time on their cruise anyway in spite of these injuries.

CHAPTER 16

2013:
COMMANDOS;
INTO THE FUTURE

*Arne & Kathie outside the prayer room at Mission Fest
in Vancouver, January, 2013*

Kathie Bryan, no spring chicken herself, always kept an eye on her indomitable husband. Theirs was a long and loving marriage, and a powerful partnership in the Lord.

One of the reasons Arne says he respected his Kathie was because she stood up to him when she disagreed with him. One of the things that Kathie disagreed with was his tendency to overwork himself. One time when he had a cold, Arne's secretary, Lanny Townsend, observed him sneak downstairs into the office to do some work when Kathie was out doing errands, chuckling to himself about it.

"When she got home," Lanny continued. "she came downstairs and demanded that he get back upstairs to rest. I thought it was pretty interesting to watch and see how that little woman was going to get that big man to do what she wanted him to do. He resisted, but not for long, because she fixed those blue eyes on him and he could see that she was not going to move until he conceded to her wishes."

Arne and Kathie didn't have the energy to take the long drives any more but Arne did not let that hinder him. He was still busy all day in his office, liaising with Lanny (his secretary since 2012), answering calls and emails, working the phones to follow up some of their original contacts. As a result new Prayer Posts were started up in B.C., Alberta and Ontario and an eighty-five-year-old lady, full of the Holy Ghost and fire, started one in Montreal.

Arne off to the rodeo, May 20, 2013 wearing the same boots that he wore 70 years before

He also called new locations. He would look up church information in a new town and phone as the Lord led, asking pastors if he could send some material on how Prayer Canada helps Christians establish prayer meetings in city halls or legislatures. They usually said yes. So he would send the material and follow up, maybe even arranging for someone to visit there on the next trip. "There should be three or four people like me phoning," said Arne. "because there are over eight hundred cities in Canada of over five thousand population and we've only touched a third of them."

And then there are the Commandos. The whole project had languished for lack of leadership until Art and Gwen Mercer heard the Lord's heart for praying young people.

Art and Gwen led the Prayer Post in Trail for several years, having been recruited by Ron Short, the Regional Director for south eastern B.C. In 2010, they shared with Arne about the stops they had just made for Prayer Canada while traveling from Sudbury, ON back to Trail.

"One thing we noticed was how many of the Prayer Partners are elderly," said Gwen. "And they're wonderful—so faithful and they really know how to pray. But, Arne, don't you think we should be training up youngsters to catch the vision?"

"You've hit the nail on the **head**!" Arne enthused. He told them about the Commandos and the Mercers shared their own vision. They were obviously the right people to head it up.

Whenever they made visits on Arne's behalf after that, they made sure that they addressed youth groups as well— an ongoing developing ministry. With more than twenty years of Sunday school experience, they grab the attention of the young people. First, wearing camouflage make-up and fatigues, they explain the importance of prayer from 2 Chronicles 7:14 and 1 Timothy 2:1-4. Then they picture the power of commando-style prayer from Joel 2:7 in the Living Bible: *"These 'soldiers' charge like infantry; they scale the walls like picked and trained commandos. Straight forward they march, never breaking ranks"* (Joel 2:7, TLB).

They involve the young people in a skit, based on Psalm 103:20–"*Bless the Lord, you mighty angels of his who carry out his orders, listening for each of his commands*" (Psalm 103:20, TLB). Art takes the role of the angel but at first he does nothing because noone is praying. Then Gwen begins to speak out God's word in prayer and Art swoops into action.

At a church in Winnipeg in May 2013, they signed up nineteen new Commandos and then another eight at a church in Surrey in July. Each one gets a special Prayer Manual for teens so they will know how to pray for the authorities. Contact is maintained through email, text, Facebook, and a link on the Prayer Canada website to their own Prayer Commandos website.

Art and Gwen Mercer now live in Kelowna and are eager to recruit more young prayer warriors. Arne is in touch with them every week.

Married 42 years on July 12, 2013

Soon after their forty-second wedding anniversary on July 12, 2013, Arne and Kathie were contemplating God's mercy. Arne was fifty-two when they married and he had already had twenty-five years of married life before that. Who would have dreamed that he and Kathie would have another twenty-five years, let alone forty-two? God has been good to them.

"The Three-Day Prayer and Fast is a key element of Prayer Canada," says Arne. "Participating in one is important for anybody who's really serious about praying for our leadership. It's **serious** business."

The Three-Day Prayer and Fast in July 2013 was in Hope again, well attended as always. Arne and Kathie invited a couple from Lloydminster, Howard and Diana Stephan, after they had been together at the Christian Heritage Party (CHP) convention in Abbotsford. They all felt unsettled that the board of directors of CHP had said no when Arne offered to wash their feet. Arne felt that the leadership had missed a very important opportunity. He says, "You can say no. But when the Lord brings you something like that, if you stop it, you are stopping a vital transition operation that would have touched those people to the heart."

Foot washing at Prayer and Fast 2013

Howard and Diana were thrilled to show everyone at the Prayer and Fast a large enamel jug that had been given to them. On one side was painted a beautiful picture of Jesus washing the disciples' feet and the scripture from John 13 was written out on the other side. He wanted Arne to be the first one to use it to wash the people's feet. No one hindered him this time.

Prayer Canada, with its international influence, was continuing and growing—praise the Lord for His sustaining power! Canada's governmental authorities were still supported with the invisible power of believing prayer and a new generation were being mentored in the work. Prayer Posts and Prayer Partners were still at work and heard Arne's encouragement on the phone, through the *Courier* and in person through volunteer travelers. Regular meetings like Prayer Breakfasts and Prayer and Fasts continued on schedule. The heartbeat of Prayer Canada continued. Would that healthy heartbeat survive two more major upheavals in Arne and Kathie's world—a serious health crisis for Kathie and a dramatic move by Arne regarding the leadership of Prayer Canada?

Through August and September 2013, Kathie suffered with increasingly bad insomnia, headaches and severe nausea. It only grew worse. Arne took her to emergency twice with violent stomach pains but, after they had endured eight or nine hours each time sitting in the waiting room, she was told it could be vertigo and was sent home to get some tests. Being Kathie, she soldiered on but only grew weaker. Her daughter, Barb, helped with shopping and anything she could do and church friends supported as well.

While this was developing, Arne was planning a Prayer Canada trip for a couple who had volunteered to drive from Ontario to B.C. and back. In 2008, a friend had introduced them to Kelvin and Faye Beckstead, of Brockville, ON. Kelvin and Faye had pastored a small independent church in the area for a few years, though Kelvin had been preaching for thirty-two years. They recognized the vital role of Prayer Canada in the country and flew to Surrey that year, for the celebration for Arne's ninetieth and Kathie's eightieth birthdays. A spiritual magnetism began. The Bryans and Becksteads stayed in contact and enjoyed every bit of distant fellowship they could squeeze in.

Kelvin & Faye Beckstead

Kelvin and Faye grasped the vision with such clarity that in the summer of 2013 they volunteered to do the long trip across Canada for Prayer Canada. God had told them to take six weeks off from their Church in September and October for the trip and they obeyed.

"That's music to my ears!" was Arne's response when Kelvin phoned with the offer. Recognizing a passion like his own, Arne set to work arranging places for them to minister and stay. In the process he would be introducing them to key prayer partners, exposing them to multiple experiences, looking for feedback from trusted colleagues. The tour included about thirty-three stops, sometimes two in a day (a dozen coming west, a few in B.C. and eighteen going back east again)—a schedule equal in intensity to any that Arne and Kathie used to relish.

The Becksteads set off and all was going well. They were well received at their first few stops and good reports came in about glorious times with them. Then in Winnipeg, six days into the trip, their commitment was tested. Faye had a phone call that her mother was dying. Rather than change the itinerary the Lord had laid out for them, Faye immediately flew home alone, leaving Kelvin to continue without her. He had "a burning desire to press on."

Arne was deeply moved by their commitment, remembering how he and Kathie had faced the same challenge in 1979 when her son had died in the middle of their long trip. He says, "The enemy will bring all kinds of stuff across your path to detour and misguide and misdirect you and many ministries are spoiled because of that."

Kelvin faithfully ministered in the Holy Spirit at all the stops and persevered with the long lonely drives, in spite of transmission problems in his van. (At every place the Prayer Partners prayed in faith for that transmission system. It would get him all the way to the west coast and all the way back home again and then still kept going.)

Saturday September 14 was Kelvin's fiftieth birthday but he didn't slow down. Arne sent him a birthday card via Harry and Gladys Rusk, who celebrated with him during a noon stop in Carrot Creek, AB before he set off to be in Clearwater, B.C. that evening.

The notes from the stops heading westward are liberally sprinkled with phrases like: "a faithful prayer warrior with whom we shared great fellowship ... spent hours talking about the Lord and His goodness ... the Holy Spirit moved in a powerful way and touched the hearts of everyone in attendance ... they were wonderful hosts and love the Lord with all their heart ... these folks love the Lord with a passion ... Prayer Canada has outstanding people in the ranks who are such an inspiration and true blessing ..."

Faye's mother passed away the day after she arrived in Ontario. "I know she is with the Lord," she says, "and am grateful she is not suffering anymore. One of these days we will all be reunited with her." After the funeral, in spite of her loss, she rejoined the tour, flying to Vancouver on Sunday September 15. Arne and Kathie brought her back to their home and Kelvin drove in the next day.

Kathie was only able to join in a little of the warm fellow-ship but by this time Arne was excited about the Becksteads' future role in Prayer Canada. However, more than a heart connection between the two couples, more than relief that someone had taken up the vision with passion and commit-ment, he had to hear a word from the Lord.

On Tuesday September 17, he and Kelvin were chatting after breakfast. Kathie was in bed and Faye was downstairs resting. Arne was sitting in his La-Z-Boy chair and Kelvin happened to be standing in front of him. Suddenly the Lord said to Arne, "That's the man!"—the man Prayer Canada had been looking for during the last ten years.

Arne looked at Kelvin and prophesied, "The Lord says, '**That's** the man!'"

Kelvin fell on his knees beside Arne and practically cried out, "Arne, before I left, the Lord told me that that's exactly what you were going to say." (On the third day of two weeks of prayer and fasting before setting off across Canada, the Lord had said to Kelvin that Arne would tell him he would be the next leader of Prayer Canada. A few days later, though Kelvin had said nothing about this to Faye, she had heard the same from the Lord herself.)

Thrilled at this awesome spiritual connection, Arne pulled out his little jar of compressed oil and anointed him right there. "Are there any examples in the Bible," Arne asks with mock innocence, "where a preacher went to the Board to ask what to do? When God tells you, you must **act**."

The next day Kelvin and Faye set off for three days on Vancouver Island: Gold River, Campbell River and Victoria, where they had a couple of days with Ray and Brenda Jansen.

While they were away, Arne and Lanny created an official certificate designating Kelvin Beckstead as the new Director of Prayer Canada. Arne signed it, rolled it up and slipped it inside a shiny baton, given to him by Faytene Grasseschi, which had been sitting in his office for some six or seven years waiting to be passed to the next runner. The baton is etched with the words, "Run With Perseverance."

The "Run With Perseverance" baton which Arne presented to Kelvin

Thursday September 19 was Kathie's eighty-fifth birthday but she stayed home in bed. On Monday the twenty-third, Barb took her to see her doctor at the request of the doctor, who had spotted something on the x-rays and thought Kathie had suffered a minor stroke. When her patient helplessly threw up in her office, the doctor called for an ambulance to take her to the Royal Columbian Hospital, although it was just across the street. That way Kathie was admitted immediately with no more delays.

His wife was in hospital but Arne had to attend to the Lord's business. He had called a board meeting for that evening "to meet the new leader of Prayer Canada" and had invited some previous board members as well. Don and Margaret Fults, Bert and Ruth Lang, Joe and Maya Pal, John and Dolores Matties, Dolphe and Gloria Hoffman, Marcus Unger and Lanny Townsend met with the Becksteads and Arne at the Knight and Day restaurant, where they had dinner together and then got down to business.

Arne presented the baton to Kelvin and Faye, opened it and showed everyone the certificate affirming them as the new leaders. Arne would no longer be the active Director; he would step back to be the Overseer and Kelvin would take over the reins immediately. They prayed together and Arne asked them all to break bread as a mark of unity and commitment. Then Arne drove off to see Kathie in hospital.

All this was very swift as Kelvin and Faye left the next morning for the return half of their trip back to Ontario. They had the certificate to show to their various hosts across the country. It was going to be an even more significant trip.

Meanwhile Kathie was experiencing the deep peace of God, like the peace He had given her when Barry and Beryl had died. Visitors could see it in her face. Arne spent many hours by her side, cheering her and reading to her. An MRI revealed the serious source of Kathie's problems—not a mini stroke but a tumour in the back of her head. The pressure of the growth was now causing double vision, so she had to wear a patch over one eye.

Arne's 95th birthday with Yani Lim by Kathie's hospital bed

On Sunday September 29, Arne celebrated his ninety-fifth birthday by Kathie's hospital bed. He found, instead of struggling to walk, he could use a hospital wheelchair to propel himself along the long corridors to her room. Pastor Yani Lim of Bethesda Ministry of Love brought a cake, sang worship songs and prayed for them both (and other patients in the room). She also did Kathie's hair and made her feel more like herself. That hospital room was filled with the gentle joyful presence of the Lord.

On Thursday October 3, Kathie had successful surgery to identify the growth. It was a lymphoma cancer, inoperable but treatable. After the surgery she began medication to reduce the tumour. Then she began a series of radiation treatments to shrink the tumour further so that eventually it would no longer cause a problem. But she began to be affected by severe pain. "Lord," she said. "You have made Heaven so beautiful. Why should I bear all this pain, when You could take me home?"

"I see the bigger picture," was the Lord's gentle answer.

She drew comfort from Psalm 139: "That psalm says that God made me. Since He made me, He is also able to fix me." She remained in hospital, quite weak and in pain, but thankful that there was no sign of cancer anywhere else in her body.

Kelvin and Faye's progress back across the country was filled with success and deeply memorable moments—awed by the Rockies, taken aback by the beauty of the prairies, inspired by vibrant fall colours along Lake Superior, they renewed friendships and made new ones, relished fabulous home cooking, sang the praises of the Lord, prayed and were prayed for, preached and prophesied all the way back home.

They met a prayer warrior who was "standing in the gap for her town like Moses of old," another who was "a strong leader like Deborah in the Bible," others who "were very devoted to Brother Arne and Sister Kathie for the wonderful leadership over the years," or "marching forward in God's great army for such a time as this."

In Kelowna they folded hundreds of Prayer Canada pamphlets with the help of Art and Gwen Mercer. In Cranbrook they met Bill Bennett, Minister of Energy and Mines, MP Dave Wilkes and the Mayor. At the Internationale Prayer Centre with eighty-five-year old Bill White, they admired his Godmobile, ministered under a heavy anointing of the Holy Spirit and prayed in faith for Kathie.

In Moose Jaw, SK their visit coincided with the noon prayer meeting in City Hall. In Winkler, MB they experienced "one of the most powerful meetings of the tour. The Prayer Post was on fire, spiritually." In Steinbach, MB they met a former Mayor, Les Magnusson, who is one of eight mayors quoted on the Prayer Canada pamphlet *How to Pray in Your City Hall and Legislature*: "Thank you for your prayers on our behalf and for fulfilling the vision God has given you to establish Prayer Posts across this nation."

Finally, Arne had arranged an overnight stay for them in Toronto with Al and Elaine Jones, the Bryans' close friends. Although not part of Prayer Canada, Al and Elaine shared Arne's passionate heart—and his sense of humour!

Arne kept in touch with them all the way and got a kick out of a couple of comments from folks who had met them: "Arne, he was here and you really must have anointed him, because he acts something like you do!"

After the trip, Arne and Kelvin continued their discussion on strategy to enable the transition. On Arne's advice, Kelvin's church became a member of the Independent Assemblies of God. It would be good to belong to a supporting group of similar churches without losing their own autonomy. Kelvin designated one of his elders to be in charge, freeing him to work full time with Prayer Canada. Arne has always maintained that travelling is the key to establishing solid commitments and he recognized that a leader based in Ontario will be better situated to build up the prayer network there and in Quebec and the Maritimes.

During this time Arne had a vision: Prayer Canada had built many prayer bases, all folded together like a sandalwood fan. Now Kelvin and Faye were going to open the fan right across Canada and beyond.

Kathie remained in hospital. She finished her course of radiation but did not regain her strength and was plagued with great pain in her hip. Arne visited as often as possible, bringing his cheerful faith to strengthen her, and the whole of Prayer Canada along with many other dear friends were praying for her.

Less than six weeks after they had left B.C., Kelvin and Faye flew back for a couple of weeks. On Thursday November 21, Arne ordained Kelvin into the Independent Assemblies of God.

"Where did you get that black eye, Arne?" people asked him on the day of the ordination.

"My wheelchair bucked me off," he joked, recalling the wild horses of his youth. In his talk to the congregation he explained what had happened with great amusement. "About ten days ago, going to the hospital to visit Kathie, I took the wheelchair out of the back of the van, put it down on the sloping sidewalk and sat in it. But I hadn't put the brakes on. So it set off rolling downhill, tipped off the edge of the sidewalk and I ended up flat on my side on the pavement."

Three young people had happened to be walking by. They kindly picked him up and wheeled him over to the hospital, as he wasn't sure what was hurt. His three rescuers took him into emergency and said, "We don't know who he is. We just picked him up off the street!" Then they went on their way and Arne didn't get their names. Arne survived with just a black eye to show for his tumble.

The next night he was leaving the hospital after visiting Kathie again. He met the same three young people going down in the elevator from the same floor. "Hi," they said. "We're the ones who picked you up yesterday. We'll wheel you down."

Arne of course got them talking and found out that the one who had come to the hospital for some treatment was a Christian.

"Well, what about you?" Arne said to the second young man. "Wouldn't you like to be a Christian?" And he led him to the Lord as the third, a girl, just stood there stunned.

"And what about you?" he asked her. "Wouldn't you like to be a Christian too?"

"Well, I suppose so..." So he led her to the Lord as well.

"God, the things You do to get people saved!" Arne prayed silently.

The night after the ordination, Prayer Canada celebrated at the thirty-sixth Anniversary Banquet, with a large and exuberant crowd of diners. Arne introduced Kelvin and Faye Beckstead as the new leaders of Prayer Canada, with the words: "I'm satisfied beyond any shadow of a doubt that this is the man. I didn't ask him what education he had, I didn't ask him his background, because when God speaks you don't even **discuss** it. I want each one of you to remember that. Be prepared to act on God's direction regardless as to how it might affect you or somebody else. If it's God's plan, we want to be obedient. Our God has got a plan for this man and He's got a plan for each of you here."

Arne and Kathie's pastor, Sam Owusu of Calvary Worship Centre, brought a deep word on prayer, challenging the older generation to cry out to God to raise up a new generation of young prayer warriors. His word was received gladly by the seasoned prayer partners there and also by some dedicated young intercessors newly attracted to Prayer Canada.

But the star of the evening was Arne Bryan, enjoying the love of so many friends and still on his mission to call God's people to greater things in the Holy Spirit.

Arne continued to spend all the hours he could with Kathie. Still extremely weak, she developed pneumonia and the antibiotics caused her throat to swell. On a drip because she couldn't swallow, she longed to go home.

Finally, after ten weeks in hospital, she went into the presence of her Lord at 8:20 pm on December 4, 2013, with her two daughters by her bedside.

Kathie had poured her heart and soul into Arne's life, into Prayer Canada, into her family and so many other lives far and wide. So it was a thankful and tender celebration of her life at Calvary Worship Centre on Monday December 9, 2013. A light snowfall fell outside on a very cold afternoon as people gathered with warm greetings, sharing memories and enjoying the glorious music from Marcus Unger on the grand piano. Beautiful hymns and special worship items would follow during the service.

Celebration of Kathie's life

A eulogy of their mother written by Brian, Brenda and Barb searched for words to describe her—"Courageous. Strong. Warm. Kind. Gracious." They ended up with the word "Love," unconditional love. "Mom loved her family," they said. "Every birth of a grandchild she was there. No matter where they were, she was right there supporting her girls. She loved her grandkids. They were her pride and joy... Everyone she met she loved like family. She was so beautiful on the inside. On the outside and on the inside.

"God was her strength and as kids we learned that. She showed us how to be strong and courageous. How to live life to the fullest and never be old in the spirit. She gave us grace and kindness... She will always be with us."

Then Ron Ward, one of Arne and Kathie's oldest friends,

looked back to 1977 when he and Vera had first met them, and described how excited Arne and Kathie were to show them the Upper Room newly opened in Surrey. "Oh you should have seen the two of them," he smiled. "They were like little children."

They had encouraged him and his wife in their ministry, Revival Centre on "Skid Row" for nearly thirty years. "I think of the many times Kathie and Arne would come down to the Revival Centre for a meeting, though some others would refuse to come because of the part of the city we were in. Kathie didn't have any fear. Kathie not only came down but she brought the grandchildren. This was Kathie."

Then Arne moved slowly to the front, stooped but still tall and imposing, and read what he called a "soliloquy," written during the evening after "Jesus wafted Kathie away to be with Him."

He thanked the Lord for His wonderful care of them since they had married. "After being alone for three years it seemed like **heaven** had opened its arms to me..." His voice was tender with grateful praise as he remembered.

"Many times I've wept over the terrible pains in her body from various maladies that had affected her," he said. "So I can rejoice she no longer has to suffer nights and days where pain takes its toll. My heart trembles when I think about the fact our partnership on this earth is over. But, who knows?" he added with a twinkle. "We may not be parted *long* at all, since I happen to be **ninety-five** years old!"

He spoke to Kathie: "I know you know the Lord is with me, dear. So I won't let sadness overtake my life. While I'm here, I'll continue to be His soldier. What greater task than being an armour bearer for the Lord? I still hear Him saying as he did in 1977: *Faithful is He who has called you, who also will do it*."

He prayed for those present: "Lord, have your way. Minister to all these people here today. Many have needs. Lord, I pray for Your love to meet their needs this day and every day and the days to come. My God is able. Thank you Lord. In Jesus' name."

He concluded: "Thank you, Kathie, for being a wonderful partner for forty-two years and I'm looking forward to those days when I'll be with you again. In Jesus' name, Amen."

Then Pastor Sam preached the gospel, eager that everybody present should be ready when the time comes.

Arne had hoped to be able to spend more time with Kathie now that the work of Prayer Canada was in safe hands. That was not to be. But Arne's work here will not be over until he too is "wafted away to be with the Lord."

EPILOGUE

This story has to end somewhere, although Arne Bryan is still on the job.

This has been the story of a resourceful Albertan cowboy, who knew at ten years old what it would take to train a wild pony—patience and guts, but mostly patience. Move steadily, stick to his father's plan, persevere through interminable repetitions and dig deep for even more patience and guts. The pattern has worked through his long life of service. He still wears his trademark bootlace necktie, cowboy belt buckle and the signet ring imprinted with a horse's head that Kathie gave him for his eightieth birthday.

As his life went on, the cowboy learned, like his faithful saddle horse Buck, to submit his daring independent nature to his heavenly Master. Arne says his life has been a God-directed pathway because of his parents, who lived the same way:

"My parents were committed Christians and through the terrible disaster of the Depression—absolutely devastating— there was no word of complaint. At one time my folks were well-off in comparison with others but, after four years of crop failure in the middle of the dust bowl, Dad gave up 640 acres of land that he'd homesteaded from 1906. They still worshiped God and Dad handled things in such a way that he achieved things I never saw anybody else do. He took apart all the granaries, moved to an irrigation area, and out of the lumber built a barn and a house and started over."

Arne's advice for Christians today faced with insurmountable challenges and devastating setbacks?

"There's only one way. You've got to turn it over to the Lord. Without the Lord's presence and power, you are powerless. You see, a person can get saved and be *useless*. You have to ask the Lord to send the Holy Spirit to grow within you and bring you all the *power* to overcome the enemy forces. When you get *passionate* enough, Deuteronomy 28:7 comes into focus and the enemy has to flee in seven directions."

This has also been the story of a sailor who signed up for commando training and never stopped living like one. His heart is to obey, absolutely and immediately, all orders from the Lord because he trusts in the One giving the orders.

That has been his unstinting message to the thousands of Christian lives he has influenced and to those he has rejoiced to call his friends.

"I have called you to demonstrate my righteousness," Arne quotes from Isaiah 42:6. "That is not a suggestion," he continues. "In the commandos you learn discipline and it's the same here. You don't *discuss* what God says. You *do* it."

That attitude equipped him to be the pioneer leader of a national ministry. Clearly Prayer Canada is the child of a commando and exhibits the same spirit.

And how important has Prayer Canada been to Canada?

"The longer I live," Arne says, "the more important I think it is. I realize it wasn't me doing it. It was God's direction so many times that only His power and authority could achieve the things. More and more people are telling me that this is the prayer network that is keeping Canada in line with godly principles. The one nation in the world that has stood up for

Israel without bending, or without consideration of what the cost might be. Why? Because people have **prayed**."

"I'm hearing from people right, left and centre: *This is God's direction for Canada*," he continues. "This is the largest and most extensive prayer network in Canada. We actually have prayer posts (that means places where people come to get direction from the Lord) in some two hundred locations across Canada, from Yukon to Newfoundland and we're building more all the time..... Prayer Canada is the chief protection over Canada right now. Not because I said so but because **dozens** of people are telling me."

Now, with the Lord's help, he will find the courage to carry on without his dear Kathie by his side. If you ask him how he is, he still answers, "I'm **blessed**!"

Optimism is in his bones. With the joy of the Lord always bubbling by the power of the Holy Spirit, conversation with him is peppered with chuckles and his cheerful merriment is contagious.

On the bulletin board in his office he pinned a hilarious cartoon with shocking pink writing on electric blue background announcing: "Everyone is entitled to my opinion!!"

The mischievous 'Doc' has become a persistent irritant to those who don't have the same vision but he gets away with it because of his lovable light-hearted approach. He and his beloved Kathie together warmed hearts with hospitality, caring, laughter and deep insight into God's heart.

Underlying everything is the call of the Lord. Recently the Lord spoke two words to him, with which this story will end:

"I'm sure you don't want to walk the last mile to heaven seeing the ravished bodies of those you could have helped and didn't."

"Regardless of the circumstances you're in, when I give you an opportunity to do something for somebody, do it."

ARNE'S LIFE
JOURNEY IN SCRIPTURE

Arne wants you to read what follows as if he is speaking to you. Hear his high-pitched, smiling voice, loud and strong on significant words, as he remembers, quotes, urges. He wrote it all out in his own handwriting so that it would be more immediate and personal. It will take you on his own life journey through the Scriptures. Let the Lord's words empower your life.

> *But seek ye first the kingdom of God and His righteousness, and all these things shall be added unto you. MATT 6:33 KJ.*

This hung in my bedroom as a boy:

"For God so loved the world He gave His only begotten Son that whosoever believeth in Him should not perish but have everlasting life" (John 3:16, KJV).

My mother told me I accepted Jesus when I was three years old. Every Sunday after dinner we had to learn a verse from the Bible.

The whole Bible was given to us by inspiration from God and is useful to teach us what is still true and to make us realize what is wrong with our lives; it straightens us out and helps us do what is right. (2 Timothy 3:16, TLB).

So God created man in His own image, in the image of God created He him, male and female created He them. And God blessed them and God said unto them, Be fruitful and multiply and replenish the earth and subdue it: and have dominion over... every living thing that moveth upon the earth (Gen 1:27-28 KJV).

...Blessed is the man who trusts in the Lord and has made the Lord his hope and confidence (Jeremiah 17:7, TLB).

The Lord gave me this following message as I was hesitating to think I was the one to pray for Canada:

Rejoice evermore. Pray without ceasing. In everything give thanks, for this is the will of God in Christ Jesus concerning you. Quench not the spirit. Despise not prophesyings. Prove all things, hold fast that which is good. Abstain from all appearance of evil. And the very God of peace sanctify you wholly, and I pray God your whole spirit and soul and body be preserved blameless unto the coming of our Lord Jesus Christ. Faithful is He that calleth you, who also will do it (1 Thessalonians 5:16-24 KJV).

When I grasped verse 24 (He will do it), I knew all my excuses were ruined.

...For we are the temple of the living God. As God said; I will live in them and walk among them, I will be their God and they will be my people
2 Cor. 6:16

Take no part in the worthless deeds of evil and darkness, but instead rebuke and expose them (Ephesians 5:11, TLB).

And I have given you authority over all the power of the enemy and to walk among snakes and scorpions and to crush them. Nothing shall injure you (Luke 10:19, TLB).

...The wicked shall not rule the godly, lest the godly be forced to do wrong (Psalm 125:3, TLB).

If my people, who are called by my name, will humble themselves and pray and seek my face and turn from their wicked ways, then I will hear from heaven and I will forgive their sin and will heal their land (2 Chronicles 7:14, NIV).

What wonderful promises the Lord gives us

Run up and down through every street in Jerusalem; search high and low, and see if you can find even one person who is fair and honest! Search every square, and

*if you find just one, I'll not destroy the city! (*Jeremiah
5:1, TLB)

Every city and village needs this protection. God's
direction is clear.

*Be sure that you select as king the man the Lord your
God shall choose. He must be an Israelite not a foreigner*
(Deuteronomy 17:15, TLB).

"A Christian not a heathen" is my translation.

*May I never forget your words for they are my only
hope. Therefore I will keep on obeying you forever and
forever, free within the limits of your laws. I will speak to
kings about their value and they will listen with interest
and respect* (Ps 119:43-46, TLB).

I have found this to be very true regarding the many
authorities I have had the privilege to speak to. Furthermore:

*...Blessings shall be showered on those who rebuke sin
fearlessly* (Proverbs 24:25, TLB).

*For the word of God is quick, and powerful, and sharper
than any two-edged sword, piercing even to the dividing
asunder of soul and spirit, and of the joints and marrow,
and is a discerner of the thoughts and intents of the
heart* (Hebrews 4:12, KJV).

I say: What greater tool do we need?

...I am convinced that nothing can ever separate us from His love. Rom 8:38 L.B.

These soldiers charge like infantry, they scale the walls like picked and trained commandos. Straight forward they march, never breaking ranks. They never crowd each other. Each is right in place. No weapon can stop them.... The Lord leads them with a shout. This is his mighty army, and they follow his orders... (Joel 2:7, 8, 11, TLB).

Feed the hungry! Help those in trouble! Then your light will shine out from the darkness and the darkness around you shall be as bright as day. And the Lord will guide you continually, and satisfy you with all good things, and keep you healthy too; and you will be like a well-watered garden, like an ever-flowing spring (Isaiah 58:10-11, TLB).

Since I was in the navy commandos for a while in the Second World War, I feel this is the kind of operation in which Prayer Canada is involved.

> Arise, my people! Let your light shine for all the nations to see! For the glory of the Lord is streaming from you. Darkness as black as night shall cover all the peoples of the earth but the glory of the Lord shall shine from you. All nations will come to your light; mighty kings will come to see the glory of the Lord upon you.
> Is 60:1-3 LB (TJ)

I the Lord have called you to demonstrate my righteousness. I will guard and support you, for I have given you to my people as the personal confirmation of my covenant with them. You shall also be a light to guide the nations unto me.

You will open the eyes of the blind and free the captives from prison. You will release those who sit in prison darkness and despair. I am the Lord. That is my name. I will not give my glory to anyone else; I will not share my praise with carved idols (Isaiah 42:6-8, TLB).

The Lord has called us to follow his example.

The Lord God has given me his words of wisdom so that I may know what to say to all these weary ones. Morning by morning He wakens me and opens my understanding to his will (Isaiah 50:4, TLB).

Because the Lord God helps me, I will not be dismayed; therefore I have set my face like flint to do his will and I know that I will triumph (Isaiah 50:7, TLB).

BIBLIOGRAPHY

The Aurora, "Prayer Canada." Labrador City, Newfoundland. July 23, 1984.

Baldrey, Keith. "Prayer room brings the Socreds to their knees" in *Sun*. Victoria, March 12, 1987.

Baldrey, Keith. "HALLELUJAH! Prayers offered up for cabinet ministers" in *Sun*, Victoria: March 19, 1987.

Bechtel. "1945 - 1959: Bringing Energy to the World." March, 2011 (http://www.bechtel.com/BAC-Chapter-3.html).

Biggs, Stan. "Lt. Governor Promotes Prayer" in *Christian Info*, April 1987.

Biggs, Stan. "Prayer Room has Pedigree" in *Christian Info*, April 10, 1987.

Canadian Press, "Vander Zalm, reporters in prayers at B.C. House" Victoria. March, 1987.

CBC Digital Archives. March, 2011 (archives.cbc.ca).

Clarke, Alison. "Prayer Canada prays for all levels of government" *in The Valley Sentinel*, August 28, 2002.

The Delia and District Historical Society. *The Delia Craigmyle Saga*. Southern Printing Company Limited, 1970.

Fieguth, Debra. "Arctic Revival" in *Faith Today*, January/February 2002.

Fleck, Peter. "Prayer key to curing nation's woes" in Alberta Sonshine News. September 1984.

Gooliaff, Vanessa. "Prayers said for local leader" in *Regina Free Press*, December 14, 1996

The Hand Hills Book Committee. *Hand Hills Heritage*. College Press, 1968.

Lake, Rhodanthe. "Prayer army travels on its knees" in *The Columbian*, June 1981.

The Leader. "Prayer Canada directors travel across the country." Surrey, BC, July 21, 1985

MacDonald, Mark. "Praying for those in authority" in *Nanaimo Daily Free Press*, July 21, 1984.

Maclean's. "An unholy prayer fight" April 13, 1987

Nanaimo Daily Free Press. "Prayer group asks guidance for city hall" January 13, 1981.

Nicol, Eric. *And crutches in the Prayer Room* March 1987.

Risdon, Anne. "Meet Arne Bryan dispensing help and comfort through Prayer Canada" in *Surrey / Delta Now*, August 27, 1986.

Prayer Post Courier, various issues. Prayer Canada.

Surrey Leader. "Signs beyond prayer" November 2, 1986.

Schweyer, Jenny. "On the front lines of Canada's spiritual battlefield" in *The Light Magazine*, March 2013.

The Vancouver Sun. "Group spends Labour Day break in three days of prayer and fast" August 30, 1980.